ACCOUNTING PRINCIPLES

FIFTH CANADIAN EDITION

→ Jerry J. Weygandt *Ph.D., C.P.A.*
University of Wisconsin—Madison

→ Donald E. Kieso *Ph.D., C.P.A.*
Northern Illinois University

→ Paul D. Kimmel *Ph.D., C.P.A.*
University of Wisconsin—Milwaukee

→ Barbara Trenholm *M.B.A., F.C.A.*
University of New Brunswick—Fredericton

→ Valerie A. Kinnear *M.Sc. (Bus. Admin.), C.A.*
Mount Royal University

In collaboration with
Joan Barlow, Mount Royal University
Brad Witt, Humber College

WILEY

John Wiley & Sons Canada, Ltd.

To our students—past, present, and future

Library and Archives Canada Cataloguing in Publication

Accounting principles / Jerry J. Weygandt... [et al.]. --

5th Canadian ed.

ISBN 978-0-470-16079-4 (pt. 1)

1. Accounting--Textbooks. I. Weygandt, Jerry J.

HF5636.A33 2009a   657'.044   C2009-903891-9

Production Credits

   Acquisitions Editor: Zoë Craig
   Vice President & Publisher: Veronica Visentin
   Vice President, Publishing Services: Karen Bryan
   Creative Director, Publishing Services: Ian Koo
   Director, Market Development: Carolyn Wells
   Marketing Manager: Aida Krneta
   Editorial Manager: Karen Staudinger
   Developmental Editor: Daleara Jamasji Hirjikaka
   Media Editor: Channade Fenandoe
   Editorial Assistant: Laura Hwee
   Design & Typesetting: OrangeSprocket Communications
   Cover Design: Natalia Burobina
   Printing & Binding: World Color Press Inc.

Printed and bound in the United States
1 2 3 4 5 WC 14 13 12 11 10

John Wiley & Sons Canada, Ltd.
6045 Freemont Blvd.
Mississauga, Ontario L5R 4J3
Visit our website at: www.wiley.ca

SELECTED CHAPTERS FROM
WEYGANDT: ACCOUNTING PRINCIPLES, FIFTH CANADIAN EDITION, PARTS 1 AND 2

A Wiley Canada Custom Publication for

Seneca College

Wiley Canada Custom Services
JOHN WILEY & SONS CANADA, LTD.

Cover Design: Natalia Burobina

Marketing Manager: Aida Krneta
Custom Coordinator: Sara Tinteri

Printed and bound in the United States of America
10 9 8 7 6 5 4 3 2 1

John Wiley & Sons Canada, Ltd
6045 Freemont Blvd.
Mississauga, Ontario
L5R 4J3
Visit our website at: www.wiley.ca

CHAPTER 1
ACCOUNTING IN ACTION

forzanigroup.com

The **Navigator** learning system encourages you to use the learning aids in the chapter and set priorities as you study.

Concepts for Review highlight concepts from your earlier reading that you need to understand before starting the new chapter.

✓ THE NAVIGATOR

- ☐ Understand *Concepts for Review*
- ☐ Read *Feature Story*
- ☐ Scan *Study Objectives*
- ☐ Read *Chapter Preview*
- ☐ Read text and answer *Before You Go On*
- ☐ Work *Demonstration Problem*
- ☐ Review *Summary of Study Objectives*
- ☐ Answer *Self-Study Questions*
- ☐ Complete assignments

CONCEPTS FOR REVIEW:

Before studying this chapter, you should understand or, if necessary, review:

a. How to use the study aids in this book. (pp. vii–xvi)

b. What the Bloom's Taxonomy classifications (K, C, AP, AN, S, and E) mean. (p. xvii)

c. How you learn best. (pp. xviii–xx)

d. The student supplements that accompany this text. (p. xxiv)

The **Feature Story** helps you see how the chapter topic fits with the real world of accounting and business. The story will be mentioned frequently throughout the chapter.

Making the Right Moves

CALGARY, Alta.—When it comes to football, everyone knows you need to "keep your eye on the ball" if you want to stay in the game. In business, as in sports, an organization needs to keep a careful eye on its financial accounting information if it wants to succeed and thrive. Consider the story of Calgary-based Forzani Group Ltd., Canada's "largest and only national sporting goods retailer."

The company kicked off in 1974 when Calgary Stampeder John Forzani and three of his teammates launched Forzani's Locker Room, a small retail operation that sold athletic footwear. Gradually, the business expanded to include clothing and sports equipment. In 1988, it launched RnR, its Relaxed and Rugged banner, specializing in leisure and recreational apparel.

Five years later, in 1993, the company went public and its shares began trading on the Toronto Stock Exchange. Expansion then continued with a series of acquisitions including Sports Experts in 1994, Coast Mountain Sports in 2000, Sport Mart in 2001, Gen-X Sports and Nevada Bob's Golf in 2004, National Sports in 2005, Fitness Source in 2006, and Athletes World in 2007. In addition, the company launched Hockey Experts and Pegasus in 2006.

Today, The Forzani Group offers a comprehensive assortment of brand-name and private-brand products, operating stores from coast to coast, under the following corporate and franchise banners: Sport Chek, Coast Mountain Sports, Sport Mart, National Sports, Athletes World, Sports Experts, Intersport, Econosports, Atmosphere, Tech Shop, Pegasus, Nevada Bob's Golf, Hockey Experts, S3, and The Fitness Source. At the end of the third quarter of its 2009 fiscal year, the company operated 335 corporate and 226 franchise stores. It also retails online at www.sportmart.ca and provides a sporting goods information site at www.sportchek.ca. For its 2009 fiscal year end, the company scored retail system sales of more than $1.3 billion and profit of almost $29.3 million.

These are rather impressive numbers for a company that started out as a single retail outlet! In fact, the spectacular growth is the result of countless decisions made along the way. Does a particular acquisition make sense financially? Should the company operate its stores under separate banners? Is e-commerce worth pursuing? While many factors have no doubt contributed to The Forzani Group's success, one thing is certain: to make these strategic decisions and others, the company's management relied on accounting information.

They're not the only ones. Over the years, other parties have used The Forzani Group's financial information, too. Its shareholders and potential investors have used it to make investment decisions, and its creditors have analyzed it to determine whether to issue loans or other forms of credit.

In short, sound accounting information lets The Forzani Group and all interested parties know exactly how the business is doing at all times—an essential part of any winning strategy!

Study Objectives show what you should be able to do after learning the specific concepts presented in the chapter.

The Navigator

STUDY OBJECTIVES:

After studying this chapter, you should be able to:

1. Identify the use and users of accounting.
2. Explain Canadian accounting standards and apply basic accounting concepts.
3. Use the accounting equation and explain the meaning of assets, liabilities, and owner's equity.
4. Analyze the effects of business transactions on the accounting equation.
5. Prepare financial statements.

The Navigator

The **Chapter Preview** outlines the major topics and subtopics you will see in the chapter.

The feature story about The Forzani Group highlights the importance of having good financial information to make good business decisions. This applies not just to companies but also to individuals. You cannot earn a living, spend money, buy on credit, make an investment, or pay taxes without receiving, using, or giving financial information. Good decision-making for companies and individuals depends on good information.

This chapter shows you that accounting is the system that produces useful financial information for decision-making. The chapter is organized as follows:

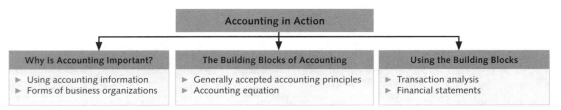

Accounting in Action

Why Is Accounting Important?	The Building Blocks of Accounting	Using the Building Blocks
▶ Using accounting information ▶ Forms of business organizations	▶ Generally accepted accounting principles ▶ Accounting equation	▶ Transaction analysis ▶ Financial statements

Why Is Accounting Important?

Essential terms are printed in blue when they first appear, and are defined in the end-of-chapter glossary.

Accounting is the information system that identifies, records, and communicates the economic events of an organization to a wide variety of interested users. The world's economic systems depend on highly transparent, relevant, understandable, and reliable financial reporting. When that does not happen, it can have disastrous results. Individuals such as financial advisers Bernard Madoff in New York and Earl Jones in Quebec concealed fraudulent investment operations, resulting in huge losses to investors, by hiding financial information regarding what was actually happening to the amounts invested by others.

A vital part of communicating economic events is the accountant's ability and responsibility to analyze and interpret the reported information. In analysis, accountants use ratios, percentages, graphs, and charts to highlight significant financial trends and relationships. In interpretation, they explain the uses, meaning, and limitations of the reported data. Accounting has long been labelled the "language of business" and has consistently ranked as one of the top career opportunities in business.

You might think this is all well and good for students who want to become accountants, but what about someone who has plans to be anything *but* an accountant?

Understanding the basics of accounting is helpful for almost every endeavour you can think of. By studying accounting, you will learn how the world of business—large and small—actually works. Whether you plan to own your own business in the future, work for someone else in their business, or invest in a business, learning how to read and interpret financial information will give you a valuable set of skills.

When you study accounting, you will also learn a lot about management, finance, and marketing, which will give you a solid foundation for your future studies. For example, you will learn how making a sale is meaningless unless it is a profitable sale and the money can eventually be collected from the customer. Marketing managers must also be able to decide pricing strategies based on costs. Accounting is what quantifies these costs and explains why a product or service costs what it does. So think of this textbook as your introduction to accounting across the organization.

It doesn't matter if you plan to become a doctor, lawyer, social worker, teacher, engineer, architect, or entrepreneur—whatever you choose, a working knowledge of accounting will be relevant and useful. Accounting is all about you. Make the most of this course—it will serve you for a lifetime in ways you cannot now imagine.

On the companion website to this text, there is more information about why accounting is important and what potential career opportunities exist. In addition, there are profiles of business people who use accounting information.

The **Web Icon** tells you about additional resources on the companion website that expand on the topic being discussed.

WILEY
PLUS
Career Paths

ACCOUNTING IN ACTION: ALL ABOUT YOU

"Bland, boring and colourless are just a few of the common stereotypes that spring to mind when describing an accountant. But these are just urban myths," an accounting magazine points out. To some entrepreneurs, the accountant is considered a hero. A survey by the Canadian Federation of Independent Business found that two thirds of companies feel that they get the most valued information from their accountant and lawyer. But what if you are not going to be an accountant—what will learning accounting do for you? Understanding the basics of accounting is helpful for almost every endeavour you can think of, including making personal investment decisions, protecting your personal resources, determining how much interest you will pay on a student loan, and deciding which company you will work for upon graduation. To demonstrate the value of accounting to you as an individual, included in each chapter is an "All About You" feature and a related activity (BYP-6) that links an accounting concept to your life as a student and to a situation you are likely to face.

Source: Yan Barcelo, "Ten Ways to Add Value," *CA Magazine*, August 2009, p. 20.

Why is understanding accounting of value to you in your personal life?

Using Accounting Information

There are two broad groups of users of accounting information: internal users and external users.

Internal Users

Internal users of accounting information plan, organize, and run companies. They work for the company. This includes finance directors, marketing managers, human resources personnel, production supervisors, and company officers. In running a business, internal users must answer many important questions, as shown in Illustration 1-1.

↑ **Accounting in Action** insights give examples of accounting situations from five different perspectives: all about you, across the organization, and in terms of business, ethics, and international concerns. At the end of the chapter, you will find answers to the questions that are asked after each insight.

← **Illustration 1-1**

Questions asked by internal users

Finance
Is there enough cash to pay the bills?

Marketing
What price should we sell iPhones for to maximize profits?

Human Resources
How many employees can we afford to hire this year?

Production
Which product line is the most profitable?

To answer these and other questions, users need detailed information on a timely basis; that is, it must be available when needed. Some examples of information that internal users need include forecasts of cash flows for the next year, projections of profit from new sales campaigns, financial comparisons of operating alternatives, analyses of salary costs, and budgeted financial statements.

External Users

There are several types of external users of accounting information. Investors use accounting information to make decisions to buy, hold, or sell their ownership interest. Creditors, such as suppliers and bankers, use accounting information to evaluate the risks of granting credit or lending money. Investors and creditors are the main external users of accounting information, but there are also many other external users with a large variety of information needs and questions.

For example, labour unions want to know whether the owners can afford to pay increased wages and benefits. Customers are interested in whether a company will continue to honour its product warranties and support its product lines. Taxing authorities, such as Canada Revenue Agency, want to know whether the company respects the tax laws. Regulatory agencies, such as provincial securities commissions that regulate companies that sell shares to the public, want to know whether the company is respecting established rules. And economic planners use accounting information to forecast economic activity.

Some questions that external users may ask about a company are shown in Illustration 1-2.

→ Illustration 1-2

Questions asked by
external users

Investors
Is the company earning enough to give me a return
on my investment?

Creditors
Will the company be able to pay its debts as they
come due?

Labour Unions
Can the company afford the pay raise we are
asking for?

Customers
Will the company stay in business long enough to
service the products I buy from it?

 ## ACCOUNTING IN ACTION: ACROSS THE ORGANIZATION INSIGHT

The Great Little Box Company, based in Vancouver, involves its employees in the company's success by regularly sharing information and acknowledging employee contributions. Every month, the company shares its corporate and financial information with all employees. These meetings ensure that everyone knows how the company is doing and what could be done to improve things. They also provide a forum for employee input and for recognizing and rewarding employees for their efforts. The company also shares 15% of its profits with employees on a monthly basis; divided equally among all eligible part-time and full-time employees. When there is a profit, the share for each employee is included in their paycheque following the monthly meeting.

Source: Industry Canada, Managing for Business Success: Great Little Box Company: A Team Approach to Success, Part 1, available at: http://www.ic.gc.ca/eic/site/mfbs-gprea.nsf/eng/lu00055.html [accessed on July 27, 2009]

What is the value of providing all of a company's employees with financial information about the company?

Ethics in Financial Reporting

In order for financial information to have value for its users, whether internal or external, it must be prepared by individuals with high standards of ethical behaviour. Ethics in accounting is of the utmost importance to accountants and decision-makers who rely on the financial information they produce.

Fortunately, most individuals in business are ethical. Their actions are both legal and responsible. They consider the organization's interests when they make decisions. Accountants and other professionals have extensive rules of conduct to guide their behaviour with each other and the public. In addition, many companies today have codes of conduct, or statements of corporate values, that outline their commitment to ethical behaviour in their internal and external relationships. The behaviour of management is critical for creating the appropriate tone from the top of the organization.

Throughout this textbook, ethical considerations will be presented to highlight the importance of ethics in financial reporting. Every chapter includes an Ethics Case in the end-of-chapter material that simulates a business situation and asks you to put yourself in the position of a key decision-maker. When you analyze these ethical situations, you should follow the steps outlined in Illustration 1-3.

Ethics in Accounting

1. Recognize an ethical situation and the ethical issues involved.

Use your personal ethics or an organization's code of ethics to identify ethical situations and issues. Some business and professional organizations provide written codes of ethics for guidance in common business situations.

2. Identify and analyze the main elements in the situation.

Identify the *stakeholders*—persons or groups who may be harmed or benefited.
Ask the question: What are the responsibilities and obligations of the parties involved?

3. Identify the alternatives, and weigh the impact of each alternative on various stakeholders.

Select the most ethical alternative, considering all the consequences. Sometimes there will be one right answer. Other situations involve more than one possible solution. These situations require an evaluation of each alternative and the selection of the best one.

↑ Illustration 1-3

Steps used to analyze ethics cases and situations

The companion website to this text includes a discussion of ethics and ethical issues that involve accounting and financial reporting.

Forms of Business Organization

As we have seen, businesses rely on accounting information to operate. Businesses can be organized in different ways. The most common examples are the proprietorship, partnership, and corporation. Illustration 1-4 compares some of the characteristics of these forms.

← Illustration 1-4

Characteristics of business organizations

	Proprietorship	Partnership	Corporation
Owners	Proprietor: one	Partners: two or more	Shareholders: one or more
Owner's liability	Unlimited	Unlimited	Limited
Private or public	Private	Usually private	Private or public
Taxation of profits	Paid by the owner	Paid by the partners	Paid by the corporation
Life of organization	Limited	Limited	Indefinite

Proprietorship

A business owned by one person is a **proprietorship**. The owner is usually the operator of the business. Small service businesses (hair stylists, plumbers, and mechanics), farms, and small retail stores (antique shops, corner grocery stores, and independent bookstores) are often proprietorships.

Often only a relatively small amount of money (capital) is needed to start in business as a proprietorship. The owner (the proprietor) receives any profits, suffers any losses, and is personally liable (responsible) for all debts of the business. This is known as **unlimited liability**.

There is no legal distinction between the business as an economic unit and the owner. Thus the life of a proprietorship is limited to the life of the owner. However, the records of the business activities must be kept separate from the personal records and activities of the owner. The profits of the business are reported and taxed on the owner's personal income tax return.

Many businesses in Canada are proprietorships, but they earn only a small percentage of the revenue earned by Canadian businesses as a whole. In this textbook, we start with proprietorships because many students organize their first business this way.

Partnership

A business owned by two or more persons who are associated as partners is a **partnership**. In most aspects, a partnership is similar to a proprietorship, except that there is more than one owner. Partnerships are often used to organize service-type businesses, including professional practices (lawyers, doctors, architects, and accountants).

Typically, a partnership agreement (written or oral) defines the initial investments of each partner, the duties of each partner, how profit (or loss) will be divided, and what the settlement will be if a partner dies or withdraws. As in a proprietorship, for accounting purposes the partnership activities must be kept separate from the personal activities of each partner. The partners' share of the profit must be reported and taxed on the partners' income tax return.

Each partner generally has unlimited liability for all debts of the partnership, even if one of the other partners created the debt. This means that any of the partners can be forced to give up his or her personal assets in order to repay the partnership debt, just as can happen to an owner in a proprietorship. We will learn more about partnerships in Chapter 12.

↓ **Helpful hints** help clarify concepts or items that are being discussed.

Helpful hint You can usually tell if a company is a corporation by looking at its name. The words *Limited (Ltd.)*, *Incorporated (Inc.)*, or *Corporation (Corp.)* usually follow its name.

Corporation

A business that is organized (incorporated) as a separate legal entity under federal or provincial corporate law is a **corporation**. A corporation is responsible for its debts and paying taxes on its profit. A corporation's ownership is divided into transferable shares. The corporation's separate legal status provides the owners of the shares (shareholders) with **limited liability** as they risk losing only the amount that they have invested in the company's shares. They are not personally liable for the debts of the corporate entity. Shareholders may sell all or part of their shares to other investors at any time. Easy changes of ownership are part of what makes it attractive to invest in a corporation. Because ownership can be transferred through the sale of shares and without dissolving the corporation, the corporation enjoys an unlimited life.

Although there are many more proprietorships and partnerships than corporations in Canada, the revenue produced by corporations is far greater. Most of the largest companies in Canada—for example, Bombardier, EnCana, Imperial Oil, Loblaw, and Magna—are corporations.

Corporations such as these are publicly traded. That is, their shares are listed on Canadian stock exchanges. Public corporations commonly distribute their financial statements to shareholders, creditors, other interested parties, and the general public upon request. Forzani is a public corporation. You can access its financial statements on its website, which is given in our feature story, as well as in Appendix A at the back of this textbook.

Other companies are private corporations, as they do not issue publicly traded shares. Some of the largest private companies in Canada include the Jim Pattison Group, the Irving Group, and McCain Foods. Like proprietorships and partnerships, these companies almost never distribute their financial statements publicly. We will discuss the corporate form of organization in Chapters 13 and 14.

Before You Go On questions at the end of major text sections are an opportunity to stop and re-examine the key points you have studied. *Related exercise material* tells you which Brief Exercises (BE) and Exercises (E) at the end of the chapter have similar study objectives.

The Navigator

BEFORE YOU GO ON . . .

→ Review It

1. Why is good accounting important?
2. How can the study of accounting benefit you?
3. Who uses accounting information? Name some specific internal and external users of accounting information.
4. Why is ethics important in terms of accounting information?
5. What are the differences between a proprietorship, partnership, and corporation?

Related exercise material: BE1–1, BE1–2, BE1–3, and E1–1.

The Building Blocks of Accounting

Financial information is communicated in accounting reports, and the most common reports are financial statements. We have included Forzani's financial statements for the year ended February 1, 2009, in Appendix A of this textbook as an example. We will refer to these statements throughout the textbook.

To make the information in financial statements meaningful, accountants have to prepare the reports in a standardized way. Every profession develops a body of theory based on principles and assumptions. Accounting is no exception.

Generally Accepted Accounting Principles

The accounting profession has developed a set of standards that are generally accepted and universally practised. This common set of standards, called **generally accepted accounting principles (GAAP)**, includes broad principles and practices, as well as rules and procedures. These standards indicate how to report economic events.

In Canada, the Accounting Standards Board (AcSB), an independent standard-setting body created by the Canadian Institute of Chartered Accountants (CICA), has the main responsibility for developing GAAP. The AcSB's most important criterion for accounting principles is this: the principle should lead to external users having the most useful financial information possible when they are making business decisions. In other words, the basic objective of financial reporting is to communicate information that is useful to investors, creditors, and other users when they make decisions.

It is important to understand that GAAP is not static and that it changes over time. The AcSB creates new standards and modifies GAAP after a long process of consultation with organizations and individuals that are interested in, or affected by, the principles. This process ensures that the main purpose of financial statements—providing information that is relevant to decision-making—continues to be met.

A recent and very dramatic change in Canadian GAAP is the implementation of two sets of standards: International Financial Reporting Standards, and Canadian GAAP for Private Enterprises.

International Financial Reporting Standards and Canadian GAAP for Private Enterprises

In its Strategic Plan, issued in January 2006, the AcSB noted that "one size does not necessarily fit all" and decided to pursue separate strategies for publicly accountable enterprises and for private enterprises. Effective January 1, 2011, all Canadian publicly accountable enterprises must follow International Financial Reporting Standards (IFRS), a set of global standards developed by the International Accounting Standards Board (IASB). **Publicly accountable enterprises** include publicly traded companies, as well as securities brokers and dealers, banks, and credit unions whose role is to hold assets for the public as part of their primary business.

Traditionally, accounting standards differed from country to country, making it difficult for investors, creditors, and others to make informed decisions about companies doing business in today's increasingly global environment. The IASB has worked, and continues to do so, with accounting standard setters across the globe to harmonize accounting standards where possible. IFRS are used as the main basis of financial reporting in more than 100 countries, including Australia, Russia, members of the European Union, and China. India and Japan, along with Canada, join in 2011. The United States is working on a convergence project with the IASB but at the time of writing had not yet set a specific date for adopting IFRS.

In Canada, the decision to adopt IFRS was made in order to enhance Canadian public companies' ability to compete in an increasingly global marketplace. When IFRS are used, the financial statements of Canadian public companies will be understood by investors and creditors throughout the world. Using IFRS will also help Canadian companies that operate in multiple countries, by allowing them to produce one set of financial statements rather than multiple sets with different accounting principles.

STUDY OBJECTIVE 2

Explain Canadian accounting standards and apply basic accounting concepts.

⬇ Alternative terminology notes give synonyms that you may hear or see in the workplace, in companies' financial statements, and occasionally in this textbook.

Alternative terminology The words *standard* and *principle* mean the same thing in accounting.

Helpful hint Accounting standards use the word "enterprise" as it is a broader term than "company" or "business." The word "enterprise" means that the accounting standard applies to the different forms of business organizations, as well as specific projects. Throughout this text, instead of using the word "enterprise," we will frequently use the words "company" or "business," as they are more common terms.

On the other hand, for many years critics have argued that traditional Canadian GAAP had too many complex standards that were not relevant for private companies. Since IFRS has even more requirements than traditional Canadian GAAP, the AcSB decided that all private companies, regardless of size, should have the choice of either adopting IFRS or following a new set of standards called Canadian GAAP for Private Enterprises.

The new Canadian GAAP for Private Enterprises requires considerably less information in financial statements than was required by traditional Canadian GAAP. A main reason for this change is that users of a private company's financial statements generally have the ability to obtain additional information from the company if required, and because these users typically require less information.

Given the differences between IFRS and GAAP for Private Enterprises, and the fact that private companies will have a choice, financial statement users will need to know which standards the company is following. Companies will be required to report this in their financial statements. In this textbook, as we proceed through the material, we will point out where there are differences in the two sets of standards. However, the two sets of standards have a great deal in common in the type of material covered in an introductory accounting textbook.

Both IFRS and Canadian GAAP for Private Enterprises are considered "principles-based" as opposed to "rules-based" standards. Principles-based standards are designed to encourage the use of professional judgement in applying basic accounting principles. As you learn more about accounting, you will see that we will frequently refer to basic principles, as opposed to detailed rules, when deciding how to account for specific events. In the following sections, we introduce a few of these basic principles and concepts.

 ACCOUNTING IN ACTION: BUSINESS INSIGHT

The new reporting requirements under International Financial Reporting Standards have made some smaller public companies consider going private. Take, for example, Calgary-based Humpty's Restaurants International Inc., which, after 19 years on the public market, decided that being private would be less costly and make the company more competitive. Humpty's estimated being private would have saved $80,000 in 2009 and the savings in 2010 would be about $120,000. This is a significant amount, considering that the restaurants' 2008 revenue was about $7 million and profit was just $503,000. Humpty's has not relied on equity financing or issued shares to raise capital or complete acquisitions for many years. It has six corporate stores and 44 franchises in Western Canada and has no plans for operational changes, though it will continue to explore franchise expansion opportunities.

Source: Dan Healing, "Humpty's Gets Cracking on Going Private," *Calgary Herald*, July 17, 2009.

Why will it be less expensive for a company like Humpty's Restaurants to use Canadian GAAP for Private Enterprises than IFRS?

Going Concern

The **going concern assumption** is the assumption that a company will continue to operate in the foreseeable future. Although some businesses fail, most companies continue operating for a long time. The going concern assumption presumes that the company will operate long enough to use its assets for their intended purpose and to complete the company's commitments.

This assumption is one of the most important assumptions in GAAP as it has implications regarding what information is useful for decision-makers and affects many of the accounting standards you will learn. If a company is a going concern, then financial statement users will find it useful for the company to report certain assets, such as land, at their cost. Land is acquired so a company can use it, not so it can be resold. Therefore, what matters is the amount the company gave up to acquire the land, not an estimate of its current worth. If a company is not a going concern, and the land is going to be sold, then financial statement users will be more interested in the land's current value.

If a company is not regarded as a going concern, or if there are significant doubts about its ability to continue as a going concern, then this must be stated in the financial statements, along with the reason why the company is not regarded as a going concern. Otherwise you can assume that the company is a going concern—even though this is not explicitly stated.

Economic Entity

The **economic entity assumption** (or entity concept) requires that an entity's business activities be kept separate and distinct from the activities of its owner and all other economic entities. An economic entity can be any organization or unit in society. It may be a company (such as The Forzani Group Ltd.), a governmental unit (such as the Province of Manitoba), a municipality (such as the Ville de Montréal), a native band council (such as the Kingsclear Indian Band), a school board (such as the Burnaby School Board), a club (such as the Melfort Rotary Club), or a proprietorship (such as Ellen's Boutique).

To illustrate, if Ellen Gélinas, owner of Ellen's Boutique, charges any of her personal living costs as expenses of Ellen's Boutique, then the economic entity assumption is being violated. This example also illustrates that an economic entity is not the same thing as a legal entity. You will recall from our earlier discussion that a proprietorship is not a separate legal entity from its owner. But the owner and the proprietorship are economically separate and must be accounted for as such.

Recognition and Measurement

Recognition is the process of recording a transaction in the accounting records. Once a transaction has been recognized or recorded, it will be included in the financial statements. **Measurement** is the process of determining the amount that should be recognized. At the time something is acquired, the transaction is first measured at the amount of cash that was paid or at the value exchanged. For example, if the Gjoa Company purchased land for $100,000, the land is recorded in Gjoa's records at $100,000. This amount is referred to as the asset's historical cost.

But what should Gjoa Company do if, by the end of the next year, the land's fair value has increased to $120,000? Under both IFRS and Canadian GAAP for Private Enterprises, historical cost is the primary basis used in financial statements, which means that Gjoa Company would continue to report the land at its historical cost of $100,000. This is often called the **cost principle**.

Cost has an important advantage over other valuations. It is reliable. Cost is definite and verifiable. The values exchanged at the time something is acquired can be objectively measured. Users can therefore rely on the information that is supplied, as they know it is based on fact.

However, critics argue that cost is often not relevant. They believe fair values provide more useful information. **Fair value** is the amount of the consideration that would be agreed upon in an arm's-length transaction between knowledgeable, willing parties who are under no compulsion to act. Fair value is not the amount that an entity would receive or pay in a forced transaction, involuntary liquidation, or distress sale.

At the time of acquisition, cost and fair value are the same. In later periods, cost and fair value differ, but the cost amount continues to be used for accounting in most circumstances. There are some exceptions that we will learn about in later chapters, and we will see that IFRS either allow or require fair value in more circumstances than Canadian GAAP for Private Enterprises.

Fundamental to this discussion is that only transactions that can be expressed as an amount of money can be included in the accounting records. This has been known as the **monetary unit assumption**. This assumption makes it possible for accounting to quantify (measure) economic events. In Canada, we mainly use the Canadian dollar to record these transactions. However, some companies report their results in U.S. dollars. In Europe, the euro (€) is used; in China, the yuan (CNY) is used; and so on.

The monetary unit assumption allows us to ignore the impact of inflation. Although inflation can be a significant accounting issue in some countries, Canada's inflation policy—set out by the federal government and the Bank of Canada—is to keep inflation at between 1% and 3% per year. Consequently, inflation is not considered an issue for accounting in Canada.

Alternative terminology
The cost principle is also known as the *historical cost principle*.

The monetary unit assumption does prevent some relevant information from being included in the accounting records. For example, the health of the owner, the quality of service, and the morale of employees would not be included, because they cannot be quantified in monetary amounts.

Other Financial Reporting Concepts

We have barely scratched the surface in terms of learning about financial reporting concepts and generally accepted accounting principles. Many other concepts and principles will be introduced as we move forward through the text. For example, in later chapters we will introduce the revenue and expense recognition criteria, the cost-benefit and materiality constraints, and concepts such as full disclosure, consistency, and comparability. Chapter 11 explores these principles in greater detail, and introduces the conceptual framework of accounting, a system that guides the development and application of accounting principles, including the relationships and hierarchy of these concepts. A conceptual framework is also important for companies to refer to when exercising professional judgement about how to apply GAAP to their specific circumstances.

BEFORE YOU GO ON . . .

→ Review It

1. What are generally accepted accounting principles?
2. What generally accepted accounting principles do companies in Canada use?
3. Explain the going concern and economic entity assumptions.
4. What is meant by recognition and measurement in accounting?
5. Explain the cost principle and the monetary unit assumptions.
6. What is the difference between cost and fair value?

The Navigator

Related exercise material: BE1–4, BE1–5, and E1–2.

Accounting Equation

STUDY OBJECTIVE 3

Use the accounting equation and explain the meaning of assets, liabilities, and owner's equity.

The categories that are used for classifying economic events are also essential building blocks of accounting. The two basic elements of a business are what it owns and what it owes. Assets are the resources owned by a business. Forzani has total assets of $689 million at February 1, 2009. Liabilities and owner's equity are the rights or claims against these resources. The claims of those who are owed money or other obligations (the creditors) are called liabilities. The claims of owners are called owner's equity. Forzani has liabilities of $356 million and owner's equity of $333 million. Illustration 1-5 shows how the relationship between assets, liabilities, and owner's equity is expressed as an equation.

→ **Illustration 1-5**

Accounting equation

Resources		Claims Against the Resources		
Assets	=	Liabilities	+	Owner's Equity
$689 million	=	$356 million	+	$333 million

Alternative terminology
The accounting equation is sometimes referred to as the *balance sheet equation.*

This equation is called the **accounting equation**. Assets must equal the sum of liabilities and owner's equity. Liabilities are shown before owner's equity in the accounting equation because creditors' claims are paid before ownership claims if a business is liquidated.

The accounting equation is the same for all economic entities regardless of their size, nature of business, or form of business organization. It applies to a small proprietorship such as a corner grocery store as much as it does to a large corporation such as The Forzani Group Ltd. This equation is the basis for recording and summarizing the economic events of a company.

Let's look at the categories in the accounting equation in more detail.

Assets

As noted earlier, **assets** are the resources owned by a business. They are used to carry out activities such as the production and distribution of merchandise. Every asset is capable of providing future services or benefits. In a company, that service potential or future economic benefit eventually results in cash inflows (receipts).

For example, imagine that a local pizza parlour, called Campus Pizza, owns a delivery truck. This truck provides economic benefits because it is used to deliver pizzas. Campus Pizza also owns other assets such as tables, chairs, a sound system, a cash register, an oven, dishes, supplies, and, of course, cash. Other common examples of assets include merchandise inventory held for resale, investments, land, buildings, equipment, patents, and copyrights. **Accounts receivable** is the asset created when a company sells services or products to customers who promise to pay cash in the future.

Liabilities

Liabilities are current obligations, arising from past events, to make a future payment of assets or services. That is, liabilities are present debts and obligations. For example, businesses of all sizes usually borrow money and purchase merchandise inventory and supplies on credit. Campus Pizza, for instance, purchases pizza ingredients and beverages on credit from suppliers. These obligations to pay cash to the supplier in the future are called **accounts payable**. Campus Pizza also has a note payable to the Bank of Montreal for the money it borrowed to purchase its delivery truck. A **note payable** is supported by a written promise to pay a specific amount, at a specific time, in the future. Campus Pizza may also have wages payable to employees, Goods and Services Taxes (GST) payable and Provincial Sales Taxes (PST) payable to the federal and provincial governments, and property taxes payable to the municipality. All of these persons or entities that Campus Pizza owes money to are called its **creditors**.

A creditor who is not paid after a certain length of time has the legal right to force the liquidation of a business. In that case, the law requires that creditor claims be paid before ownership claims are paid.

Owner's Equity

The owner's claim on the assets of the company is known as **owner's equity**. It is equal to total assets minus total liabilities. Here is why: As shown in the accounting equation, assets are resources that can be claimed by either creditors or owners. To find out what belongs to owners, we subtract creditors' claims (the liabilities) from assets. The remainder—owner's equity—is the owner's claim on the assets of the business. This amount is also called **net assets**. Since the claims of creditors must be paid before ownership claims, the owner's equity is often called residual equity. If the equity is negative—that is, if total liabilities are more than total assets—the term "owner's deficiency" (or deficit) describes the shortage.

In a proprietorship, owner's equity is increased by investments made by the owner and decreased by withdrawals made by the owner. Owner's equity is also increased when a company generates a profit from business activities. Let's look at each of these equity components in more detail.

Investments. **Investments by the owner** are recorded as increases to what is known as the owner's capital account. Investments may be cash or other assets (e.g., a vehicle or computer) that are contributed by the owner. Accordingly, investments such as these result in an increase in an asset and an increase in owner's equity.

Drawings. An owner may withdraw cash (or other assets) for personal use. These drawings could be recorded as a direct decrease of owner's equity. However, it is generally considered better to use a separate account classification called **drawings** so that the total withdrawals for the accounting period can be determined. Drawings result in a decrease in an asset and a decrease in owner's equity.

Alternative terminology
Profit is also sometimes called *net income* or *earnings* or *net earnings*.

Profit. Revenues increase owner's equity, and expenses decrease owner's equity. **Profit** results when revenues are greater than expenses. Owner's equity then increases correspondingly. Conversely, if expenses are greater than revenues, a **loss** results and owner's equity decreases.

Revenues. **Revenues** result from business activities that are done to earn profit. Generally, revenues result from performing services, selling merchandise inventory, renting property, and lending money.

Revenues result in an increase in an asset (or a decrease in a liability when a customer has paid in advance) and an increase in owner's equity. They come from different sources and are given different names, depending on the type of business. Campus Pizza, for instance, has two categories of revenues: pizza sales and beverage sales. Common sources of revenue include sales, fees, services, commissions, interest, and rent.

Expenses. **Expenses** are the costs of assets that are consumed and services that are used in a company's ordinary business activities. Expenses result in a decrease in owner's equity and a corresponding decrease in an asset or an increase in a liability. Like revenues, there are many kinds of expenses and they are identified by various names, depending on the type of asset consumed or service used. For example, Campus Pizza recognizes (records) the following expenses: cost of ingredients (meat, flour, cheese, tomato paste, mushrooms, etc.), cost of beverages, wages expense, utility expense (electricity, gas, and water expense), telephone expense, delivery expense (gasoline, repairs, licences, insurance, etc.), supplies expense (napkins, detergents, aprons, etc.), rent expense, insurance expense, and interest expense.

Illustration 1-6 summarizes the transactions that change owner's equity.

→ Illustration 1-6

Transactions that increase and decrease owner's equity

Increases in owner's equity	Decreases in owner's equity
Investments by the owner	Drawings by the owner
Revenues	Expenses

In Illustration 1-7, we have expanded the basic accounting equation in Illustration 1-5 to show the different parts of owner's equity. This illustration shows the relationship between revenues, expenses, profit (or loss), and owner's equity.

→ Illustration 1-7

Expanded accounting equation

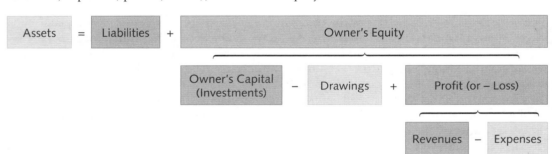

Accounting Differences by Type of Business Organization

Previously, you were introduced to different forms of business organizations: the proprietorship, partnership, and corporation. In the early chapters of this text, we focus mostly on proprietorships. Partnerships and corporations will be discussed in more detail in later chapters. Until that time, you need only a general understanding of the accounting distinctions between these types of organization.

Accounting for assets, liabilities, revenues, and expenses is the same, regardless of the form of business organization. The main distinction between the forms of organizations is found in (1) the terminology that is used to name the equity section, and (2) the accounting and reporting of the owner's investments and withdrawals. In Illustration 1-8, we summarize these differences.

	Proprietorship	Partnership	Corporation
Equity section called:	Owner's equity	Partners' equity	Shareholders' equity
Investments by owners added to:	Owner's capital	Partners' capital	Share capital
Profits added to:	Owner's capital	Partners' capital	Retained earnings
Withdrawals by owners called:	Drawings	Drawings	Dividends
Withdrawals deducted from:	Owner's capital	Partners' capital	Retained earnings

Illustration 1-8

Accounting differences by type of business organization

In a proprietorship, equity is summarized and reported in a one-line capital account. In a partnership, equity is summarized and reported in separate one-line capital accounts for each partner. In a corporation, investments by all of the shareholders are grouped together and called *share capital*. In a corporation, regardless of the number of shareholders, one account called Retained Earnings is used to record the accumulated profit (or earnings) of the company that have been retained (i.e., not paid out to shareholders) in the company.

In Illustration 1-5, when the assets, liabilities, and equity were reported for The Forzani Group, the equity was identified as owner's equity to keep the illustration simpler. Technically, since Forzani is a corporation, this equity should have been called *shareholders' equity*, as shown in Illustration 1-8.

BEFORE YOU GO ON . . .

Review It

1. What is the accounting equation?
2. What are assets, liabilities, and owner's equity?
3. Identify some of the assets that you own personally and some of the liabilities that you owe.
4. What are the different types of equity reported by each form of business organization?

Do It

Classify the following items as assets, liabilities, or owner's equity: (1) cash, (2) service revenue, (3) drawings, (4) accounts receivable, (5) accounts payable, and (6) salaries expense. For any items that affect owner's equity, please indicate whether these items increase or decrease equity.

Action Plan

- Understand that assets are resources owned by a business.
- Understand that liabilities are amounts owed by a business.
- Understand the items that affect owner's equity. Investments and revenues increase owner's equity. Drawings and expenses decrease owner's equity.

Solution

1. Cash is classified as an asset.
2. Service revenue is classified as revenue, which increases profit and ultimately owner's equity.
3. Drawings decrease owner's equity.
4. Accounts receivable are amounts that are due from customers, and are classified as an asset.
5. Accounts payable are amounts that are owed to creditors, and are classified as a liability.
6. Salaries expense is classified as an expense, which decreases profit and ultimately owner's equity.

Related exercise material: BE1–6, BE1–7, BE1–8, BE1–9, E1–3, E1–4, E1–5, E1–6, and E1–7.

Sometimes **Review It** questions are alone; other times they come with practice exercises. The **Do It** exercises like the one here ask you to put your new knowledge to work. They also outline an Action Plan you need to follow to do the exercise.

The Navigator

Using the Building Blocks

Transaction Analysis

We began the chapter by telling you that accounting is the information system that identifies, records, and communicates the economic events of an organization. The first step in accounting is to determine what the company should record. Not all events are recorded and reported as accounting transactions. Only events that cause changes in assets, liabilities, or owner's equity should be recorded. For example, suppose a new employee is hired. Should this event be recorded in the company's accounting records? The answer is no. While the hiring of an employee will lead to future accounting transactions (e.g., the payment of a salary after the work has been completed), no accounting transaction has occurred at the time of hiring.

An **accounting transaction** occurs when assets, liabilities, or owner's equity items change as the result of some economic event. Illustration 1-9 summarizes the process that is used to decide whether or not to record an event.

→ Illustration 1-9

Transaction identification process

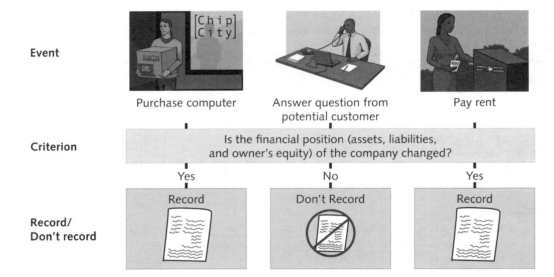

Once a transaction has been identified, it must be analyzed for its effect on the components of the accounting equation before it can be recorded. This analysis must identify the specific items that are affected and the amount of change in each item.

Each transaction must have a dual effect on the equation for the two sides of the accounting equation to be equal. For example, if an asset is increased, there must be a corresponding

1. decrease in another asset, or
2. increase in a liability, or
3. increase in owner's equity.

Two or more items could be affected when an asset is increased. For example, as one asset is increased by $10,000, another asset could decrease by $6,000, and a liability could increase by $4,000. Any change in a liability or owner's equity item also has to be analyzed like this.

As a general example, we will now look at transactions incurred by a computer programming business during its first month of operations. You should study these transactions until you are sure you understand them. They are not difficult, but they are important to your success in this course. Being able to analyze how transactions affect the accounting equation is essential for understanding accounting.

Transaction (1): Investment by Owner. Marc Doucet decides to open a computer programming business, which he names Softbyte. On September 1, 2011, he invests $15,000 cash in the business, which he deposits in a bank account opened under the name of Softbyte. This transaction results in an equal increase in both assets and owner's equity for Softbyte. In this case, there is an increase in the asset account, Cash, $15,000, and an equal increase in the owner's equity account, M. Doucet, Capital, $15,000. The effect of this transaction on the basic equation is:

	Assets	=	Liabilities +	Owner's Equity
				M. Doucet,
	Cash	=		Capital
(1)	+$15,000	=		+$15,000

When a specific **account title** is used, the account name is capitalized. The exception to this is in financial statements (introduced in the next section).

Notice that the two sides of the basic equation remain equal. Note also that investments by an owner are **not** revenues. The increase therefore has to be recorded as an investment in the owner's capital account rather than as revenue from operations.

Transaction (2): Purchase of Equipment for Cash. Softbyte purchases computer equipment for $7,000 cash. This transaction results in an equal increase and decrease in total assets, though the composition of assets changes. Cash is decreased by $7,000, and the asset account Equipment is increased by $7,000. The specific effect of this transaction and the cumulative effect of the first two transactions are:

		Assets			=	Liabilities	+	Owner's Equity
		Cash	+	Equipment	=			M. Doucet, Capital
	Old Balances	$15,000			=			$15,000
(2)		−7,000		+$7,000				
	New Balances	$ 8,000	+	$7,000	=			$15,000
			$15,000				$15,000	

Notice that total assets are still $15,000, and that Doucet's equity also remains at $15,000, the amount of his original investment.

Transaction (3): Purchase of Supplies on Credit. Softbyte purchases $1,600 of computer paper and other supplies that are expected to last several months from the Chuah Supply Company. Chuah Supply agrees to allow Softbyte to pay this bill next month (in October). This transaction is referred to as a purchase on account, or a credit purchase. Assets are increased because of the expected future benefits of using the paper and supplies. Liabilities are increased by the amount that is due to Chuah Supply Company. So, the asset Supplies is increased by $1,600 and the liability Accounts Payable is increased by the same amount. The effect on the equation is:

		Assets					=	Liabilities	+	Owner's Equity
								Accounts		M. Doucet,
		Cash	+	Supplies	+	Equipment	=	Payable	+	Capital
	Old Balances	$8,000			+	$7,000	=			$15,000
(3)				+$1,600				+$1,600		
	New Balances	$8,000	+	$1,600	+	$7,000	=	$1,600	+	$15,000
				$16,600					$16,600	

Total assets are now $16,600. This total is matched by a $1,600 creditor's claim and a $15,000 ownership claim.

Transaction (4): Services Provided for Cash. Softbyte receives $1,200 cash from customers for programming services it has provided. This transaction is Softbyte's main revenue-producing activity. Remember that revenue increases profit, which then increases owner's equity. Cash is increased by $1,200, and Service Revenue is increased by $1,200. We don't have room to give details for each individual revenue and expense account in this illustration, so revenues (and expenses when we get to them) will be summarized under one column heading for Revenues and one for Expenses. However, it is important to keep track of the account titles that are affected (e.g., Service Revenue), as they will be needed when financial statements are prepared in the next section. The new balances in the equation are:

		Assets			=	Liabilities +	Owner's Equity	
		Cash +	Supplies +	Equipment	=	Accounts Payable +	M. Doucet, Capital +	Revenues
	Old Balances	$8,000 +	$1,600 +	$7,000	=	$1,600 +	$15,000	
(4)		+1,200						+$1,200
	New Balances	$9,200 +	$1,600 +	$7,000	=	$1,600 +	$15,000 +	$1,200
		$17,800					$17,800	

The two sides of the equation balance at $17,800.

Transaction (5): Purchase of Advertising on Credit. Softbyte receives a bill for $250 from the local newspaper for advertising the opening of its business. It postpones payment of the bill until a later date. This transaction results in an increase in liabilities, through the Accounts Payable account, and a decrease in owner's equity, through the Advertising Expense account. The cost of advertising is an expense, and not an asset, because the benefits have already been used.

Note that owner's equity decreases because an expense is incurred, which in turn reduces profit and owner's equity. Here is the effect on the accounting equation:

		Assets			= Liabilities +	Owner's Equity		
		Cash +	Supplies +	Equipment =	Accounts Payable +	M. Doucet, Capital +	Revenues −	Expenses
	Old Balances	$9,200 +	$1,600 +	$7,000 =	$1,600 +	$15,000 +	$1,200	
(5)					+$250			−$250
	New Balances	$9,200 +	$1,600 +	$7,000 =	$1,850 +	$15,000 +	$1,200 −	$250
		$17,800				$17,800		

The two sides of the equation still balance at $17,800.

Expenses do not have to be paid in cash at the time they are incurred. When payment is made on the later date, the liability Accounts Payable will be decreased and the asset Cash will also be decreased [see transaction (8)].

Transaction (6): Services Provided for Cash and Credit. Softbyte provides $3,500 of programming services for customers. Cash of $1,500 is received from customers, and the balance of $2,000 is billed to customers on account. This transaction results in an equal increase in assets and owner's equity. Three specific items are affected: Cash is increased by $1,500; Accounts Receivable is increased by $2,000; and Service Revenue is increased by $3,500. The new balances are as follows:

		Assets				= Liabilities +	Owner's Equity		
		Cash +	Accounts Receivable +	Supplies +	Equipment =	Accounts Payable +	M. Doucet, Capital +	Revenues −	Expenses
	Old Balances	$ 9,200		+ $1,600 +	$7,000 =	$1,850 +	$15,000 +	$1,200 −	$250
(6)		+1,500	+$2,000					+3,500	
	New Balances	$10,700 +	$2,000 +	$1,600 +	$7,000 =	$1,850 +	$15,000 +	$4,700 −	$250
		$21,300					$21,300		

You might wonder why owner's equity is increased by $3,500 when only $1,500 has been collected. The reason is that the assets from earning revenues do not have to be in cash. Owner's equity is increased when revenues are earned. In Softbyte's case, revenues are earned when the service is provided. When collections on account are received at a later date, Cash will be increased and Accounts Receivable will be decreased [see transaction (9)].

Transaction (7): Payment of Expenses. The expenses paid in cash for September are store rent, $600; salaries of employees, $900; and utilities, $200. These payments result in an equal decrease in assets and owner's equity. Cash is decreased by $1,700 in total ($600 + $900 + $200) and expense accounts are increased by the same amount, which then decreases owner's equity. Here is the effect of these payments on the equation:

		Assets				=	Liabilities	+			Owner's Equity		
			Accounts						Accounts		M. Doucet,		
		Cash +	Receivable +	Supplies +	Equipment	=	Payable +		Capital	+	Revenues –	Expenses	
	Old Balances	$10,700 +	$2,000 +	$1,600 +	$7,000	=	$1,850 +		$15,000	+	$4,700 –	$ 250	
(7)		−600										−600	
		−900										−900	
		−200										−200	
	New Balances	$ 9,000 +	$2,000 +	$1,600 +	$7,000	=	$1,850 +		$15,000	+	$4,700 –	$1,950	
			$19,600							$19,600			

The two sides of the equation now balance at $19,600. Three lines are now needed in the analysis in order to show the different types of expenses that have been paid.

Transaction (8): Payment of Accounts Payable. Softbyte pays its $250 advertising bill in cash. Remember that the bill was previously recorded in transaction (5) as an increase in Accounts Payable and a decrease in owner's equity. This payment on account decreases the asset Cash by $250 and also decreases the liability Accounts Payable. The effect of this transaction on the equation is:

		Assets				=	Liabilities	+			Owner's Equity		
			Accounts						Accounts		M. Doucet,		
		Cash +	Receivable +	Supplies +	Equipment	=	Payable +		Capital	+	Revenues –	Expenses	
	Old Balances	$9,000 +	$2,000 +	$1,600 +	$7,000	=	$1,850 +		$15,000	+	$4,700 –	$1,950	
(8)		−250					−250						
	New Balances	$8,750 +	$2,000 +	$1,600 +	$7,000	=	$1,600 +		$15,000	+	$4,700 –	$1,950	
			$19,350							$19,350			

Notice that the payment of a liability for an expense that has previously been recorded does not affect owner's equity. This expense was recorded in transaction (5) and should not be recorded again.

Transaction (9): Receipt of Cash on Account. The sum of $600 in cash is received from some customers who were billed for services in transaction (6). This transaction does not change total assets, but it does change the composition of those assets. Cash is increased by $600, and Accounts Receivable is decreased by $600. The new balances are:

		Assets				=	Liabilities	+			Owner's Equity		
			Accounts						Accounts		M. Doucet,		
		Cash +	Receivable +	Supplies +	Equipment	=	Payable +		Capital	+	Revenues –	Expenses	
	Old Balances	$8,750 +	$2,000 +	$1,600 +	$7,000	=	$1,600 +		$15,000	+	$4,700 –	$1,950	
(9)		+600	−600										
	New Balances	$9,350 +	$1,400 +	$1,600 +	$7,000	=	$1,600 +		$15,000	+	$4,700 –	$1,950	
			$19,350							$19,350			

Note that a collection on account for services that were billed and recorded earlier does not affect owner's equity. Revenue was already recorded in transaction (6) and must not be recorded again.

Transaction (10): Signed Contract to Rent Equipment in October. Marc Doucet and an equipment supplier sign a contract for Softbyte to rent equipment for the months of October and November at the rate of $250 per month. Softbyte is to pay each month's rent at the start of the month. There is no effect on the accounting equation because the assets, liabilities, and owner's equity have not changed. An accounting transaction has not occurred. At this point Softbyte has not paid for anything, nor has it used the equipment and therefore has not incurred any expenses.

		Assets			=	Liabilities +		Owner's Equity		
		Accounts				Accounts	M. Doucet,			
	Cash +	Receivable +	Supplies +	Equipment	=	Payable +	Capital	+ Revenues	− Expenses	
Old Balances	$9,350 +	$1,400 +	$1,600 +	$7,000	=	$1,600 +	$15,000	+ $4,700	− $1,950	
(10) No entry										
New Balances	$9,350 +	$1,400 +	$1,600 +	$7,000	=	$1,600 +	$15,000	+ $4,700	− $1,950	
			$19,350					$19,350		

Note that the new balances are all identical to the old balances as nothing has changed.

Transaction (11): Withdrawal of Cash by Owner. Marc Doucet withdraws $1,300 in cash from the business for his personal use. This transaction results in an equal decrease in assets and owner's equity. The asset Cash is decreased by $1,300, and Drawings is increased by $1,300, which then decreases owner's equity, as follows:

		Assets			=	Liabilities +		Owner's Equity		
		Accounts				Accounts	M. Doucet,	M. Doucet,		
	Cash +	Receivable +	Supplies +	Equipment	=	Payable +	Capital	− Drawings	+ Revenues	− Expenses
Old Balances	$9,350 +	$1,400 +	$1,600 +	$7,000	=	$1,600 +	$15,000		+ $4,700	− $1,950
(11)	−1,300							−$1,300		
New Balances	$8,050 +	$1,400 +	$1,600 +	$7,000	=	$1,600 +	$15,000	− $1,300	+ $4,700	− $1,950
			$18,050					$18,050		

Note that both drawings and expenses reduce owner's equity, as shown in the accounting equation above. However, an owner's drawings are not expenses. Expenses are incurred for the purpose of earning revenue. Drawings do not generate revenue. They are a *disinvestment*; that is, the effect of an owner's cash withdrawal is the opposite of the effect of an owner's investment. Like owner's investments, drawings are not included when profit is determined.

Summary of Transactions

Softbyte's transactions are summarized in Illustration 1-10 to show their cumulative effect on the accounting equation. The transaction number and the specific effects of each transaction are indicated.

	Assets				=	Liabilities +		Owner's Equity			
		Accounts				Accounts	M. Doucet,	M. Doucet,			
	Cash +	Receivable +	Supplies +	Equipment	=	Payable +	Capital –	Drawings +	Revenues –	Expenses
(1)	+$15,000						+$15,000			
(2)	–7,000			+$7,000						
(3)			+$1,600			+$1,600				
(4)	+1,200								+$1,200	
(5)						+250				–$ 250
(6)	+1,500	+$2,000							+3,500	
(7)	–600									–600
	–900									–900
	–200									–200
(8)	–250					–250				
(9)	+600	–600								
(10)	No entry									
(11)	–1,300							–$1,300		
	$ 8,050 +	$1,400 +	$1,600 +	$7,000	=	$1,600 +	$15,000 –	$1,300 +	$4,700 –	$1,950
		$18,050						$18,050		

The illustration demonstrates some significant facts.

↑ Illustration 1-10

Tabular summary of Softbyte transactions

1. Each transaction must be analyzed for its effects on:
   (a) the three components (assets, liabilities, and owner's equity) of the accounting equation, and
   (b) specific items within each component.
2. The two sides of the equation must always be equal.

This section on transaction analysis is not the formal method of recording transactions. We will start illustrating that in Chapter 2. But understanding how transactions change assets, liabilities, and owner's equity is fundamental to understanding accounting and also business in general. No matter what area of an organization you work in, you will need to understand the impact of transactions on the organization if you want to move into more senior positions.

BEFORE YOU GO ON . . .

➡ Review It

1. Provide examples of two kinds of transactions: (a) an economic event that should be recorded; and (b) an event that should not be recorded.
2. If an asset increases, what are the three possible effects on the accounting equation? What are the possible effects if a liability increases?

➡ Do It

Transactions for the month of August by Verma & Co., a public accounting firm, are shown below. Prepare a tabular analysis (i.e., make a table) that shows the effects of these transactions on the accounting equation, like what is shown in Illustration 1-10.

1. The owner, Anil Verma, invested $25,000 of cash in the business.
2. Office equipment was purchased on credit, $7,000.
3. Services were performed for customers for $8,000. Of this amount, $2,000 was received in cash and $6,000 is due on account.
4. Rent of $850 was paid for the month.
5. Customers on account paid $4,000 (see transaction 3).
6. The owner withdrew $1,000 of cash for personal use.

Action Plan

- Analyze the effects of each transaction on the accounting equation.
- Use appropriate account names for the account titles (not descriptions).
- Keep the accounting equation in balance.

Solution

		Assets			=	Liabilities +		Owner's Equity			
	Cash	+	Accounts Receivable	+	Office Equipment	=	Accounts Payable	+	A. Verma, Capital	−	A. Verma, Drawings	+ Revenues − Expenses

	Cash	Accounts Receivable	Office Equipment	Accounts Payable	A. Verma, Capital	A. Verma, Drawings	Revenues	Expenses
1.	+$25,000				+$25,000			
2.			+$7,000	+$7,000				
3.	+2,000	+$6,000					+$8,000	
4.	−850							−$850
5.	+4,000	−4,000						
6.	−1,000					−$1,000		
	$29,150 +	$2,000 +	$7,000	= $7,000 +	$25,000 −	$1,000 +	$8,000 −	$850
		$38,150				$38,150		

The Navigator

Related exercise material: BE1–10, BE1–11, E1–8, E1–9, E1–10, and E1–11.

Financial Statements

Helpful hint The income statement, statement of owner's equity and cash flow statement all report information for a period of time. The balance sheet reports information at a point in time.

The next step in accounting is to communicate the information that has been identified, recorded, and summarized. The information from the summarized accounting data is communicated in four financial statements:

1. Income statement. An **income statement** presents the revenues and expenses, and the resulting profit or loss for a specific period of time.
2. Statement of owner's equity. A **statement of owner's equity** summarizes the changes in owner's equity for a specific period of time.
3. Balance sheet. A **balance sheet** reports the assets, liabilities, and owner's equity at a specific date.
4. Cash flow statement. A **cash flow statement** summarizes information about the cash inflows (receipts) and outflows (payments) for a specific period of time.

Each statement gives management, owners, and other interested parties relevant financial data. The financial statements of Softbyte and how they relate to each other are shown in Illustration 1-11. You will see that the statements are interrelated: (1) Profit of $2,750 shown on the income statement is added to the beginning balance of owner's capital in the statement of owner's equity. (2) Owner's capital of $16,450 at the end of the reporting period in the statement of owner's equity is also reported on the balance sheet. (3) Cash of $8,050 on the balance sheet is also reported on the cash flow statement.

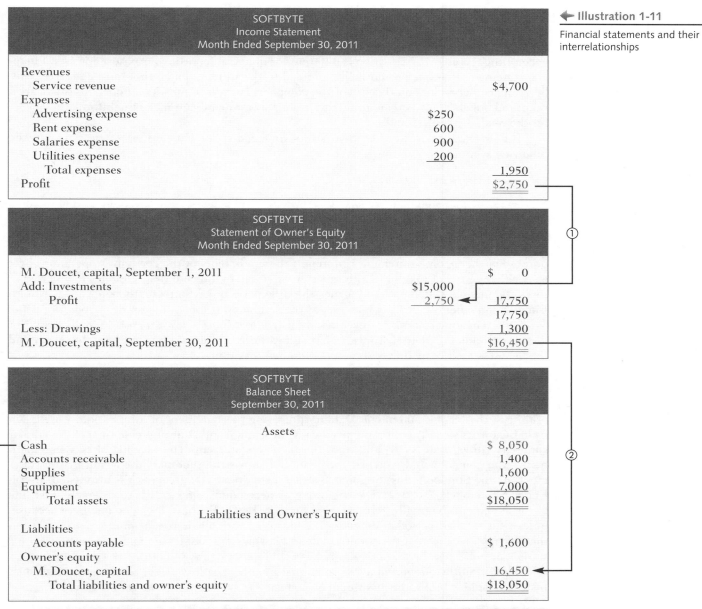

SOFTBYTE
Income Statement
Month Ended September 30, 2011

Revenues		
Service revenue		$4,700
Expenses		
Advertising expense	$250	
Rent expense	600	
Salaries expense	900	
Utilities expense	200	
Total expenses		1,950
Profit		$2,750

SOFTBYTE
Statement of Owner's Equity
Month Ended September 30, 2011

M. Doucet, capital, September 1, 2011		$ 0
Add: Investments	$15,000	
Profit	2,750	17,750
		17,750
Less: Drawings		1,300
M. Doucet, capital, September 30, 2011		$16,450

SOFTBYTE
Balance Sheet
September 30, 2011

Assets		
Cash		$ 8,050
Accounts receivable		1,400
Supplies		1,600
Equipment		7,000
Total assets		$18,050
Liabilities and Owner's Equity		
Liabilities		
Accounts payable		$ 1,600
Owner's equity		
M. Doucet, capital		16,450
Total liabilities and owner's equity		$18,050

SOFTBYTE
Cash Flow Statement
Month Ended September 30, 2011

Operating activities		
Cash receipts from customers	$ 3,300	
Cash payments for operating expenses	(1,950)	
Net cash provided by operating activities		$ 1,350
Investing activities		
Purchase of equipment	$ (7,000)	
Net cash used by investing activities		(7,000)
Financing activities		
Investments by owner	$15,000	
Drawings by owner	(1,300)	
Net cash provided by financing activities		13,700
Net increase in cash		8,050
Cash, September 1, 2011		0
Cash, September 30, 2011		$ 8,050

◄ **Illustration 1-11**

Financial statements and their interrelationships

① ② ③

Helpful hint 1. Profit is calculated first and is needed to determine the ending balance in owner's capital. 2. The ending balance in owner's capital is needed for preparing the balance sheet. 3. The cash shown on the balance sheet is needed for preparing the cash flow statement.

To keep it simple, we did not include cents in the dollar amounts we recorded in the Softbyte example in the previous section of the chapter. In reality, it is important to understand that cents should be, and are, used when transactions are recorded in a company's internal accounting records. The situation is different for financial reporting purposes, however. Financial statement amounts are normally rounded to the nearest dollar, thousand dollars, or million dollars, depending on the size of the company. Forzani rounds its numbers to the nearest thousand dollars. This is done to remove unimportant detail and make the information easier for the reader to understand.

The essential features of Softbyte's four financial statements are briefly described in the following sections.

Income Statement

Alternative terminology
The income statement is
sometimes called the
statement of earnings or
statement of operations.

Softbyte's income statement reports the revenues and expenses for a specific period of time. The income statement is prepared from the data in the owner's equity columns (specifically the Revenues and Expenses columns) of Illustration 1-10. The statement's heading names the company and type of statement, and shows the time period covered by the statement. The main purpose of the income statement is to report the profitability of the company's operations over a specified period of time (a month, quarter, or year). To indicate that it applies to a period of time, the income statement date names the time period. For Softbyte, this appears as Month Ended September 30, 2011, which means the statement is for a one-month period.

On the income statement, revenues are listed first, followed by expenses. Finally, profit (or loss) is determined. Note that investment and withdrawal transactions between the owner and the business are not included in the measurement of profit.

Statement of Owner's Equity

Softbyte's statement of owner's equity reports the changes in owner's equity for the same period of time as the income statement. Data for preparing the statement of owner's equity are taken from the owner's equity columns (specifically the Capital and Drawings columns) of the tabular summary (Illustration 1-10) and from the income statement. The heading of this statement names the company and type of statement, and shows the time period covered by the statement. As the time period is the same as it is for the income statement, it is also dated Month Ended September 30, 2011. The beginning owner's equity amount is shown on the first line of the statement. Normally, zero balances are not shown. We have included one here because, unless it is the first period of operations, companies normally have a beginning balance. Then the owner's investments, the profit, and the drawings are identified. The information in this statement indicates why owner's equity has increased or decreased during the period.

What if Softbyte reported a loss in its first month? The loss would reduce owner's capital. Instead of adding profit, the loss would be deducted in the same section as owner's drawings.

Balance Sheet

Alternative terminology
The balance sheet is sometimes called the *statement of financial position.*

Softbyte's balance sheet reports the assets, liabilities, and owner's equity at a specific date. The balance sheet is prepared from the Assets and Liabilities column headings and the month-end data shown in the last line of the tabular summary (Illustration 1-10). The heading of a balance sheet must identify the company, statement, and date. The balance sheet is like a snapshot of the company's financial condition at a specific moment in time (usually the end of a month, quarter, or year). To indicate that the balance sheet is at a specific point in time, the date only mentions the point in time (there is no indication of a time period). For Softbyte, the date is September 30, 2011. Sometimes, the words "as at" precede the balance sheet date. Notice that the assets are listed at the top, followed by liabilities and owner's equity. Total assets must equal total liabilities and owner's equity. In other words, the balance sheet must balance.

Cash Flow Statement

Softbyte's cash flow statement gives information about the cash receipts and cash payments for a specific period of time. To help investors, creditors, and others analyze a company's cash, the cash flow statement reports the following: (1) the cash effects of the company's operating activities during a period; (2) the cash inflows and outflows from investing transactions (e.g., the purchase and sale of land, buildings, and equipment); (3) the cash inflows and outflows from financing transactions (e.g., borrowing and repayments of debt, and investments and withdrawals by the owner); (4) the net increase or decrease in cash during the period; and (5) the cash amount at the end of the period.

Reporting the sources, uses, and change in cash is useful because investors, creditors, and others want to know what is happening to a company's most liquid resource, its money. The cash flow statement gives answers to the following simple but important questions:

1. Where did the cash come from during the period?
2. What was the cash used for during the period?
3. What was the change in the cash balance during the period?

Softbyte's cash flow statement, shown in Illustration 1-11, is for the same period of time as the income statement and the statement of owner's equity. Note that the positive numbers indicate cash inflows or increases. Numbers in parentheses indicate cash outflows or decreases. Parentheses are often used in financial statements to indicate negative, or opposite, numbers. As shown in the statement, cash increased by $8,050 during the month. Operating activities increased cash by $1,350. Investing activities decreased cash by $7,000. Financing activities increased cash by $13,700. At this time, you do not need to know how these amounts are determined. In Chapter 17 we will look at the cash flow statement in detail.

Using the Information in the Financial Statements

Illustration 1-11 introduced the financial statements for Softbyte. Every set of financial statements also has explanatory notes and supporting schedules that are an essential part of the statements. For example, as previously mentioned, at the very least a company will have to indicate if it is following IFRS or Canadian GAAP for Private Enterprises.

Public corporations issue their financial statements and supplementary materials in an annual report. The **annual report** is a document that includes useful non-financial information about the company, as well as financial information.

Non-financial information may include a management discussion of the company's mission, goals, and objectives; market position; and the people involved in the company. Financial information may include a review of current operations and a historical summary of key financial figures and ratios, in addition to comparative financial statements. Public company financial statements are audited and include the auditors' report. There is also a statement of management responsibility for the statements.

Now is a good time to go to Appendix A at the end of this textbook, where you will find The Forzani Group Ltd.'s financial statements taken from its annual report. Carefully examine the format and content of each financial statement outlined earlier in Illustration 1-11. What similarities can you find between the financial statements in Illustration 1-11 and the more complicated financial statements for Forzani?

You will see that The Forzani Group's transactions have been accumulated for the year ended February 1, 2009, and grouped together in categories. When similar transactions are grouped together, they are being reported in aggregate. By presenting recorded data in aggregate, the accounting information system simplifies a large number of transactions. As a result, the company's activities are easier to understand and are more meaningful. This simplification does mean less detail, however. The Forzani Group's financial statements are highly condensed and some critics would argue that the statements are too simple. Still, Forzani is not the only organization that reports in this way. Most companies report condensed information for two reasons: it's simpler, and it also avoids revealing significant details to competitors.

We will ask you to look at Forzani's statements at different times throughout the text. At this point, they will probably look complex and confusing to you. By the end of this course, however, you'll be surprised at your ability to understand and interpret them.

Alternative terminology
The cash flow statement is sometimes called the *statement of cash flows*.

For **Review It** questions about The Forzani Group, you need to use Forzani's financial statements in Appendix A at the end of this textbook.

The Navigator

BEFORE YOU GO ON . . .

→ Review It

1. Describe the income statement, statement of owner's equity, balance sheet, and cash flow statement.
2. Why does it matter in which order the financial statements are prepared?
3. Explain how Forzani's financial statements are interrelated: identify specific accounts and amounts. The answer to this question is given at the end of the chapter.
4. What information is normally found in an annual report?

Related exercise material: BE1–12, BE1–13, BE1–14, BE1–15, BE1–16, BE1–17, BE1-18, E1–12, E1–13, E1–14, E1–15, and E1–16.

Demonstration Problem

Demonstration Problems

The **Demonstration Problem** is a final review before you work on the assignment material. The problem-solving strategies in the margins give you tips about how to approach the problem. The solutions show both the form and the content of complete answers.

Action Plan

• Make sure that assets equal liabilities plus owner's equity in each transaction.
• Investments and revenues increase owner's equity. Withdrawals and expenses decrease owner's equity.

Raman Balakra opens his own law office on July 1, 2011. During the first month of operations, the following transactions occurred:
1. Invested $11,000 in cash in the law practice.
2. Hired a legal assistant to work part-time for $500 per month.
3. Paid $800 for July rent on office space.
4. Purchased office equipment on account, $3,000.
5. Provided legal services to clients for cash, $1,500.
6. Borrowed $700 cash from a bank on a note payable.
7. Provided legal services to a client on account, $2,000.
8. Collected $500 of the amount owed by a client on account (see transaction 7).
9. Paid monthly expenses: salaries, $500; utilities, $300; and telephone, $100.
10. Withdrew $1,000 cash for personal use.

Instructions
(a) Prepare a tabular analysis of the transactions.
(b) Prepare the income statement, statement of owner's equity, and balance sheet for Raman Balakra, Barrister & Solicitor.

Solution to Demonstration Problem

(a)

Transaction	Assets			=	Liabilities			Owner's Equity				
	Cash	+ Accounts Receivable	+ Equipment	=	Note Payable	+ Accounts Payable	+	R. Balakra Capital	− R. Balakra, Drawings	+ Revenues	− Expenses
(1)	+$11,000							+$11,000			
(2) No Entry											
(3)	−800										−$800
(4)			+$3,000			+$3,000					
(5)	+1,500									+$1,500	
(6)	+700				+$700						
(7)		+$2,000								+2,000	
(8)	+500	−500									
(9)	−500										−500
	−300										−300
	−100										−100
(10)	−1,000								−$1,000		
	$11,000 +	$1,500 +	$3,000	=	$700 +	$3,000 +		$11,000 −	$1,000 +	$3,500 −	$1,700

$15,500 $15,500

(b)

RAMAN BALAKRA, BARRISTER & SOLICITOR
Income Statement
Month Ended July 31, 2011

Revenues		
Fees earned		$3,500
Expenses		
Rent expense	$800	
Salaries expense	500	
Utilities expense	300	
Telephone expense	100	
Total expenses		1,700
Profit		$1,800

RAMAN BALAKRA, BARRISTER & SOLICITOR
Statement of Owner's Equity
Month Ended July 31, 2011

R. Balakra, capital, July 1, 2011		$ 0
Add: Investments	$11,000	
Profit	1,800	12,800
		12,800
Less: Drawings		1,000
R. Balakra, capital, July 31, 2011		$11,800

RAMAN BALAKRA, BARRISTER & SOLICITOR
Balance Sheet
July 31, 2011

Assets	
Cash	$11,000
Accounts receivable	1,500
Equipment	3,000
Total assets	$15,500
Liabilities and Owner's Equity	
Liabilities	
Note payable	$ 700
Accounts payable	3,000
Total liabilities	3,700
Owner's equity	
R. Balakra, capital	11,800
Total liabilities and owner's equity	$15,500

Action Plan (continued)

- Prepare the financial statements in the order listed.
- The income statement shows revenues and expenses for a period of time.
- Profit (or loss) is calculated on the income statement and carried forward to the statement of owner's equity.
- The statement of owner's equity shows the changes in owner's equity for the same period of time as the income statement.
- The owner's capital at the end of the period is carried forward from the statement of owner's equity to the balance sheet.
- The balance sheet reports assets, liabilities, and owner's equity at a specific date.

The Navigator

Summary of Study Objectives

1. *Identify the use and users of accounting.* Accounting is the information system that identifies, records, and communicates the economic events of an organization to a wide variety of interested users. Good accounting is important to people both inside and outside the organization. Internal users, such as management, use accounting information to plan, control, and evaluate business operations. External users include investors and creditors, among others. Accounting data are used by investors (owners) to decide whether to buy, hold, or sell their financial interests. Creditors (suppliers and bankers) evaluate the risks of granting credit or lending money based on the accounting information. Other groups that use accounting information are taxing authorities, regulatory agencies, customers, labour unions, and economic planners. For our economic system to function smoothly, reliable and ethical accounting and financial reporting are critical. The most common examples of business organizations are proprietorship, partnership, and corporation.

2. *Explain Canadian accounting standards and apply basic accounting concepts.* Generally accepted accounting principles are a common set of guidelines that are used to prepare and report accounting information. In Canada, as of 2011 there are two sets of standards or GAAP. Publicly accountable enterprises follow International Financial Reporting Standards (IFRS) and private enterprises have the choice of following IFRS or Canadian GAAP for Private Enterprises.

The going concern assumption presumes that a business will continue operations for enough time to use its assets for their intended purpose and to complete its commitments. The economic entity assumption requires the activities of each economic entity to be kept separate from the activities of its owner and other economic entities. Recognition is the process of recording items and measurement is the process of determining the amount that should be recognized. The cost principle states that assets should be recorded at their historical (original) cost. The monetary unit assumption requires that only transaction data that can be expressed as an amount of money be included in the accounting records, and it assumes that the monetary unit is stable.

3. *Use the accounting equation and explain the meaning of assets, liabilities, and owner's equity.* The accounting equation is: Assets = Liabilities + Owner's Equity. Assets are resources owned by a business that are capable of providing future services or benefits.

Liabilities are current obligations arising from past events to make future payments of assets or services. Owner's equity is the owner's claim on the company's assets and is equal to total assets minus total liabilities. Owner's equity is increased by investments by the owner and by revenues. It is decreased by drawings and expenses. Revenues are the increase in assets, or decrease in liabilities, that result from business activities that are done to earn profit. Expenses are the cost of assets consumed or services used in a company's ordinary business activities. Drawings are withdrawals of cash or other assets from the business for the owner's personal use.

4. *Analyze the effects of business transactions on the accounting equation.* Each business transaction must have a dual effect on the accounting equation. For example, if an individual asset is increased, there must be a corresponding (1) decrease in another asset, (2) increase in a liability, and/or (3) increase in owner's equity.

5. *Prepare financial statements.* An income statement presents the revenues and expenses, and the resulting profit or loss, of a company for a specific period of time. A statement of owner's equity summarizes the changes in owner's equity that have occurred for a specific period of time. A balance sheet reports the assets, liabilities, and owner's equity of a business at a specific date. A cash flow statement summarizes information about the cash inflows (receipts) and outflows (payments) for a specific period of time.

The Navigator

Glossary

WILEY PLUS Glossary
Key Term Matching Activity

Accounting   The information system that identifies, records, and communicates the economic events of an organization to a wide variety of interested users. (p. 2)

Accounting equation   Assets = Liabilities + Owner's Equity. (p. 10)

Accounting transaction   An economic event that is recorded in the accounting records because it changed the assets, liabilities, or owner's equity items of the organization. (p. 14)

Accounts payable   A liability created by buying services or products on credit. It is an obligation to pay cash to a supplier in the future. (p. 11)

Accounts receivable   An asset created when selling services or products to customers who promise to pay cash in the future. (p. 11)

Annual report   Information that a company gives each year to its shareholders and other interested parties about its operations and financial position. It includes the financial statements and auditors' report, in addition to information and reports by management. (p. 23)

Assets   Resources owned by a business that are capable of providing future services or benefits. (p. 11)

Balance sheet   A financial statement that reports the assets, liabilities, and owner's equity at a specific date. (p. 20)

Cash flow statement   A financial statement that provides information about the cash inflows (receipts) and cash outflows (payments) for a specific period of time. (p. 20)

Corporation   A business organized as a separate legal entity under corporation law, with ownership divided into transferable shares. (p. 6)

Cost principle   An accounting principle that states that assets should be recorded at their historical (original) cost. (p. 9)

Creditors   All of the persons or entities that a company owes money to. (p. 11)

Drawings Withdrawals of cash or other assets from an unincorporated business for the owner's personal use. Drawings reduce owner's equity. (p. 11)

Economic entity assumption An assumption that requires the activities of the entity to be kept separate and distinct from the activities of its owner and of all other economic entities. (p. 9)

Expenses The cost of assets consumed or services used in a company's ordinary business activities. Expenses result in a reduction of owner's equity. (p. 12)

Fair value The amount of the consideration that would be agreed upon in an arm's-length transaction between knowledgeable, willing parties who are under no compulsion to act. (p. 9)

Generally accepted accounting principles (GAAP) An accepted set of accounting standards that includes broad principles, practices, as well as rules and procedures. These standards indicate how to report economic events. (p. 7)

Going concern assumption An assumption that a company will continue to operate in the foreseeable future. (p. 8)

Income statement A financial statement that presents the revenues and expenses and resulting profit (or loss) for a specific period of time. (p. 20)

Investments by the owner The increase in owner's equity that results from assets put into the business by the owner. (p. 11)

Liabilities Current obligations, arising from past events, to make future payments of assets or services. (p. 11)

Limited liability The legal principle that the owners' liability for the debts of the business is limited to the amount they invested in the business. (p. 6)

Loss The amount by which expenses are greater than revenues. A loss decreases owner's equity. (p. 12)

Measurement The process of determining the amount that should be recognized. (p. 9)

Monetary unit assumption An assumption that states that only transaction data that can be expressed as an amount of money may be included in the accounting records. It is also assumed that the monetary unit is stable. (p. 9)

Net assets Total assets minus total liabilities; equal to owner's equity. (p. 11)

Note payable A liability supported by a written promise to pay a specific amount, at a specific time, in the future. (p. 11)

Owner's equity The owner's claim on the assets of the company, which is equal to total assets minus total liabilities. (p. 11)

Partnership An association of two or more persons to carry on as co-owners of a business for profit. (p. 6)

Profit The amount by which revenues are greater than expenses. Profit increases owner's equity. (p. 12)

Proprietorship A small business owned by one person. (p. 5)

Publicly accountable enterprises Publicly traded companies as well as securities brokers and dealers, banks, and credit unions whose role is to hold assets for the public as part of their primary business. (p. 7)

Recognition The process of recording a transaction in the accounting records. (p. 9)

Revenues The increase in assets, or decrease in liabilities, that results from business activities that are done to earn profit. (p. 12)

Statement of owner's equity A financial statement that summarizes the changes in owner's equity for a specific period of time. (p. 20)

Unlimited liability The principle that the owners of a business are personally liable (responsible) for all debts of the business. (p. 5)

Self-Study Questions

Answers are at the end of the chapter.

(SO 1) K 1. Which of the following statements about users of accounting information is incorrect?
   (a) Management is an internal user.
   (b) Taxing authorities are external users.
   (c) Creditors are external users.
   (d) Regulatory authorities are internal users.

2. Which of the following characteristics are related (SO 1) K to corporations as opposed to partnerships and proprietorships?
   (a) Simple to form, unlimited legal liability, limited life
   (b) Limited legal liability, limited life, income taxes on profit paid by the organization
   (c) More than one owner, income taxes on profit paid by the owners, unlimited legal liability
   (d) Income taxes paid by the organization, limited legal liability, indefinite life

(SO 2) K   3. Which of the following statements about International Financial Reporting Standards (IFRS) is correct?
   (a) Canada is following the lead of the United States in adopting IFRS.
   (b) Under IFRS, companies that operate in more than one country must produce separate financial statements for each of those countries.
   (c) All Canadian publicly accountable enterprises must use IFRS effective January 1, 2011.
   (d) Canadian private enterprises are not allowed to use IFRS. They must use Canadian GAAP for Private Enterprises.

(SO 2) C   4. Which of the following statements is incorrect?
   (a) Under the going concern assumption, it is assumed that a company ends its operations once a year for reporting purposes.
   (b) The economic entity assumption states that the activities of the entity should be kept separate from those of its owner and other entities.
   (c) Under the cost principle, assets continue to be recorded at their historical (original) cost, even if the fair value has increased.
   (d) An important part of the monetary unit assumption is that the monetary unit is assumed to remain stable.

(SO 3) AP   5. As at December 31, after its first year of operations, Stoneland Company has assets of $8,500; revenues of $6,000; expenses of $3,500; owner's capital of $5,000; and drawings of $500. What are the liabilities for Stoneland Company as at December 31?
   (a) $1,500
   (b) $2,500
   (c) $500
   (d) $3,500

(SO 3) C   6. Profit will result during a time period when:
   (a) assets are greater than liabilities.
   (b) assets are greater than revenues.
   (c) expenses are greater than revenues.
   (d) revenues are greater than expenses.

(SO 4) AP   7. The effects on the accounting equation of performing services on account are:
   (a) increased assets and decreased owner's equity.
   (b) increased assets and increased owner's equity.
   (c) increased assets and increased liabilities.
   (d) increased liabilities and increased owner's equity.

(SO 5) AP   8. Genesis Company buys a $10,000 machine on credit. Initially, this transaction will only affect the:
   (a) income statement.
   (b) balance sheet.
   (c) income statement and statement of owner's equity.
   (d) income statement, statement of owner's equity, and balance sheet.

(SO 5) K   9. The financial statement that reports assets, liabilities, and owner's equity is the:
   (a) income statement.
   (b) statement of owner's equity.
   (c) balance sheet.
   (d) cash flow statement.

(SO 5) C   10. Which of the following items is *not* reported on the statement of owner's equity?
   (a) Investments by the owner
   (b) Drawings
   (c) Profit
   (d) Cash flow from operating activities

The Navigator

Questions

(SO 1) C   1. "Accounting is ingrained in our society and it is vital to our economic system." Do you agree? Explain.

(SO 1) C   2. Why should everyone study accounting whether they are going to be an accountant or not?

(SO 1) C   3. (a) Distinguish between internal and external users of accounting data. (b) How does accounting provide relevant data for these users?

(SO 1) C   4. Why is ethics important to the accounting profession? To statement users?

(SO 1) C   5. Explain the differences between the following forms of business organization: (a) proprietorship, (b) partnership, (c) public corporation, and (d) private corporation.

(SO 2) C   6. Veronica argues that all Canadian companies should follow the same set of generally accepted accounting principles. Explain to Veronica why there are two sets of standards in Canada and how she can tell what standards the company is using.

(SO 2) C   7. Explain the going concern assumption and how a user of financial statements can tell if the company is a going concern or not.

(SO 2) C   8. How does the going concern assumption support the cost principle?

(SO 2) K   9. What is the economic entity assumption?

(SO 2) C 10. What is the monetary unit assumption? What type of information is not included in the financial statements because of this assumption?

(SO 3) K 11. What is the accounting equation? What is the expanded accounting equation?

(SO 3) K 12. (a) Define assets, liabilities, and owner's equity. (b) What items increase and decrease owner's equity?

(SO 3) K 13. What is the difference between Accounts Payable and Accounts Receivable? Between Accounts Payable and Notes Payable?

(SO 3) K 14. Explain the difference in accounting for the three forms of a business organization: (a) a proprietorship, (b) a partnership, and (c) a corporation.

(SO 4) C 15. Are the following events recorded in the accounting records? Explain your answer in each case.
(a) The owner of the company dies.
(b) Supplies are purchased on account.
(c) An employee is terminated.
(d) The company wins an award as one of the top 50 companies in Canada to work for.

(SO 4) C 16. Can a business have a transaction in which only the left (assets) side of the accounting equation is affected? If yes, give an example.

(SO 4) AP 17. Explain how the following transactions affect the accounting equation:
(a) Paid cash for employees' salaries.
(b) Purchased equipment and signed a note payable for the amount owing.

(c) Owner withdrew cash from the business.
(d) Performed services on account.
(e) Collected amount owing from a customer for services previously provided.

(SO 4) AP 18. Paul Dumas withdrew $10,000 from his business, Dumas Pharmacy, which is organized as a proprietorship. Dumas' accountant recorded this withdrawal as an increase in an expense and a decrease in cash. Is this treatment correct? Why or why not?

(SO 5) C 19. A company's profit appears directly on the income statement and the statement of owner's equity. It is also included indirectly in the company's balance sheet. Do you agree or disagree? Explain.

(SO 5) C 20. Explain how the following pairs of financial statements are interrelated: (a) income statement and statement of owner's equity, (b) statement of owner's equity and balance sheet, and (c) balance sheet and cash flow statement.

(SO 5) C 21. André is puzzled as he reads Forzani's financial statements. He notices that the numbers have all been rounded to the nearest thousand. He thought financial statements were supposed to be accurate and he is now wondering what happened to the rest of the money. Respond to André's concern.

(SO 5) C 22. Forzani's year end is not a fixed date; rather, it can vary slightly from one year to the next. What possible problems does this create for financial statement users?

When the financial results of **real companies** are used in the end-of-chapter material, the company's name is shown in red.

Brief Exercises

BE1-1 A list of decisions made by different users of accounting information follows:

1. Decide whether the company pays fair wages.
2. Decide whether the company can pay its obligations.
3. Decide whether a marketing proposal will be cost-effective.
4. Decide whether the company's profit will permit an increase in drawings.
5. Decide how the company should finance its operations.

Identify users of accounting information.
(SO 1) K

The different users are identified in the table that follows. (a) Insert the number (1–5) of the kind of decision described above that each user would likely make. (b) Indicate whether the user is internal or external.

User	(a) Kind of Decision	(b) Internal or External User
Owner		
Marketing manager		
Creditor		
Chief financial officer		
Labour union		

Discuss ethical issues.
(SO 1) AN

BE1–2   Imagine and describe an ethical dilemma that each of the following individuals might encounter:

1. A student in an introductory accounting course
2. A production supervisor
3. A salesperson
4. A banker
5. The prime minister of Canada

Identify forms of business organization.
(SO 1) C

BE1–3   Match each of the following forms of business organization with the correct set of characteristics: proprietorship (PP), partnership (P), and corporation (C).

(a) ___ Shared control; combined skills and resources
(b) ___ Easier to transfer ownership and raise funds; no personal liability; entity pays income tax
(c) ___ Simple to set up; founder keeps control

Identify application of IFRS and Canadian GAAP for Private Enterprises.
(SO 2) C

BE1–4   For each of the following statements related to International Financial Reporting Standards (IFRS) and/or Canadian GAAP for Private Enterprises, indicate whether the statement is true or false by placing a T or an F in the blank at the start of each statement.

(a) ___ All publicly accountable enterprises must follow IFRS as of 2011.
(b) ___ All private enterprises must follow Canadian GAAP for Private Enterprises as of 2011.
(c) ___ Under both IFRS and Canadian GAAP for Private Enterprises, there are more requirements to provide information in the financial statements than there were under traditional Canadian GAAP.
(d) ___ Private companies that are larger than the prescribed threshold will have to use IFRS.
(e) ___ Companies will be required to include a note in their financial statements stating if they are using IFRS or Canadian GAAP for Private Enterprises
(f) ___ Using IFRS may help Canadian public companies attract investors from around the globe.

Identify GAAP concepts.
(SO 2) C

BE1–5   Match each of the following terms with the best description below:

1. Generally accepted accounting principles
2. Going concern assumption
3. Economic entity assumption
4. Cost principle
5. Monetary unit assumption

(a) ___ Transactions are recorded in terms of units of money.
(b) ___ Transactions are recorded based on the actual amount received or paid.
(c) ___ Accounting for a business excludes any personal transactions of the owner and the transactions of any other entity.
(d) ___ These are the broad principles and practices, as well as rules and procedures, that indicate how to report economic events.
(e) ___ Businesses are expected to continue operating indefinitely.

Solve accounting equation.
(SO 3) AP

BE1–6   Presented below is the accounting equation. Determine the missing amounts:

Assets	=	Liabilities	+	Owner's Equity
$95,000		$54,000		(a)
(b)		$120,000		$71,000
$49,000		(c)		$22,000

Solve accounting equation.
(SO 3) AP

BE1–7   Use the accounting equation to answer each of the following questions:

(a) Cai Company has liabilities of $220,000. The balance in M. Cai, Capital is $100,000; in drawings, $40,000; revenues, $440,000; and expenses, $330,000. What is the amount of Cai Company's total assets?

(b) Pereira Company has total assets of $80,000. The balance in Karen Pereira's Capital is $30,000; in drawings, $7,000; revenues, $55,000; and expenses, $45,000. What is the amount of the company's total liabilities?

(c) Yellow Co. has total assets of $800,000 and its liabilities are equal to one quarter of its total assets. What is the amount of Yellow Co.'s owner's equity?

BE1–8 At the beginning of the year, Lam Company had total assets of $750,000 and total liabilities of $500,000. Answer each of the following independent questions:

Solve accounting equation.
(SO 3) AP

(a) If total assets increased by $120,000 during the year and total liabilities decreased by $90,000, what is the amount of owner's equity at the end of the year?

(b) During the year, total liabilities decreased by $85,000. The company incurred a loss of $50,000. Lifei Lam made an additional investment of $100,000 and made no withdrawals. What is the amount of total assets at the end of the year?

(c) Total assets increased by $90,000 during the year. Profit was $175,000. There were no additional owner's investments, but Lifei Lam withdrew $60,000. What is the amount of total liabilities at the end of the year?

(d) Total assets increased by $25,000, and total liabilities decreased by $50,000. There were no additional owner's investments, and Lifei Lam withdrew $40,000. What is the amount of profit or loss for the year?

BE1–9 Indicate whether each of the following items is an asset (A), a liability (L), or part of owner's equity (OE):

Identify assets, liabilities, and owner's equity.
(SO 3) AP

(a) ___ Cash
(b) ___ Accounts payable
(c) ___ Drawings
(d) ___ Accounts receivable
(e) ___ Supplies
(f) ___ Equipment
(g) ___ E. Johnston, drawings
(h) ___ Salaries payable
(i) ___ Service revenue
(j) ___ E. Johnston, capital
(k) ___ Rent expense
(l) ___ Note payable

BE1–10 Presented below are eight business transactions. Indicate whether the transactions increased (+), decreased (–), or had no effect (NE) on each element of the accounting equation.

Determine effects of transactions on accounting equation.
(SO 4) AP

1. Purchased $250 of supplies on account.
2. Performed $500 of services on account.
3. Paid $300 of operating expenses.
4. Paid $250 cash on account for the supplies purchased in item 1 above.
5. Invested $1,000 cash in the business.
6. Owner withdrew $400 cash.
7. Hired an employee to start working the following month.
8. Received $500 from a customer who had been billed previously in item 2 above.

Use the following format, in which the first one has been done for you as an example:

Transaction	Assets	Liabilities	Owner's Equity Capital	Drawings	Revenues	Expenses
1.	+$250	+$250	NE	NE	NE	NE

BE1–11 Classify each of the following items as owner's investments (I), drawings (D), revenue (R), expenses (E), or as having no effect on owner's equity (NE):

Determine effects of transactions on owner's equity.
(SO 4) AP

(a) ___ Costs incurred for advertising

(b) ___ Commission earnings
(c) ___ Equipment received from the company owner
(d) ___ Amounts paid to employees
(e) ___ Cash paid to purchase equipment
(f) ___ Services performed on account
(g) ___ Rent received
(h) ___ Utilities incurred
(i) ___ Cash distributed to company owner
(j) ___ Collection of an account receivable

Classify accounts.
(SO 3, 5) C

BE1–12   Below are some items found in the financial statements of Kaustev Sen, M.D. Indicate (a) whether each of the following items is an asset (A), liability (L), or part of owner's equity (OE); and (b) which financial statement—income statement (IS), statement of owner's equity (OE), or balance sheet (BS)—it would be reported on. The first one has been done for you as an example.

	(a)	(b)
1. Accounts receivable	A	BS
2. Wages payable	___	___
3. Wages expense	___	___
4. Office supplies	___	___
5. Supplies expense	___	___
6. K. Sen, capital (opening balance)	___	___
7. K. Sen, capital (ending balance)	___	___
8. Service revenue	___	___
9. Equipment	___	___
10. Note payable	___	___
11. Cash	___	___
12. K. Sen, drawings	___	___

Determine missing items in owner's equity.
(SO 3, 5) AP

BE1–13   Presented below is information from the statements of owner's equity for Kirkham Consulting for the first three years of operation. Determine the missing amounts:

	2010	2011	2012
P. Kirkham, capital, January 1	$ 0	$63,000	(c)
Investment in the year	50,000	0	20,000
Profit (loss) for the year	25,000	(b)	17,000
Drawings in the year	(a)	25,000	12,000
P. Kirkham, capital, December 31	63,000	53,000	(d)

Identify elements of financial statements.
(SO 5) C

BE1–14   The Calgary Exhibition and Stampede Limited has the following selected accounts in its corporate financial statements. In each case, identify whether the item would appear on the balance sheet (BS) or income statement (IS).

(a) ___ Accounts receivable
(b) ___ Inventory
(c) ___ Interest expense
(d) ___ Share capital
(e) ___ Equipment
(f) ___ Stampede revenue
(g) ___ Agricultural activities revenue
(h) ___ Accounts payable and accrued liabilities
(i) ___ Cash and short-term deposits
(j) ___ Administration, marketing, and park services expenses
(k) ___ Food and beverage revenue

BE1–15 Schwinghamer Enterprises had a capital balance of $125,000 at the beginning of the period. At the end of the accounting period, the capital balance was $150,000.

Calculate profit.
(SO 5) AP

(a) If there were no additional investments or withdrawals, what is the profit for the period?

(b) Assuming there was an additional investment of $5,000 but no withdrawals, what is the profit for the period?

(c) Assuming there was an additional investment of $10,000 and a withdrawal of $7,000, what is the profit for the period?

BE1–16 Portage Company is owned and operated by Nate Hudson. In alphabetical order below are the financial statement items for Portage Company. Using the appropriate items, prepare an income statement for the month ended August 31, 2011.

Prepare an income statement.
(SO 5) AP

Accounts payable	$90,000	N. Hudson, capital, August 1, 2011	$26,000
Accounts receivable	72,500	N. Hudson, drawings	3,000
Advertising expense	1,200	Rent expense	1,300
Cash	49,000	Service revenue	11,000

BE1–17 Refer to the data in BE1–16. Using these data and the information from Portage's income statement, prepare a statement of owner's equity.

Prepare a statement of owner's equity.
(SO 5) AP

BE1–18 Refer to the data in BE1–16. Using these data and the information from Portage's statement of owner's equity prepared in BE1–17, prepare a balance sheet for Portage Company.

Prepare a balance sheet.
(SO 5) AP

Exercises

E1–1 Roots Canada Ltd. is known around the world for its clothing and accessories. It has more than 120 stores in Canada and the United States, and more than 60 locations in Asia.

Identify users and uses of accounting information.
(SO 1) C

Instructions

(a) Identify two internal users of Roots' accounting information. Write a question that each user might try to answer by using accounting information.

(b) Identify two external users of Roots' accounting information. Write a question that each user might try to answer by using accounting information.

E1–2 Marietta Company, a proprietorship, had the following selected business transactions during the year:

Identify GAAP.
(SO 2) C

(a) Land with a cost of $208,000 was reported at its fair value of $260,000.

(b) A lease agreement to rent equipment from an equipment supplier starting next year was signed. The rent is $500 per month and the lease is for two years. Payments are due at the start of each month. Nothing was recorded in Marietta Company's accounting records when the lease was signed.

(c) Marietta paid the rent for an apartment for the owner's personal use and charged it to Rent Expense.

(d) Marietta wanted to make its profit look worse than it really was, so it adjusted its expenses upward to include the effects of inflation.

(e) Marietta included a note in its financial statements stating the company was a going concern and is following GAAP for Private Enterprises.

Instructions

(a) In each situation, identify whether the accounting treatment is correct or not, and why.

(b) If it is incorrect, state what should have been done.

Match words with
descriptions.
(SO 1, 2, 3) K

E1–3   Here are some terms from the chapter:

1. Accounts payable
2. Expenses
3. Creditor
4. International Financial Reporting Standards (IFRS)
5. Profit

6. Assets
7. Corporation
8. Generally accepted accounting principles
9. Accounts receivable
10. Owner's equity

Instructions

Match each term with the best description that follows:

(a) ___ A company that raises money by issuing shares
(b) ___ An accepted set of accounting standards that includes broad principles, practices, rules, and procedures
(c) ___ Obligations to suppliers of goods
(d) ___ Amounts due from customers
(e) ___ Equal to net assets
(f) ___ A party that a company owes money to
(g) ___ Resources owned by a business that have the ability to provide a future benefit
(h) ___ The set of accounting standards that all publicly accountable enterprises in Canada have to follow
(i) ___ Results when revenues exceed expenses
(j) ___ The cost of assets consumed or services used in a company's ordinary business activities

Relate concepts to forms of
business organization.
(SO 1, 3) C

E1–4   Listed below are several statements regarding different forms of business organization.

Instructions

For each statement, indicate if that statement is true or false for each of the forms of business organizations by placing a T or an F in each column.

	Proprietorship	Partnership	Corporation
1. Owners have limited liability	____	____	____
2. Withdrawals of assets by owners are called drawings	____	____	____
3. Ownership claim on assets is called partners' equity	____	____	____
4. Entity pays income taxes on its profits	____	____	____
5. Withdrawals of assets by owners reduce Retained Earnings	____	____	____
6. Owners are called shareholders	____	____	____
7. Need to have a minimum of two owners	____	____	____
8. Entity has a limited life	____	____	____
9. The entity has a separate legal existence from its owners	____	____	____

Classify accounts and prepare
accounting equation.
(SO 3) AP

E1–5   The following items (in U.S. millions) were taken from a recent balance sheet of Nike, Inc. Nike is the largest seller of athletic apparel and footwear in the world.

Accounts payable	$1,031.9	Notes payable	$ 812.1
Accounts receivable	2,883.9	Other assets	2,595.9
Cash	2,291.1	Other liabilities	2,712.5
Inventories	2,357.0	Retained earnings	5,451.4
Investments	1,164.0	Share capital	3,241.7
Land, buildings, and equipment	1,957.7		

Instructions

(a) Classify each of the above items as an asset (A), liability (L), or shareholders' (owner's) equity (SE) item.

(b) Show the amounts in Nike's accounting equation by calculating the value of Nike's total assets, total liabilities, and total shareholders' equity.

E1–6 The summaries of balance sheet and income statement data for three proprietorships follow. Three items are missing from each summary.

Determine missing items.
(SO 3) AP

	Wyatt Company	Maxim Enterprises	Distasi Services
Beginning of year:			
Total assets	$ 85,000	$134,000	(g)
Total liabilities	62,000	(d)	$30,000
Total owner's equity	(a)	52,000	33,000
End of year:			
Total assets	110,000	(e)	79,000
Total liabilities	(b)	61,000	42,000
Total owner's equity	60,000	44,000	(h)
Changes during year in owner's equity:			
Investments by owner	(c)	0	5,000
Drawings	18,000	(f)	25,000
Total revenues	175,000	99,000	85,000
Total expenses	140,000	48,000	(i)

Instructions

Determine the missing amounts.

E1–7 The Depeau Company had the following assets and liabilities on the dates indicated:

Calculate profit (or loss).
(SO 3) AP

December 31	Total Assets	Total Liabilities
2009	$350,000	$200,000
2010	420,000	265,000
2011	510,000	330,000

Don Depeau began business on January 1, 2009, with an investment of $100,000.

Instructions

Use the accounting equation and the change in owner's equity during the year to calculate the profit (or loss) for:

(a) 2009, assuming Don Depeau's drawings were $60,000 for the year.

(b) 2010, assuming Don Depeau made an additional investment of $50,000 and had no drawings in 2010.

(c) 2011, assuming Don Depeau made an additional investment of $10,000 and his drawings were $40,000 for the year.

E1–8 A list of effects on the accounting equation follows. For each effect, give an example of a transaction that would cause it.

Give examples of transactions.
(SO 4) C

1. Increases an asset and increases a liability.
2. Increases an asset and increases owner's equity.
3. Decreases an asset and decreases a liability.
4. Decreases owner's equity and decreases an asset.
5. Increases a liability and decreases owner's equity.
6. Increases one asset and decreases another asset.

Analyze effects of transactions for new company.
(SO 4) AP

E1–9 Here are the transactions for Lush Lawn Care during its first month of operations:

1. Rudy Holland, the owner, made a $15,000 cash investment to start business.
2. Paid monthly rent, $600.
3. Purchased equipment for $5,000. Paid $1,000 cash and signed a note for the balance.
4. Purchased supplies for cash, $500.
5. Billed customers for services performed, $2,500.
6. Rudy Holland withdrew cash for his personal use, $1,000.
7. Received $1,500 from customers billed in transaction 5.
8. Incurred advertising expense on account, $500.
9. Received $1,000 cash from customers for services performed.
10. Paid $300 on account for advertising expense incurred in transaction 8.

Instructions

Prepare a tabular analysis of the above transactions, as shown in Illustration 1-10 in the text.

Analyze effects of transactions for an existing company.
(SO 4) AP

E1–10 Paterson Computer Company had Cash of $8,000, Accounts Receivable of $20,000, Accounts Payable of $3,000, and B. Paterson, Capital of $25,000 at the beginning of May. During the month of May, the following transactions occurred:

1. Purchased computer equipment for $19,000 from Digital Equipment. Paid $2,000 cash and signed a note payable for the balance.
2. Received $5,000 from customers for contracts billed in April.
3. Paid $4,000 for May rent of office space.
4. Paid $2,000 of the amounts owing to suppliers at the beginning of May.
5. Provided computer services to Brieske Construction Company for $3,000 cash.
6. Paid NB Power $1,000 for energy used in May.
7. Ms. Paterson invested an additional $10,000 in the business.
8. Paid Digital Equipment $1,100 on account of the note payable issued for the computer equipment purchased in transaction 1. Of this, $100 was for interest expense.
9. Hired an employee to start working in June.
10. Incurred advertising expense on account for May, $2,000.

Instructions

Prepare a tabular analysis of the above transactions, as shown in Illustration 1-10 in the text. The first row is the amounts the company had at the beginning of May.

Analyze transactions. Calculate profit and increase in owner's equity.
(SO 4) AP

E1–11 An analysis of the transactions for Bnita & Co., a public accounting firm, for its first month of operation s, August 2011, follows:

	Cash	+	Accounts Receivable	+	Supplies	+	Office Equipment	–	Accounts Payable	+	B. Bnita, Capital	–	B. Bnita, Drawings	+	Revenues	–	Expenses
1.	+$10,000						+$5,000				+$15,000						
2.	–2,000						+5,000		+$3,000								
3.					+$750				+750								
4.	+2,700		+$3,400												+$6,100		
5.	–1,500								–1,500								
6.	–2,200												–$2,200				
7.	–750																–750 Rent
8.	+1,450		–1,450														
9.	–2,900																–2,900 Salaries
10.									+550								–550 Utilities

Instructions

(a) Describe each transaction that occurred in the month.
(b) Calculate the increase in owner's equity for the month.
(c) Calculate the amount of profit for the month.

E1–12 Below are some items found in the financial statements of Petr Zizler, Orthodontist. Indicate (a) whether each of the following items is an asset (A), liability (L), or part of owner's equity (OE); and (b) which financial statement—income statement (IS), statement of owner's equity (OE), or balance sheet (BS)—it would be reported on. The first one has been done for you as an example.

Classify accounts.
(SO 3, 5) C

	(a)	(b)
1. Accounts payable	L	BS
2. Accounts receivable	___	___
3. Cash	___	___
4. Dental equipment	___	___
5. Furniture and fixtures	___	___
6. Interest payable	___	___
7. Interest revenue	___	___
8. Interest expense	___	___
9. Investment by the owner	___	___
10. Orthodontist fees earned	___	___
11. P. Zizler, capital (opening balance)	___	___
12. P. Zizler, drawings	___	___
13. Salaries expense	___	___
14. Supplies	___	___
15. Supplies expense	___	___

E1–13 An analysis of transactions for Bnita & Co. for August 2011 was presented in E1–11.

Prepare financial statements.
(SO 5) AP

Instructions

Prepare an income statement and statement of owner's equity for August and a balance sheet at August 31.

E1–14 Atlantic Cruise Co. is owned by Irina Sail. The following information is an alphabetical listing of financial statement items for the company for the year ended July 31, 2011:

Prepare income statement and statement of owner's equity.
(SO 5) AP

Accounts payable	$ 50,000	Interest expense	$ 20,000
Accounts receivable	42,000	Investments by owner	5,000
Advertising expense	3,500	Maintenance expense	83,000
Cash	27,000	Notes payable	400,000
Equipment	120,000	Salaries expense	128,000
Food, fuel, and other expenses	65,500	Ships	550,000
I. Sail, capital, August 1, 2010	279,000	Supplies	15,000
I. Sail, drawings	35,000	Ticket revenue	355,000

Instructions

Prepare an income statement and a statement of owner's equity for the year.

E1–15 Refer to the financial information in E1–14 for the Atlantic Cruise Company at July 31, 2011.

Prepare balance sheet.
(SO 5) AP

Instructions

Prepare the balance sheet.

E1–16 Judy Cumby is the sole owner of Deer Park, a public camping ground near Gros Morne National Park. Judy has gathered the following financial information for the year ended December 31, 2011:

Calculate profit and owner's equity and prepare balance sheet.
(SO 5) AP

Revenues—camping fees	$160,000	Revenues—general store	$ 40,000
Operating expenses	150,000	Cash on hand	10,000
Supplies on hand	2,500	Original cost of equipment	110,000

Fair value of equipment	$125,000	Notes payable	$70,000
Accounts payable	11,500	J. Cumby, capital, January 1	17,000
Accounts receivable	21,000	J. Cumby, drawings	5,000

Instructions

(a) Calculate Deer Park's profit for the year.
(b) Calculate Judy's owner's equity at December 31.
(c) Prepare a balance sheet at December 31.

Problems: Set A

Identify financial statements for decision-making.
(SO 1) S

P1–1A   Financial decisions often depend more on one type of financial statement than others. Consider the following independent, hypothetical situations:

1. The South Face Co. is thinking about extending credit to a new customer. The terms of credit would require the customer to pay within 45 days of receipt of the goods.
2. An investor is considering purchasing a company called Music Online Co. The investor plans on owning the company for at least five years.
3. The president of Tech Toy Limited is trying to determine whether the company is generating enough cash to increase the amount of dividends paid to shareholders and still have enough cash to buy additional equipment when needed.
4. Caisse d'Économie Base Montréal is thinking about extending a loan to a small company. The company would be required to make interest payments at the end of each year for five years, and to repay the loan at the end of the fifth year.

Taking It Further is an extra question at the end of each problem designed to challenge students to think beyond the basics concepts covered in the problem, and to provide written explanations. Your instructor may assign problems with or without this extra element.

Instructions

In each situation, state whether the individual making the decision would depend mostly on information in the income statement, balance sheet, or cash flow statement. Briefly justify your choice.

Taking It Further   Why is it important to users of financial statements to know that the statements have been prepared by individuals who have high standards of ethical behaviour?

Determine forms of business organization.
(SO 1) AP

P1–2A   Five independent situations follow:

1. Dawn Addington, a student looking for summer employment, opened a vegetable stand along a busy local highway. She buys produce from local farmers each morning and then sells it in the afternoon as people return home from work.
2. Joseph Counsell and Sabra Surkis each own a bike shop. They have decided to combine their businesses and try to expand their operations to include snowboards. They expect that in the coming year they will need funds to expand their operations.
3. Three chemistry professors have formed a business that uses bacteria to clean up toxic waste sites. Each has contributed an equal amount of cash and knowledge to the venture. The use of bacteria in this situation is experimental, and legal obligations could result.
4. Abdur Rahim has run a successful but small organic food store for over five years. The increased sales at his store have made him believe the time is right to open a chain of organic food stores across the country. Of course, this will require a substantial investment for inventory and store equipment, as well as for employees and other resources. Abdur has minimal personal savings.
5. Mary Emery, Richard Goedde, and Jigme Tshering have law degrees and recently passed their bar exams. They have decided to start a law practice in their hometown.

Instructions

In each case, explain what form of organization the business is likely to take: proprietorship, partnership, or corporation. Give reasons for your choice.

Taking It Further   Frequently, individuals start a business as a proprietorship and later incorporate the business. What are some of the advantages of doing this?

P1–3A   Five independent situations follow:

1. Human Solutions Incorporated believes its people are its most significant asset. It estimates and records their value on its balance sheet.
2. Barton Co. is carrying equipment at its current fair value of $100,000. The equipment had an original cost of $75,000.
3. Steph Wolfson, owner of the Sound Effects Company, bought a computer for her personal use. She paid for the computer with company funds and debited the Computers account.
4. West Spirit Oil Corp. is a very small oil and gas company that is listed on the Alberta Stock Exchange. The president asked each of the shareholders to approve using Canadian GAAP for Private Enterprises instead of IFRS to reduce expenses for accounting services. He received 100% approval and has advised the company accountant to prepare the 2011 financial statements accordingly.
5. White Wall Tire Company is potentially on the verge of bankruptcy and the accountant is preparing its financial statements. The accountant advises the owner that it will be necessary to include a note to this effect in the financial statements.

Assess accounting treatment. (SO 2) C

Instructions

(a) For each of the above situations, determine if the accounting treatment of the situation is correct or incorrect. Explain why.
(b) If the accounting treatment is incorrect, explain what should be done.

Taking It Further   Why is it important for companies to follow generally accepted accounting principles when preparing their financial statements?

P1–4A   The following selected data are for Jaroslawsky Trading Company for its first three years of operations:

Determine missing items. (SO 3, 4) AP

January 1:	2010	2011	2012
Total assets	$ 40,000	$ (f)	$ (j)
Total liabilities	0	45,000	(k)
Total owner's equity	(a)	65,000	(l)
December 31:			
Total assets	(b)	140,000	155,000
Total liabilities	45,000	(g)	85,000
Total owner's equity	(c)	75,000	(m)
Changes during year in owner's equity:			
Investments by owner during the year	9,000	0	(n)
Drawings by owner during the year	12,000	(h)	36,000
Profit or loss for the year	(d)	40,000	(o)
Total revenues for the year	125,000	(i)	155,000
Total expenses for the year	(e)	105,000	126,000

Instructions

Determine the missing amounts.

Taking It Further   What information does the owner of a company need in order to decide whether he or she is able to withdraw cash from the business?

P1–5A   On April 1, Angela Loken established the Loken Travel Agency. The following transactions are for her first month of operations:

Analyze transactions and calculate owner's equity. (SO 3, 4) AP

Apr. 1   Deposited $12,000 in the agency's bank account at the CIBC.
    2   Paid rent for the month, $1,100.

Apr. 2   Purchased office equipment for $7,500, paying $2,000 cash and signing a note payable for the balance.

7   Incurred $300 of advertising costs, on account.

8   Paid $725 for office supplies.

11   Earned $9,000 for services provided, with $1,000 paid in cash and the remainder on account.

17   Paid the amount due in the April 7 transaction.

25   Withdrew $500 for personal use.

30   Paid employee salaries, $3,500.

30   Received a bill for utilities for the month, $400.

30   Received $5,000 from customers who were billed in the April 11 transaction.

Instructions

(a) Prepare a tabular analysis of the effects of the above transactions on the accounting equation.

(b) From an analysis of the owner's equity, calculate the account balance in A. Loken, Capital, at April 30.

Taking It Further   Assume that on April 28, Loken Travel Agency received a $500 advance cash payment from a customer for services to be provided in May. Should this be recorded as revenue in April when the cash is received? Why or why not?

Classify accounts and prepare accounting equation.
(SO 3, 5) AP

P1–6A   Listed in alphabetical order, the following selected items (in thousands) were taken from Capital Aviation's December 31 financial statements:

1.	L BS	Accounts payable	$1,197	11. ___ ___	Notes payable	$2,536
2.	___ ___	Accounts receivable	547	12. ___ ___	Other assets	1,270
3.	___ ___	Aircraft fuel expense	432	13. ___ ___	Other expenses	650
4.	___ ___	Airport fee expense	309	14. ___ ___	Other liabilities	1,436
5.	___ ___	Cargo revenues	161	15. ___ ___	Other revenue	230
6.	___ ___	Cash	632	16. ___ ___	Passenger revenues	1,681
7.	___ ___	C. Chung, capital, January 1	1,160	17. ___ ___	Property and equipment	3,561
8.	___ ___	C. Chung, drawings	14	18. ___ ___	Salaries expense	596
9.	___ ___	Interest expense	75	19. ___ ___	Spare parts and supplies	237
10.	___ ___	Maintenance expense	78			

Instructions

(a) In each case, identify on the blank line in the first column whether the item is an asset (A), liability (L), capital (C), drawings (D), revenue (R), or expense (E) item. The first one has been done for you as an example.

(b) Indicate on the blank line in the second column which financial statement—income statement (IS), statement of owner's equity (OE), or balance sheet (BS)—each item would be reported on. The first one has been done for you as an example.

(c) Show the amounts in Capital Aviation's accounting equation by calculating the value of total assets, total liabilities, and total owner's equity at December 31.

Taking It Further   Is it important for Capital Aviation to keep track of its different types of revenues as separate items? Explain.

Analyze transactions and prepare balance sheet.
(SO 4, 5) AP

P1–7A   The following events concern Anita LeTourneau, a Manitoba law school graduate, for March 2011:

1. On March 4, she spent $10 on a lottery ticket.

2. On March 7, she won $250,000 in the lottery and immediately quit her job as a junior lawyer.

3. On March 10, she decided to open her own law practice, and deposited $40,000 of her winnings in a business chequing account.

4. On March 14, she purchased a new condominium with a down payment of $100,000 from her personal funds plus a home mortgage of $200,000.

5. On March 15, Ms. LeTourneau signed a rental agreement for her law office space for $1,000 a month, starting March 15. She paid the first month's rent, as it is due on the 15th of each month.

6. On March 19, she hired a receptionist. He will be paid $500 a week and will begin working on March 24.

7. On March 20, she purchased office furniture for her law practice from a company that had just declared bankruptcy. The furniture was worth at least $12,000 but Anita was able to buy it for only $8,000.

8. On March 21, she purchased $500 of office supplies on account.

9. On March 24, she purchased $6,500 of computer and other equipment for her law practice for $2,000 plus a $4,500 note payable due in six months.

10. On March 31, she performed $3,000 of legal services on account.

11. On March 31, she paid her receptionist $500 for the week.

12. On March 31, she paid $300 for the supplies purchased on account on March 21.

Instructions

(a) Prepare a tabular analysis of the effects of the above transactions on the accounting equation.

(b) Calculate profit and owner's equity for the month ended March 31.

(c) Prepare a balance sheet at March 31.

Taking It Further   How should Anita determine which transactions should be recorded and which ones should not be recorded?

P1–8A   Tony Tiberio opens a law office under the name Tony Tiberio, Barrister & Solicitor, on July 1, 2011. On July 31, the balance sheet showed Cash $4,000; Accounts Receivable $1,900; Supplies $500; Office Equipment $5,000; Accounts Payable $5,500; and T. Tiberio, Capital $5,900. During August, the following transactions occurred:

Analyze transactions and prepare financial statements. (SO 4, 5) AP

Aug. 4   Collected $1,200 of accounts receivable.

5   Earned fees of $6,500, of which $3,000 was collected from clients and the remainder was on account.

7   Paid $2,100 on accounts payable.

12   Purchased additional office equipment for $1,600, paying $400 cash and leaving the balance on account.

15   Paid salaries, $3,500; rent for August, $1,100; and advertising expenses, $275.

18   Collected the balance of the accounts receivable from July 31.

20   Withdrew $500 for personal use.

26   Borrowed $2,000 from the Bank of Montreal on a note payable.

28   Signed a contract to provide legal services to a client in September for $4,500. The client will pay the amount owing after the work has been completed.

29   Received telephone bill for August, $275.

30   Billed a client $1,000 for services provided in August.

Instructions

(a) Beginning with the July 31 balances, prepare a tabular analysis of the effects of the August transactions on the accounting equation.

(b) Prepare an income statement and statement of owner's equity for August, and a balance sheet at August 31.

Taking It Further   What are the differences between purchasing an item on account and signing a note payable for the amount owing?

Prepare financial statements.
(SO 5) AP

P1–9A   Bennett's Home Renovations was started in 2005 by Jim Bennett. Jim operates the business from an office in his home. Listed below, in alphabetical order, are the company's assets and liabilities as at December 31, 2011, and the revenues, expenses, and drawings for the year ended December 31, 2011:

Accounts payable	$ 9,240	Note payable	$ 30,800
Accounts receivable	10,080	Office supplies	595
Cash	7,700	Office supplies expense	2,975
Equipment	29,400	Renovation fee revenue	154,700
Insurance expense	3,375	Salaries expense	87,430
Interest expense	1,190	Truck	42,000
J. Bennett, drawings	44,800	Truck operating expenses	19,545

Jim's capital at the beginning of 2011 was $54,350. He made no investments during the year.

Instructions

Prepare an income statement, statement of owner's equity, and balance sheet.

Taking It Further   Why is it necessary to prepare the income statement first, then the statement of owner's equity, and the balance sheet last?

Determine missing amounts, and comment.

(SO 5) AN

The pencil icon means that you have to write a detailed answer.

P1–10A   Here are incomplete financial statements for Wu Company:

WU COMPANY
Balance Sheet
January 31, 2011

Assets		Liabilities and Owner's Equity	
Cash	$10,000	Liabilities	
Accounts receivable	(i)	Notes payable	$ (iii)
Land	15,000	Accounts payable	18,500
Building and equipment	45,000	Total liabilities	45,000
Total assets	$ (ii)	W. Wu, capital	(iv)
		Total liabilities and owner's equity	$85,000

WU COMPANY
Income Statement
Year Ended January 31, 2011

Revenues		
Fees earned		$75,000
Expenses		
Salaries expense	$30,000	
Other expenses	28,000	
Supplies expense	(v)	
Total expenses		64,000
Profit		$ (vi)

WU COMPANY
Statement of Owner's Equity
Year Ended January 31, 2011

W. Wu, capital, February 1, 2010	$14,000
Add: Investments	(vii)
Profit	(viii)
	40,000
Less: W. Wu, drawings	(ix)
W. Wu, capital, January 31, 2011	$ (x)

Instructions

(a) Calculate the missing amounts (i) to (x).

(b) Write a memo explaining (1) the sequence for preparing the financial statements, and (2) the interrelationships between the income statement, statement of owner's equity, and balance sheet.

Taking It Further   Why isn't the balance sheet dated the same way as the income statement and statement of owner's equity: "Year Ended January 31, 2011"?

P1–11A   The balance sheet of Confucius Book Shop at April 30, 2011, is as follows:

Discuss errors and prepare corrected balance sheet.
(SO 2, 3, 5) AP

CONFUCIUS BOOK SHOP				
Balance Sheet				
April 30, 2011				
Assets			**Liabilities and Owner's Equity**	
Building	$110,000	Accounts payable		$ 15,000
C. Cai, capital	85,000	Accounts receivable		37,000
Cash	10,000	Equipment and furnishings		58,000
Land	50,000	Supplies		4,000
Notes payable	120,000	"Plug"		261,000
	$375,000			$375,000

Cenhai Cai, the owner of the book shop, willingly admits that he is not an accountant. In fact, he couldn't get the balance sheet to balance without "plugging" the numbers (making up numbers to give the desired result). He gives you the following additional information:

1. A professional real estate appraiser estimated the value of the land at $50,000. The actual cost of the land was $36,000.

2. Accounts receivable includes amounts due from customers in China for 35,000 yuan, which is about $5,000 Canadian. Cenhai didn't know how to convert the currency for reporting purposes so he added the 35,000 yuan to the $2,000 due from Canadian customers. He thought it more important to know how much he was owed by each customer in the currency they would likely pay him with anyway. Cenhai also believes that Accounts Receivable is a liability. He sees it as bad for the business that he doesn't have the cash from his customers yet.

3. Cenhai reasons that equipment and furnishings are a liability because it will cost him money in the future to maintain these items.

4. Cenhai reasons that the note payable must be an asset because getting the loan was good for the business. If he had not obtained the loan, he would not have been able to purchase the land and buildings.

5. Cenhai believes that his capital account is also an asset. He has invested in the business, and investments are assets; therefore his capital account is an asset.

Instructions

(a) Identify any corrections that should be made to the balance sheet, and explain why by referring to the appropriate accounting concept.

(b) Prepare a corrected balance sheet for Confucius Book Shop at April 30. (*Hint*: The capital account may need to be adjusted in order to balance.)

Taking It Further   Explain to Cenhai why all transactions affect at least two financial statement items.

Problems: Set B

Identify financial statements for decision-making.
(SO 1) S

P1–1B   Financial decisions often depend more on one type of financial statement than on others. Consider the following independent, hypothetical situations:

1. An Ontario investor is considering purchasing a company called Fight Flab Co., which operates a chain of 13 fitness centres in the greater Toronto area. The investor plans on owning the company for a minimum of five years.
2. The Backroads Company is considering extending credit to a new customer. The terms of credit would require the customer to pay within 45 days of receipt of the goods.
3. The senior partner of Private Label Enterprises is trying to determine if the company is generating enough cash to increase the partners' drawings and still ensure the company has enough cash for the company to expand its operations.
4. Laurentian Bank is thinking about extending a loan to a small company. The company would be required to make interest payments at the end of each year for three years, and to repay the loan at the end of the third year.

Instructions

In each situation, state whether the individual making the decision would depend mostly on information in the income statement, balance sheet, or cash flow statement. Briefly justify your choice.

Taking It Further   Why is it important to users of financial statements to know that the statements have been prepared by individuals who have high standards of ethical behaviour?

Determine forms of business organization.
(SO 1) AP

P1–2B   Five independent situations follow:

1. Three computer science professors have formed a business to sell software to reduce and control spam e-mail. Each has contributed an equal amount of cash and knowledge to the venture. While their software looks promising, they are concerned about the legal liabilities that their business might confront.
2. Joseph LeBlanc, a student looking for summer employment, opened a bait shop in a small shed on a local fishing dock.
3. Robert Steven and Tom Cheng each own a snowboard manufacturing business and have now decided to combine their businesses. They expect that in the next year they will need funds to expand their operations.
4. Darcy Becker, Ellen Sweet, and Meg Dwyer recently graduated with marketing degrees. Friends since childhood, they have decided to start a consulting business that focuses on branding strategies for small and medium-sized businesses.
5. Hervé Gaudet wants to rent DVD players and DVDs in airports across the country. His idea is that customers will be able to rent equipment and DVDs at one airport, watch the DVDs on their flights and return the equipment and DVDs at their destination airport. Of course, this will require a substantial investment for equipment and DVDs, as well as employees and space in each airport.

Instructions

In each case, explain what form of organization the business is likely to take: proprietorship, partnership, or corporation. Give reasons for your choice.

Taking It Further   What are the advantages of two individuals first forming a partnership to run a business, and later incorporating?

P1–3B Five independent situations follow:

Assess accounting treatment. (SO 2) C

1. In preparing its financial statements, Karim Company estimated and recorded the impact of the recent death of its president.
2. Paradis Company recently purchased a powerboat. It plans on inviting clients for outings occasionally, so the boat was paid for with company funds and recorded in the company's records. Marc Paradis' family will use the boat whenever it is not being used to entertain clients. It is estimated that the boat will be used by the family about 75% of the time.
3. Because of a "flood sale," equipment worth $300,000 was purchased by Montigny Company for only $200,000. The equipment was recorded at $300,000 on Montigny's books.
4. Vertical Lines Company was on the verge of filing for bankruptcy, but a turnaround in the economy has resulted in the company being very healthy financially. The company president insists that the accountant put a note in the financial statements that states the company is a real going concern now.
5. Three Green Thumbs is a landscaping business operated as a partnership. The partners plan on incorporating and going public in three years. They agree that the company should use International Financial Reporting Standards (IFRS) and also agree that they do not need to put that information in the financial statements as they are currently a private company.

Instructions

(a) For each of the above situations, determine if the accounting treatment of the situation is correct or incorrect. Explain why.
(b) If the accounting treatment is incorrect, explain what should be done.

Taking It Further Why is it important for private and public companies to follow generally accepted accounting principles when preparing their financial statements?

P1–4B The following selected data are for Siksika Trading Company for its first three years of operations:

Determine missing items. (SO 3, 4) AP

January 1:	2010	2011	2012
Total assets	$ (a)	$ 80,000	$135,000
Total liabilities	0	(e)	(k)
Total owner's equity	50,000	(f)	(l)
December 31:			
Total assets	80,000	(g)	170,000
Total liabilities	(b)	75,000	(m)
Total owner's equity	40,000	(h)	80,000
Changes during year in owner's equity:			
Investments by owner during the year	5,000	(i)	0
Drawings by owner during the year	0	10,000	(n)
Profit or loss for the year	(c)	25,000	60,000
Total revenues for the year	(d)	(j)	155,000
Total expenses for the year	110,000	105,000	(o)

Instructions

Determine the missing amounts.

Taking It Further What information does the owner of a company need in order to decide whether he or she needs to invest additional cash in the business?

Analyze transactions and
calculate owner's equity.
(SO 3, 4) AP

P1–5B   Jaeger's Repair Shop was started on May 1 by R. Jaeger. A summary of the May transactions follows:

May 1   Invested $15,000 to start the repair shop.
2   Purchased equipment for $8,000, paying $2,000 cash and signing a note payable for the balance.
5   Paid rent for the month, $940.
7   Purchased $850 of supplies on account.
9   Received $2,100 in cash from customers for repair services.
16   Provided repair services on account to customers, $1,800.
26   Collected $500 on account for services billed on May 16.
27   Paid for supplies purchased on May 7.
28   Paid $220 for advertising.
30   Withdrew $500 for personal use.
31   Received May telephone bill, $100.
31   Paid part-time employee salaries, $1,000.
31   Billed a customer $350 for repair services.

Instructions

(a) Prepare a tabular analysis of the effects of the above transactions on the accounting equation.
(b) From an analysis of the owner's equity, calculate the account balance in R. Jaeger, Capital at May 31.

Taking It Further   Assume that on May 28, Jaeger Repair Shop received a $500 advance cash payment from a customer for work to be performed in June. Should this be recorded as revenue in May? Why or why not?

Classify accounts and prepare
accounting equation.
(SO 3, 5) AP

P1–6B   Listed in alphabetical order, the following selected items (in thousands) were taken from Happy Valley Hotel & Resorts' December 31 financial statements:

1.	_L_	BS	Accounts payable	$ 159	9. ___ ___	Operating expenses	$661
2.	___	___	Accounts receivable	90	10. ___ ___	Other assets	512
3.	___	___	Cash	100	11. ___ ___	Other liabilities	256
4.	___	___	Hotel real estate and		12. ___ ___	Other revenue	37
			equipment	1,435	13. ___ ___	Revenues from	
5.	___	___	Interest expense	33		hotel operations	841
6.	___	___	Investments	150	14. ___ ___	Salaries payable	35
7.	___	___	Non-hotel real estate	100	15. ___ ___	T. Waye, capital, January 1	966
8.	___	___	Notes payable	802	16. ___ ___	T. Waye, drawings	15

Instructions

(a) In each case, identify on the blank line, in the first column, whether the item is an asset (A), liability (L), capital (C), drawings (D), revenue (R), or expense (E) item. The first one has been done for you as an example.
(b) Indicate on the blank line, in the second column, which financial statement—income statement (IS), statement of owner's equity (OE), or balance sheet (BS)—each item would be reported on. The first one has been done for you as an example.
(c) Show the amounts in Happy Valley Hotel & Resorts' accounting equation by calculating the value of total assets, total liabilities, and total owner's equity at December 31.

Taking it Further   Is it important for Happy Valley Hotel & Resorts to keep track of its different types of expenses as separate items? Explain.

Analyze transactions and
prepare balance sheet.
(SO 4, 5) AP

P1–7B   Lynn Barry started her own consulting firm, Barry Consulting, on June 1, 2011. The following transactions occurred during the month of June:

June 1   Barry sold her shares in Big Country Airlines for $5,000, which she deposited in her personal bank account.

1   Barry transferred $4,500 from her personal account to a business account in the name of Barry Consulting.

2   Paid $750 for office rent for the month.

3   Purchased $475 of supplies on account.

5   Paid $80 to advertise in the *County News*.

9   Received $2,175 for services provided.

12   Withdrew $400 for personal use.

15   Performed $3,000 of services on account.

17   Paid $1,500 for employee salaries.

21   Received $2,400 for services provided on account on June 15.

22   Paid for the supplies purchased on account on June 3.

25   Signed a contract to provide consulting services to a client for $5,500. Services will be performed and paid for in July.

26   Borrowed $4,000 from the bank and signed a note payable.

29   Used part of the cash borrowed from the bank on June 26 to purchase office equipment for $1,650.

30   Paid $150 for telephone service for the month.

Instructions

(a) Prepare a tabular analysis of the effects of the above transactions on the accounting equation.

(b) Calculate profit and owner's equity for the month ended June 30.

(c) Prepare a balance sheet at June 30.

Taking It Further   How should Lynn determine which transactions should be recorded and which ones should not be recorded?

P1–8B   Brian Fraser opened the Fraser Veterinary Clinic in Regina on August 1, 2011. On August 31, the balance sheet showed Cash $4,500; Accounts Receivable $1,800; Supplies $400; Office Equipment $6,500; Accounts Payable $3,200; and B. Fraser, Capital $10,000. During September, the following transactions occurred:

Analyze transactions and prepare financial statements. (SO 4, 5) AP

Sept. 1   Paid $2,800 of the accounts payable.

1   Paid $800 rent for September.

4   Collected $1,450 of the accounts receivable.

5   Hired a part-time office assistant at $75 per day to start work the following week.

8   Purchased additional office equipment for $5,000, paying $1,000 cash and signing a note payable for the balance.

14   Performed $500 of veterinary services on account.

15   Paid $200 for advertising.

18   Collected $500 from customers who received services on September 14.

20   Paid $250 for Brian's daughter and friends to go horseback riding on her birthday.

25   Borrowed $7,500 from the Western Bank on a note payable.

26   Sent a statement reminding a customer that he still owed the company money from August.

28   Earned revenue of $4,300, of which $2,900 was paid in cash and the balance was due in October.

29   Paid the part-time office assistant $675 for working nine days in September.

30   Received the telephone bill for the month, $175.

30   Withdrew $750 cash for personal expenses.

Instructions

(a) Beginning with the August 31 balances, prepare a tabular analysis of the effects of the September transactions on the accounting equation.

(b) Prepare an income statement and statement of owner's equity for September, and a balance sheet at September 30.

Taking It Further   Explain the correct accounting treatment of the transaction on August 20.

Prepare financial statements.
(SO 5) AP

P1–9B   Judy Johansen operates an interior design business, Johansen Designs. Listed below, in alphabetical order, are the company's assets and liabilities as at December 31, 2011, and the revenues, expenses, and drawings for the year ended December 31, 2011:

Accounts payable	$ 5,840	J. Johansen, drawings	$35,000
Accounts receivable	7,645	Note payable	5,950
Cash	10,390	Office supplies	525
Computer equipment	8,050	Office supplies expense	2,625
Design fee revenue	122,395	Rent expense	16,800
Furniture	11,730	Salaries expense	66,360
Interest expense	315	Telephone expense	5,320

Judy's capital at the beginning of 2011 was $30,575. She made no investments during the year.

Instructions

Prepare an income statement, statement of owner's equity, and balance sheet.

Taking It Further   Why is the balance sheet prepared after the statement of owner's equity?

Determine missing amounts, and comment.

(SO 5) AN

P1–10B   Here are incomplete financial statements for Baxter Company:

BAXTER COMPANY
Balance Sheet
November 30, 2011

Assets		Liabilities and Owner's Equity	
Cash	$ 5,000	Liabilities	
Accounts receivable	10,000	Notes payable	$59,600
Land	(i)	Accounts payable	(ii)
Building and equipment	45,000	Total liabilities	66,500
Total assets	$110,000	Owner's equity	
		B. Baxter, capital	(iii)
		Total liabilities and owner's equity	$ (iv)

BAXTER COMPANY
Income Statement
Year Ended November 30, 2011

Revenues		
Fees earned		$80,000
Expenses		
Salaries expense	$37,500	
Other expenses	(v)	
Supplies expense	6,000	
Total expenses		62,500
Profit		$ (vi)

BAXTER COMPANY Statement of Owner's Equity Year Ended November 30, 2011	
B. Baxter, capital, December 1, 2010	$35,000
Add: Investments	(vii)
Profit	(viii)
	57,500
Less: B. Baxter, drawings	(ix)
B. Baxter, capital, November 30, 2011	$ (x)

Instructions

(a) Calculate the missing amounts (i) to (x).

(b) Write a memo explaining (1) the sequence for preparing the financial statements, and (2) the interrelationships between the income statement, statement of owner's equity, and balance sheet.

Taking It Further   Why aren't the income statement and the statement of owner's equity dated the same way as the balance sheet: "November 30, 2011"?

P1–11B   GG Company was formed on January 1, 2011. On December 31, Guy Gélinas, the owner, prepared a balance sheet:

Discuss errors and prepare corrected balance sheet. (SO 2, 5) AP

GG COMPANY Balance Sheet December 31, 2011			
Assets		**Liabilities and Owner's Equity**	
Cash	$ 15,000	Accounts and notes payable	$ 45,000
Accounts receivable	55,000	Boat loan payable	13,000
Supplies	20,000	G. Gélinas, capital	25,000
Boat	18,000	Profit for 2011	25,000
	$108,000		$108,000

Guy willingly admits that he is not an accountant by training. He is concerned that his balance sheet might not be correct. He gives you the following additional information:

1. The boat actually belongs to Guy Gélinas, not to GG Company. However, because he thinks he might take customers out on the boat occasionally, he decided to list it as an asset of the company. To be consistent, he also listed as a liability of the company the personal bank loan that he took out to buy the boat.

2. Guy spent $15,000 to purchase more supplies than he usually does, because he heard that the price of the supplies was expected to increase. It did, and the supplies are now worth $20,000. He thought it best to record the supplies at $20,000, as that is what it would have cost him to buy them today.

3. Guy has signed a contract to purchase equipment in January 2012. The company will have to pay $5,000 cash for the equipment when it arrives and the balance will be payable in 30 days. Guy has already reduced Cash by $5,000 because he is committed to paying this amount.

4. The balance in G. Gélinas, Capital is equal to the amount Guy originally invested in the company when he started it on January 1, 2011.

5. Guy combined notes payable of $15,000 with accounts payable of $30,000 as he thought this was more efficient.

6. Guy knows that a balance sheet needs to balance but on his first attempt he had $108,000 of assets and $83,000 of liabilities and owner's equity. He reasoned that the difference was the amount of profit the company earned this year and added that to the balance sheet as part of owner's equity.

Instructions

(a) Identify any corrections that should be made to the balance sheet, and explain why by referring to the appropriate accounting concepts, assumption or principle.

(b) Prepare a corrected balance sheet for GG Company. (*Hint*: To get the balance sheet to balance, adjust owner's equity.)

Taking It Further   Assume that Guy did not make any withdrawals from the company in 2011, nor any investments other than his initial investment of $25,000. What was the actual profit for the year?

Continuing Cookie Chronicle

The **Continuing Cookie Chronicle** starts in this chapter and continues in every chapter throughout the book. This feature chronicles the growth of a hypothetical small business to show how the concepts you learn in each chapter can be applied in the real world.

Natalie Koebel spent much of her childhood learning the art of cookie-making from her grandmother. They passed many happy hours mastering every type of cookie imaginable and later creating new recipes that were both healthy and delicious. Now at the start of her second year in college, Natalie is investigating various possibilities for starting her own business as part of the requirements of the Entrepreneurship program she is taking. A long-time friend insists that Natalie has to somehow include cookies in her business plan and, after a series of brainstorming sessions, Natalie settles on the idea of operating a cookie-making school. She will start on a part-time basis and offer her services in peoples' homes. Now that she has started thinking about it, the possibilities seem endless. During the fall, she will concentrate on Christmas cookies. She will offer group sessions (which will probably be more entertainment than education for the participants) and individual lessons. Natalie also decides to include children in her target market. The first difficult decision is coming up with the perfect name for her business. In the end, she settles on "Cookie Creations" and then moves on to more important issues.

Instructions

(a) What form of business organization—proprietorship, partnership, or corporation—do you recommend that Natalie use for her business? Discuss the benefits and weaknesses of each form and give the reasons for your choice.

(b) Will Natalie need accounting information? If yes, what information will she need and why? How often will she need this information?

(c) In addition to Natalie, who do you anticipate to be the users of Natalie's accounting information? What information will these identified users need and why?

(d) Which set of accounting standards will Natalie likely adopt when compiling her accounting information? Why?

(e) Identify specific asset, liability, and equity accounts that Cookie Creations will likely use to record its business transactions.

(f) Should Natalie open a separate bank account for the business? Why or why not?

Financial Reporting and Analysis

Financial Reporting Problem

BYP1–1 The Forzani Group Ltd.'s financial statements have been reproduced in Appendix A at the back of the textbook.

Instructions

(a) How many notes to the financial statements are presented for The Forzani Group? How many pages of the financial statement package do these notes use? How many pages do the financial statements themselves use?

(b) Notice that the dates on the financial statements are February 1, 2009, and February 3, 2008. What is The Forzani Group's fiscal year end? (See note 2 (j) to the financial statements.)

(c) What were The Forzani Group's total assets as at February 1, 2009? As at February 3, 2008?

(d) What is the amount of change in The Forzani Group's profit (Forzani calls this "net earnings") from 2008 to 2009?

(e) What amount of cash did The Forzani Group have on February 1, 2009? On February 3, 2008?

(f) In the notes to the financial statements (note 2), the company highlights a number of accounting policies. At the end of this note, it also discusses its planned change to International Financial Reporting Standards (IFRS). When is the company required to change to IFRS? Will it show a comparative prior year based on prior Canadian GAAP or based on IFRS? For Forzani, which year ends will be shown in its first report under IFRS?

Interpreting Financial Statements

BYP1–2 Research In Motion Limited (RIM) is a Canadian company that designs, manufactures, and markets mobile communications solutions. RIM's award-winning products include the BlackBerry wireless platform, software development tools, and software/hardware licensing agreements. In the assets section of its 2009 balance sheet, the following data were presented:

Assets	2009	2008
RESEARCH IN MOTION LIMITED. Balance Sheet (partial) February 28, 2009 (in U.S. thousands)		
Cash	$ 835,546	$1,184,398
Short term investments	682,666	420,709
Trade receivables	2,112,117	1,174,692
Other receivables	157,728	74,689
Inventory	682,400	396,267
Other current assets	187,257	135,849
Deferred income tax asset—current	183,872	90,750
Long term investments	720,635	738,889
Capital assets	1,334,648	705,955
Intangible assets	1,066,527	469,988
Goodwill	137,572	114,455
Deferred income tax asset—non-current	404	4,546
Total assets	$8,101,372	$5,511,187

Instructions

(a) For a company such as RIM, what do you think its most important economic resources (assets) would be? Where are these recorded on the balance sheet? At what value (if any) should they be shown?

(b) Does the balance sheet tell you what RIM is worth? What information does the balance sheet give you about the company's value?

(c) Why do you think a Canadian company such as RIM would prepare its financial statements in U.S. dollars?

Critical Thinking

Collaborative Learning Activity

Note to instructor: Additional instructions and material for this group activity can be found on the Instructor Resource Site.

WILEY PLUS
Working in Groups

BYP1–3   In this group activity, you will analyze and record the transactions for a service company.

Instructions

(a) Complete the transaction table supplied by your instructor without consulting your classmates.

(b) Your instructor will divide the class into groups. One member of your group will take on the role of recorder as the group completes a new transaction table. You can refer to your individual transaction table for answers during the group activity but you should not change your individual answers. When your answers differ, you must explain your reasoning to the other members of the group.

(c) Each group will hand in the group transaction table along with the individual transaction tables of each member.

Communication Activity

BYP1–4 Robert Joote is the owner of Peak Company. Robert has prepared the following balance sheet:

PEAK COMPANY Balance Sheet Month Ended December 31, 2011	
Assets	
Equipment	$20,500
Cash	10,500
Supplies	2,000
Accounts payable	(5,000)
Total assets	$28,000
Liabilities and Owner's Equity	
R. Joote, capital	$21,000
Accounts receivable	(3,000)
R. Joote, drawings	(2,000)
Notes payable	12,000
Total liabilities and owner's equity	$28,000

Robert didn't know how to determine the balance for his capital account so he just "plugged" the number (he made up a number that would give him the result that he wanted). He had heard somewhere that assets had to equal the total of liabilities and owner's equity so he made up a number for capital so that these would be equal.

Instructions

In a memo, explain to Robert (a) how to determine the balance for his capital account, (b) why his balance sheet is incorrect, and (c) what he should do to correct it. Include in your explanation how the financial statements are interrelated, and why the order of preparation is important.

Ethics Case

BYP1–5 Chief executive officers (CEOs) and chief financial officers (CFOs) of publicly traded companies must personally certify that their companies' financial statements and other financial information contain no untrue statements and do not leave out any important facts. After many corporate scandals, the certification requirement was introduced as a way to hold top executives personally responsible for the integrity of their company's financial information.

Khan Corporation just hired a new management team, and its members say they are too new to the company to know whether the most recent financial reports are accurate or not. They refuse to sign the certification.

Instructions

(a) Who are the stakeholders in this situation?
(b) Should the CEO and CFO sign the certification? Explain why or why not.
(c) What are the CEO's and CFO's alternatives?

"All About You" Activity

BYP1–6 In the "All About You" feature, we introduced the idea that having a background in accounting is of value not just to accountants but to you as an individual. Accounting is all about providing and using information for decisions that you face either as a student or after graduation. Following are three such decisions.

1. You have $5,000 to invest and you are trying to decide if you should invest in Company A or Company B.
2. You will be graduating this year and have received job offers from Company C and Company D. You are deciding which company you should work for and you want to accept a position in a company that is financially stable and has growth potential.
3. Your brother owns his own landscaping business that has been operating for two years. He wants to buy some more equipment for the business and asked you to loan him $5,000.

Instructions

(a) For each decision, indicate what information you would want to have in order to make an optimal decision.
(b) Based on what you have learned in Chapter 1, how will learning about accounting help you with the above decisions?

ANSWERS TO CHAPTER QUESTIONS

Answers to Accounting in Action Insight Questions

All About You Insight, p. 3

Q: Why is understanding accounting of value to you in your personal life?

A: How do you make sure that the balance shown by the bank is the right amount in your bank account? Learning accounting will provide you with tools that will help you track your transactions and ensure that the bank balance is correct. You will learn how to calculate how much your paycheque should be. Examining your potential employer's financial statements will help you predict if the company will have enough cash to pay you now and if the company has growth potential. Stay tuned to the "All About You" features and related activities for more!

Across the Organization Insight, p. 4

Q: What is the value of providing all of a company's employees with financial information about the company?

A: Financial information shows the results of the employees' work. When employees are provided with this information, it increases their understanding of how the business functions and what their role is in the company's success or failure. Sharing financial information can assist in educating employees, managing costs and relationships, building team spirit, and setting goals, among other things.

Business Insight, p. 8

Q: Why will it be less expensive for a company like Humpty's Restaurants to use Canadian GAAP for Private Enterprises than IFRS?

A: IFRS requires significantly more financial information in financial statements than Canadian GAAP for Private Enterprises. Researching and reporting this information is a significant time commitment, which means a company needs more employees working in accounting. Also, these individuals must be able to deal with more complex reporting requirements and thus are likely to be relatively well paid, increasing the company's salary costs.

Answer to Forzani Review It Question 3, p. 24

The net earnings amount of $29,325 thousand (also known as *profit*) on the statement of operations (also known as the *income statement*) is included on the statement of retained earnings to determine the ending balance in retained earnings of $178,754 thousand. A statement of retained earnings is prepared by corporations, and is similar to the statement of owner's equity prepared by proprietorships.

The ending retained earnings balance of $178,754 thousand on Forzani's statement of retained earnings is also reported on the balance sheet. Finally, the $3,474 thousand ending cash balance reported as an asset on the balance sheet is explained on the statement of cash flows (also known as the cash flow statement), which ends with this same ending cash balance.

Answers to Self-Study Questions

1. d   2. d   3. c   4. a   5. a   6. d   7. b   8. b   9. c   10. d

Remember to go back to the beginning of the chapter to check off your completed work!

←

CHAPTER 2
THE RECORDING PROCESS

✔ THE NAVIGATOR

☐ Understand *Concepts for Review*

☐ Read *Feature Story*

☐ Scan *Study Objectives*

☐ Read *Chapter Preview*

☐ Read text and answer *Before You Go On*

☐ Work *Demonstration Problem*

☐ Review *Summary of Study Objectives*

☐ Answer *Self-Study Questions*

☐ Complete assignments

CONCEPTS FOR REVIEW:

Before studying this chapter, you should understand or, if necessary, review:

a. Why assets equal liabilities plus owner's equity. (Ch. 1, p. 10)

b. What assets, liabilities, owner's capital, drawings, revenues, and expenses are. (Ch. 1, pp. 11–12)

c. What transactions are, and how they affect the basic accounting equation. (Ch. 1, pp. 14–19)

Dancing to Her Own Business Tune

CALGARY, Alta.—At the Prestige Dance Academy, tiny pink ballerinas admire themselves before the mirrors. Their energetic teacher, Amanda Hunsley, dances along with them, encouraging them to express themselves through music.

Even when she was a young child taking dance lessons, Ms. Hunsley knew she wanted to run her own business. At just 19, while in her second year of studies at Mount Royal College, she opened her own dance school. Seven years later, the Prestige Dance Academy has a part-time staff of nine teaching some 800 students tap, jazz, ballet, creative performing arts, lyrical, preschool, mom and me, hip-hop, and intensive dance.

"I combined my love for kids and for business," she says. "I get to come to work every day and have this place that is mine and teach the kids what I love."

Ms. Hunsley takes care of hiring and scheduling the staff, registrations and any other administrative work, and advertising and marketing. To ensure the business's finances don't fall through the cracks, a bookkeeper helps with her record keeping.

While the dance academy provides birthday parties and summer camps, the bulk of the business is weekly dance lessons that run from September to June. Parents register their children in the fall, providing postdated cheques or a lump-sum payment for the entire year. Ms. Hunsley recently began accepting credit or debit cards for the lump-sum payments.

Using QuickBooks accounting software, Ms. Hunsley creates an account for each student registered and tracks their payments. Not surprisingly, September is the busiest time for creating new accounts and entering the initial monthly payments, as well as the lump-sum payments. At the beginning of each month, Ms. Hunsley records the payment of the postdated cheques then deposits the money in the bank. Expenses, such as lease payments (including heat, light, and water), phone and Internet bills, and staff salaries, are also entered into the system.

When she receives her bank statement at month end, Ms. Hunsley reconciles it with her own records. Her bookkeeper then produces three reports—an income statement, statement of retained earnings, and a balance sheet—so she can see how the business is doing. The bookkeeper also files quarterly sales tax reports and produces the T4s. At year end, Ms. Hunsley saves her QuickBooks file to disk and passes it on to her accountant, who looks for any problems and produces a final set of financial statements.

"I don't think you could run a business properly without being so on top of the finances," she stresses. "That's why I have a bookkeeper… You can't put some of that stuff off."

Good record keeping also allows Ms. Hunsley more time for what she enjoys most. Despite the tremendous growth of the business, she still taught about 15 hours a week while expecting a baby girl. Though she didn't plan to teach immediately after the baby was born, she would continue running the business, and planned to return to teaching within a few months. "Teaching and working with kids is my favourite part," she says.

The Navigator

STUDY OBJECTIVES:

After studying this chapter, you should be able to:

1. Define debits and credits and illustrate how they are used to record transactions.

2. Describe the accounting cycle and the steps in the recording process.

3. Explain what a journal is, and journalize transactions.

4. Explain what a ledger is, and post journal entries.

5. Explain the purpose of a trial balance, and prepare one.

The Navigator

In Chapter 1, we used the accounting equation to analyze transactions. The combined effects of these transactions were presented in a tabular form. This method could work for small companies like Softbyte (the fictitious company discussed in Chapter 1) because they have relatively few transactions. But imagine Prestige Dance in the feature story using the same tabular format as Softbyte. With 800 students, the dance academy has too many transactions to record each one this way. Instead, a set of procedures and records are used to keep track of transaction data more easily.

This chapter introduces and illustrates the basic procedures and records. It is organized as follows:

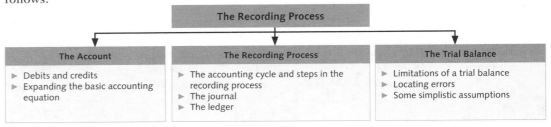

The Recording Process		
The Account	**The Recording Process**	**The Trial Balance**
▶ Debits and credits	▶ The accounting cycle and steps in the recording process	▶ Limitations of a trial balance
▶ Expanding the basic accounting equation	▶ The journal	▶ Locating errors
	▶ The ledger	▶ Some simplistic assumptions

The Account

STUDY OBJECTIVE 1

Define debits and credits and illustrate how they are used to record business transactions.

An **account** is an individual accounting record of increases and decreases in a specific asset, liability, or owner's equity item. For example, Softbyte has separate accounts called Cash, Accounts Receivable, Accounts Payable, Service Revenue, Salaries Expense, and so on.

In its simplest form, an account has three parts: (1) the title of the account, (2) a left or a debit side, and (3) a right or a credit side. Because these parts of an account are positioned like the letter T, it is called a **T account**. The basic form of an account is shown in Illustration 2-1.

Illustration 2-1 ➡

Basic form of T account

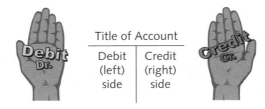

Title of Account	
Debit (left) side	Credit (right) side

The actual form that is used in real life is more complex than the above T, which account that will be explained later in the chapter. The T account format is a learning tool that will be used throughout the book to explain basic accounting relationships. It is also a form used by professional accountants for analytical purposes.

Debits and Credits

Tutorials:
Accounting Cycle Tutorial

The term **debit** means left. The term **credit** means right. These terms are often abbreviated Dr. for debit and Cr. for credit. Debit and credit are simply directional signals that describe where entries are made in the accounts. Entering an amount on the left side of an account is called debiting the account. Entering an amount on the right side is called crediting the account.

When the totals of the two sides are compared, an account will have a debit balance if the total of the debit amounts exceeds the credits. On the other hand, an account will have a credit balance if the credit amounts are more than the debits.

The recording of debits and credits in an account is shown below for Softbyte's cash transactions. The data are taken from the Cash column of the tabular summary in Illustration 1-10.

Tabular Summary Cash		Account Form			
			Cash		
		(Debits)		(Credits)	
+$15,000		15,000		7,000	
-7,000		1,200		600	
+1,200		1,500		900	
+1,500		600		200	
-600				250	
-900				1,300	
-200		Balance	8,050		
-250					
+600					
-1,300					
$ 8,050					

In the tabular summary, every positive item is a receipt of cash. Every negative amount is a payment of cash. Notice that in the account format the increases in cash are recorded as debits, and the decreases in cash are recorded as credits. The account balance, a debit of $8,050, indicates that Softbyte had $8,050 more increases than decreases in cash. We will learn in the next section why debits and credits are used in this way.

Debit and Credit Procedure

In Chapter 1, you learned that each transaction must affect two or more accounts to keep the basic accounting equation in balance. We will also see that, for each transaction, debits must equal credits. The equality of debits and credits is the basis for the double-entry system of recording transactions.

In the **double-entry system**, the dual (two-sided) effect of each transaction is recorded in the appropriate accounts. This system is used all over the world and gives a logical method for recording transactions and ensuring the amounts are recorded accurately. If every transaction is recorded with equal debits and credits, then the sum of all the debits to the accounts must equal the sum of all the credits.

Assets and Liabilities. In the Softbyte illustration, increases in Cash—an asset account—were entered on the left side, and decreases in Cash were entered on the right side. Why did we do this instead of the opposite? First, we know that in the basic accounting equation (assets = liabilities + owner's equity), assets are on the left or debit side of the equation. So, to be consistent, when the double-entry system was created, it was decided that the normal balance of asset accounts should also be on the left side. Second, there are usually more increases in asset accounts than decreases. Logically, then, for the balance in an asset account to be on the debit side, increases also need to be recorded on that side. This is why asset accounts normally show debit balances.

So remember this: increases in assets must be entered on the left or debit side, and decreases in assets must be entered on the right or credit side.

Similarly, because liabilities are on the right or credit side of the accounting equation, liability accounts normally show credit balances. Credits to a liability account should be more than the debits to that account. Increases in liabilities must be entered on the right or credit side, and decreases in liabilities must be entered on the left or debit side.

To summarize, because assets are on the opposite side of the accounting equation from liabilities, increases and decreases in assets are recorded opposite from increases and decreases in liabilities. In this way, the total amount of debits always equals the total amount of credits and the equation stays in balance. The effects that debits and credits have on assets and liabilities and the normal balances are as follows:

Helpful hint Increases in accounts are always on the same side as the normal balance for that account.

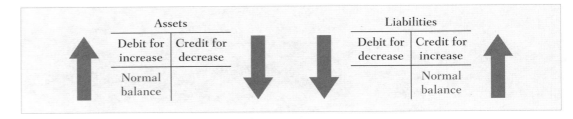

Knowing the normal balance in an account may also help you find errors. In automated systems, the computer is programmed to find these normal balance exceptions and to print out error or exception reports. In manual systems, a careful inspection of the accounts has to be done to find balances that are not normal. For example, a credit balance in an asset account such as Land or a debit balance in a liability account such as Wages Payable probably means there was a recording error. Occasionally, an abnormal balance may be correct. The Cash account, for example, will have a credit balance when a company has overdrawn its bank balance.

Owner's Equity. As explained in Chapter 1, owner's equity is increased by owner's investments and revenues. It is decreased by owner's drawings and expenses. Separate accounts are kept for each of these types of transactions.

Owner's Capital. Investments by owners are credited to the owner's capital account. Like liability accounts, the owner's capital account is increased by credits and decreased by debits. For example, when cash is invested in the business, the Cash account is debited and Owner's Capital is credited.

The rules of debit and credit for the Owner's Capital account and the normal balance are as follows:

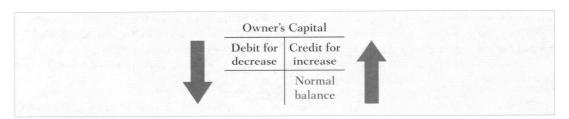

As liabilities and owner's equity are on the same side of the accounting equation, the rules of debit and credit are the same for these two types of accounts.

Owner's Drawings. An owner may withdraw cash or other assets for personal use. Withdrawals should be recorded as debits because withdrawals decrease owner's equity. Withdrawals could be debited directly to Owner's Capital. However, it is better to have a separate account, called Drawings, as we did in Chapter 1. The separate account makes it easier to add up the total withdrawals for the accounting period and to prepare the statement of owner's equity. Because the drawings account decreases owner's equity, the account has a normal debit balance. Note that increases and decreases are recorded opposite to how they are recorded in Owner's Capital, which increases owner's equity. Credits to an owner's drawings account are unusual, but might be used to correct a withdrawal recorded in error, for example.

The rules of debit and credit for the Drawings account and the normal balance are as follows:

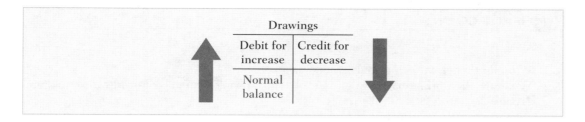

Revenues and Expenses. When revenues are earned, owner's equity is increased. Accordingly, the effect of debits and credits on revenue accounts is the same as their effect on Owner's Capital. Revenue accounts are increased by credits and decreased by debits.

Expenses have the opposite effect: expenses decrease owner's equity. As a result, expenses are recorded as debits because debits decrease owner's equity. Since expenses are the negative factor in calculating profit, and revenues are the positive factor, it is logical that the increase and decrease sides of expense accounts should be the reverse of revenue accounts. Thus, expense accounts are increased by debits and decreased by credits.

Credits to revenue accounts should exceed the debits. Debits to expense accounts should exceed the credits. Thus, revenue accounts normally show credit balances. Expense accounts normally show debit balances.

The effect of debits and credits on revenues and expenses and the normal balances are as follows:

Expanding the Basic Accounting Equation

You have already learned the basic accounting equation. Illustration 2-2 expands this equation to show the accounts that form owner's equity. In addition, the debit/credit rules and effects on each type of account are shown. Study this diagram carefully. It will help you to understand the basics of the double-entry system. Like the basic equation, the expanded basic equation must always be in balance (total debits must equal total credits).

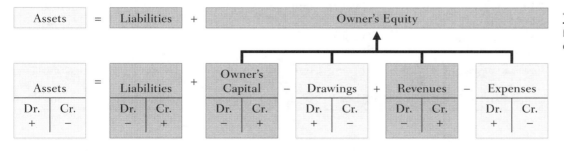

← **Illustration 2-2**

Expanded basic equation and debit/credit rules and effects

Remember, the normal balance of each account is on its increase side. So assets, drawings, and expense accounts have a normal debit balance, while liabilities, owner's capital, and revenue accounts have a normal credit balance.

BEFORE YOU GO ON . . .

➔ Review It

1. What do the terms "debit" and "credit" mean?
2. What are the normal balances of asset, liability, owner's capital, drawings, revenue, and expense accounts?
3. What are the effects of debits and credits on the asset, liability, and owner's capital accounts?
4. What are the effects of debits and credits on the revenue, expense, and drawings accounts?
5. What are the normal balances for these Forzani accounts: Accounts Receivable; Accounts Payable and Accrued Liabilities; Retail Revenue; and Store Operating Expense? The answer to this question is at the end of this chapter.

➔ Do It

Eszter Schwenke has just rented space in a shopping mall where she will open a beauty salon called Hair It Is. Eszter has determined that the company will need the following accounts:

1.	Accounts Payable	6.	Rent Expense
2.	Cash	7.	Salon Equipment
3.	E. Schwenke, Capital	8.	Service Revenue
4.	E. Schwenke, Drawings	9.	Supplies
5.	Notes Payable	10.	Wages Expense

(a) Indicate whether each of these accounts is an asset, liability, or owner's equity account. If it is an owner's equity account, indicate what type it is (e.g., owner's capital, drawings, revenue, or expense).
(b) What is the normal balance of these accounts?
(c) Will a debit increase or decrease these accounts?

Action Plan

- Use the expanded accounting equation to determine the type of account.
- Remember that the normal balance of an account is on its increase side.
- Remember that assets are increased by debits, and that liabilities and owner's equity are increased by credits.

Solution

Account	(a) Type of Account	(b) Normal Balance	(c) Debit Effect
Accounts Payable	Liability	Credit	Decrease
Cash	Asset	Debit	Increase
E. Schwenke, Capital	Owner's Equity	Credit	Decrease
E. Schwenke, Drawings	Owner's Equity (drawing)	Debit	Increase
Notes Payable	Liability	Credit	Decrease
Rent Expense	Owner's Equity (expense)	Debit	Increase
Salon Equipment	Asset	Debit	Increase
Service Revenue	Owner's Equity (revenue)	Credit	Decrease
Supplies	Asset	Debit	Increase
Wages Expense	Owner's Equity (expense)	Debit	Increase

The Navigator

Related exercise material: BE2–1, BE2–2, BE2–3, BE2–4, BE2–5, BE2–6, BE2–7, E2–2, E2–3, and E2–4.

The Recording Process

We could record transaction information directly into the accounts, but important information would be lost and the number of errors would increase. Instead, accountants follow systematic procedures to ensure transactions are correctly recorded, summarized, and reported to financial statement users. In the following sections we explain the recording process.

The Accounting Cycle and Steps in the Recording Process

STUDY OBJECTIVE 2

Describe the accounting cycle and the steps in the recording process.

The procedures used in recording transaction information is part of a series of steps, called the **accounting cycle**, which accountants follow in preparing financial statements as shown in Illustration 2-3.

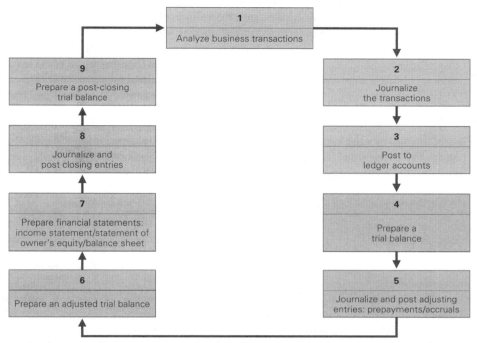

← Illustration 2-3

The accounting cycle

The steps in the recording process are the first three steps in the accounting cycle:

1. Analyze each transaction for its effects on the accounts.
2. Record the transaction in a journal (book of original entry).
3. Transfer the journal information to the correct accounts in the ledger (book of accounts).

The fourth step will be discussed later in the chapter. The remaining steps, 5 through 9, will be discussed in the next two chapters.

The recording process begins with analyzing the transaction. Deciding what to record is the most critical point in the accounting cycle. Recall from Chapter 1 that a transaction is recorded only if it causes the company's financial position (assets, liabilities, and owner's equity) to change.

Documents, such as a sales slip, cheque, bill, cash register tape, or bank statement, are analyzed to determine the effects of the transaction on specific accounts. Ms. Hunsley's Prestige Dance Academy in the feature story uses customers' payments and the company's cheques written for expenses to begin its recording process.

Then the transaction is entered in the journal. After that, the information in the journal entry is transferred to the correct accounts in the ledger. The sequence of events in the recording process is shown in Illustration 2-4.

← Illustration 2-4

The recording process

Analyze each transaction   Record transaction in a journal   Transfer journal information
to ledger accounts

The steps in the recording process are repeated again and again in every company, whether a computerized or manual accounting system is used. However, the first two steps—the analysis and entering of each transaction—must be done by a person even when a computerized system is used. The major difference between a computerized and a manual accounting system is in transferring information from the journal to the ledger. In computerized systems, this is done automatically by the computer, which substantially reduces the possibility of making mistakes. In order to understand how computerized systems do this, we need to understand the manual way of processing accounting data. We will focus on the manual approach in this chapter.

BEFORE YOU GO ON . . .

→ **Review It**

1. What is the accounting cycle?
2. What are the three steps in the recording process?
3. What is the main advantage of a computerized accounting system?

Related exercise material: BE2-8

The Navigator

The Journal

Transactions are first recorded in chronological (date) order in a **journal** and then transferred to the accounts. For this reason, the journal is referred to as the book of original entry. For each transaction, the journal shows the debit and credit effects on specific accounts. Companies can use various kinds of journals, but every company has the most basic form of journal, a **general journal**. Whenever we use the term "journal" in this textbook without a description of it, we mean the general journal.

The journal makes some important contributions to the recording process:

- It discloses the complete effect of a transaction in one place.
- It provides a chronological record of transactions.
- It helps to prevent and locate errors, because the debit and credit amounts for each entry can be easily compared.
- It gives an explanation of the transaction and, if there is one, identifies the source document.

Journalizing

The second step in the accounting cycle, entering transaction data in the journal, is known as **journalizing**. A separate journal entry is made for each transaction. A complete entry consists of the following: (1) the date of the transaction, (2) the accounts and amounts to be debited and credited, and (3) a brief explanation of the transaction.

To illustrate the technique of journalizing, let's look at the first two transactions of Softbyte from Chapter 1. These transactions were (1) September 1, Marc Doucet invested $15,000 cash in the business, and (2) computer equipment was purchased for $7,000 cash (we will assume that this transaction also occurred on September 1). In tabular form, these transactions appeared in Chapter 1 as follows:

	Assets		=	Liabilities	+	Owner's Equity
						M. Doucet,
	Cash	+ Equipment				Capital
(1)	+$15,000					+$15,000
(2)	−7,000	+$7,000				

In journal form, these transactions would appear as follows:

Date	Account Titles and Explanation	Ref.	Debit	Credit
GENERAL JOURNAL				J1
2011 Sept. 1	Cash		15,000	
	M. Doucet, Capital			15,000
	Invested cash in business.			
1	Equipment		7,000	
	Cash			7,000
	Purchased equipment for cash.			

A	=	L	+	OE
+15,000				+15,000

↑ Cash flows: +15,000

A	=	L	+	OE
+7,000				
−7,000				

↓ Cash flows: −7,000

Since this is the first page of Softbyte's general journal, it is numbered J1. As illustrated in the previous illustration, the standard form and content of journal entries are as follows:

1. The date of the transaction is entered in the Date column.
2. The account to be debited is entered first at the left margin of the column headed Account Titles and Explanation. The account to be credited is then entered on the next line and indented from the left margin. The indentation visually separates the accounts to be debited and credited, so there is less chance of switching the debits and credits.
3. The amounts for the debits are recorded in the Debit (left) column and the amounts for the credits are recorded in the Credit (right) column.
4. A brief explanation of the transaction is given on the line below the credit account title. To simplify the illustrations in this textbook, journal entry explanations are often left out. Remember, however, that in real life, explanations are essential for every journal entry.
5. A blank row can be left between journal entries. This makes the journal easier to read.
6. The column titled Ref. (which stands for "reference") is left blank when the journal entry is made. This column is used later, when the journal entries are transferred to the ledger accounts. At that time, the ledger account number is placed in the Reference column to indicate where the amount in the journal entry was transferred to.

Students often find it difficult to decide what account title to use. To make the decision easier, the main thing to consider is that each title has to accurately describe the account's content. For example, the account title used for the computer equipment purchased by Softbyte may be Equipment, Computer Equipment, Computers, or Office Equipment. However, once a company chooses the specific title to use, all transactions for the account should be recorded under that account title.

When you complete the assignments in this text, if specific account titles are given, you should use those. If account titles are not given, you should create account titles that identify the nature and content of each account. The account titles used in journalizing should not contain explanations (such as Cash Paid or Cash Received).

If an entry affects only two accounts, one debit and one credit, it is considered a simple journal entry. Some transactions, however, involve more than two accounts. When three or more accounts are required in one journal entry, the entry is called a **compound entry**. To illustrate, recall from Chapter 1 that Softbyte provided $3,500 of programming services to customers (assume this was on September 9). It received $1,500 cash from the customers for these services. The balance, $2,000, was owed on account. The compound entry to record this transaction is as follows:

Date	Account Titles and Explanation	Ref.	Debit	Credit
GENERAL JOURNAL				J1
2011 Sept. 9	Cash		1,500	
	Accounts Receivable		2,000	
	Service Revenue			3,500
	Performed services for cash and credit.			

A	=	L	+	OE
+1,500				+3,500
+2,000				

↑ Cash flows: +1,500

In a compound entry, just as in a simple entry, the total debit and credit amounts must be equal. Also, all of the debits are listed before the credits are listed.

ACCOUNTING IN ACTION: BUSINESS INSIGHT

As Mississauga, Ontario–based Magellan Aerospace has recently experienced, incorrect and unrecorded transactions can have a serious impact on profit. The company launched an internal investigation of one of its divisions after overvalued accounts receivable were found on the company's books during bill collection. The investigation found unsupported and unrecorded transactions—accounting irregularities that increased the aircraft parts company's 2007 loss to $11.3 million. Correcting the misstatements, which took place from 2003 to 2007, resulted in pre-tax losses of $5.8 million after estimated insurance recoveries. The losses occurred "as the overstated carrying values of the assets were written down to their appropriate values," the company said.

Source: CBC News, "After fixing bad accounting, Magellan loses $11.3 million" (April 1, 2008), < http://www.cbc.ca/money/story/2008/04/01/magellan-loss.html> (accessed on February 9, 2009).

How can unrecorded accounts receivable transactions increase a loss on the income statement?

BEFORE YOU GO ON . . .

→ Review It

1. What is the purpose of the journal in the recording process?
2. What is the standard form and content of a journal entry in the general journal?
3. What is a compound journal entry and what are the debit and credit rules for compound entries?

→ Do It

In starting her beauty salon, Hair It Is, Eszter Schwenke did the following:

May 1   Opened a bank account in the name of Hair It Is and deposited $20,000 of her own money in this account as her initial investment.

3   Purchased equipment on account (to be paid in 30 days), for a total cost of $4,800.

7   Hired a stylist and agreed to pay her $500 per week.

(a) In what form (type of record) should Eszter first record these three activities?
(b) Prepare the entries to record the transactions.

Action Plan
• Understand which activities need to be recorded and which do not.
• Analyze the effects of the transactions on asset, liability, and owner's equity accounts.
• Apply the debit and credit rules.
• Record the transactions in the general journal following the formatting rules.

Solution
(a) Each transaction that is recorded is entered in the general journal.
(b)

May 1	Cash	20,000	
	E. Schwenke, Capital		20,000
	Invested cash in the business.		
3	Equipment	4,800	
	Accounts Payable		4,800
	Purchased equipment on account.		
7	No entry because no transaction has occurred.		

The Navigator

Related exercise material: BE2–9, BE2–10, E2–4, E2–5, and E2–6.

The Ledger

The entire group of accounts maintained by a company is called the ledger. The **ledger** keeps all the information about changes in each account in one place.

STUDY OBJECTIVE 4

Explain what a ledger is, and post journal entries.

Companies can use different kinds of ledgers, but every company has a **general ledger**. A general ledger contains all the asset, liability, and owner's equity accounts. Whenever we use the term "ledger" on its own in this textbook, we mean the general ledger.

A business can use a loose-leaf binder or card file for the ledger, with each account kept on a separate sheet or card. However, most companies use a computerized accounting system that keeps each account in a separate file. In a computerized system, such as the QuickBooks accounting software used by Prestige Dance Academy in the feature story, each account is numbered so that it is easier to identify.

The ledger should be arranged in the same order that is used to present the accounts in the financial statements, beginning with the balance sheet accounts. The asset accounts come first, followed by liability accounts, owner's capital, drawings, revenues, and expenses. The ledger gives the balance in each account. The ledger will also show all of the increases and decreases that have been made to each account.

Standard Form of Account

The simple T account form used in accounting textbooks is often very useful for illustrations and for learning accounting. In reality, however, the account forms that are used in ledgers are designed to include additional information. A very popular form in both manual and computerized systems, using the data (and assumed dates) from Softbyte's Cash account, follows:

GENERAL LEDGER					
CASH					
Date	Explanation	Ref.	Debit	Credit	Balance
2011					
Sept. 1			15,000		15,000
1				7,000	8,000
3			1,200		9,200
9			1,500		10,700
17				600	10,100
17				900	9,200
20				200	9,000
25				250	8,750
30			600		9,350
30				1,300	8,050

This form is often called the three-column form of account because it has three money columns: debit, credit, and balance. The balance in the account is determined after each transaction. Note that the explanation space and reference columns make it possible to give information about the transaction. In manual accounting systems, the explanation space is usually left blank because it is too time-consuming to copy explanations from the general journal. Computerized accounting systems will automatically include in the ledger the explanation that was originally recorded in the journal entry.

Posting

The procedure of transferring journal entries to the ledger accounts is called **posting**. It is the third step in the accounting cycle. Posting has the following steps:

1. General Ledger. In the ledger, enter the date, journal page, and debit or credit amount shown in the journal in the correct columns of each affected account.
2. General Journal. In the reference column of the journal, write the account numbers to which the debit and credit amounts were posted in the ledger.

Illustration 2-5 ➜

Posting a journal entry

These steps are shown in Illustration 2-5 using Softbyte's first journal entry.

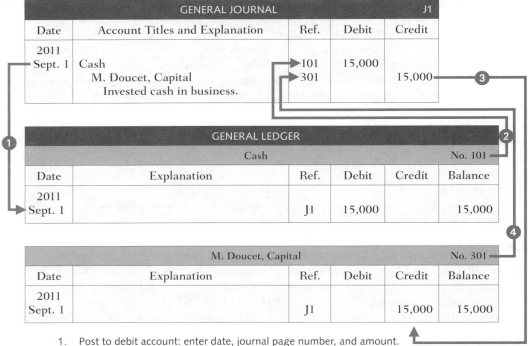

1. Post to debit account: enter date, journal page number, and amount.
2. Enter debit account number in journal reference column.
3. Post to credit account: enter date, journal page number, and amount.
4. Enter credit account number in journal reference column.

The reference column in the journal has several purposes. The numbers in this column indicate the entries that have been posted. After the last entry has been posted, this column should be looked at carefully to see that all postings have been made. The references also show the account numbers to which the amounts have been posted. The reference column of a ledger account indicates the journal page where the transaction was posted from.

Posting should be done in chronological order. That is, all the debits and credits of one journal entry should be posted before going to the next journal entry. Postings should be made on a timely basis—normally monthly—to keep the ledger up to date. In a computerized accounting system, posting usually occurs automatically right after each journal entry is prepared.

Chart of Accounts

The first step in designing an accounting system—whether computerized or manual—is to create a **chart of accounts**. The chart of accounts is the framework for the entire database of accounting information. It lists the account names and numbers of all the accounts in the ledger. The numbering system that is used to identify the accounts usually starts with the balance sheet accounts. The income statement accounts come next.

Because each company is different, the types of accounts they have and how many they have are also different. The number of accounts depends on the amount of detail that management wants. The management of one company may want one account for all types of utility expense. Another company may keep separate expense accounts for each type of utility expense, such as gas, electricity, and water.

ACCOUNTING IN ACTION: ACROSS THE ORGANIZATION

The numbering system used to identify accounts can be quite sophisticated or relatively simple. For example, Goodyear Canada Inc. uses an eight-digit system. The first three digits identify the account classification as follows:

100–199 Assets	300–399 Revenues
200–299 Liabilities and Owner's Equity	400–599 Expenses

The balance of the numbering system can be used to describe location, but is usually used to facilitate reporting requirements (at a more detailed level) or to segregate activities in order to ensure that account reconciliations can be done efficiently.

In contrast, a small company, Beanz Espresso Bar in Charlottetown, uses the basic four-digit numbering system set up by its accounting software, Simply Accounting. There is no need for other digits describing location as there is only one store and the basic system provides all the detail that the owner needs.

When deciding how to create a chart of accounts, whom should an accountant consult with?

In this and the next two chapters, we will show the accounting cycle for a service company named Pioneer Advertising Agency. Accounts 100–199 indicate asset accounts; 200–299 indicate liabilities; 300–399 indicate owner's equity accounts; 400–499, revenues; and 500–999, expenses. The chart of accounts for Pioneer Advertising Agency, owned by Clarence Byrd, is shown in Illustration 2-6.

Accounts shown in red are used in this chapter; accounts shown in black are explained in later chapters. From your study of transaction analysis in Chapter 1, you will be familiar with all of the accounts shown in red except for Unearned Revenue and Prepaid Insurance. These two new accounts will be introduced in the next section in Transactions 3 and 5, respectively.

PIONEER ADVERTISING AGENCY
Chart of Accounts

Assets		Owner's Equity	
101.	Cash	301.	C. Byrd, Capital
112.	Accounts Receivable	306.	C. Byrd, Drawings
129.	Advertising Supplies	350.	Income Summary
130.	Prepaid Insurance		
151.	Office Equipment	**Revenues**	
152.	Accumulated Depreciation—	400.	Service Revenue
	Office Equipment		
		Expenses	
Liabilities		611.	Advertising Supplies Expense
200.	Notes Payable	711.	Depreciation Expense
201.	Accounts Payable	722.	Insurance Expense
209.	Unearned Revenue	726.	Salaries Expense
212.	Salaries Payable	729.	Rent Expense
230.	Interest Payable	905.	Interest Expense

← Illustration 2-6

Chart of accounts

You will notice that there are gaps in the numbering system of the chart of accounts for Pioneer Advertising. Gaps make it possible to insert new accounts whenever they are needed.

WILEY PLUS

Chart of Accounts

The Recording Process Illustrated

In the following section, we show the basic steps in analyzing and recording the October 2011 transactions of the Pioneer Advertising Agency. The agency's accounting period is one month. A basic analysis and a debit/credit analysis are done before each transaction is journalized and posted. For simplicity, the illustrations show the T account form instead of the standard account form.

Study these transaction analyses carefully. The purpose of transaction analysis is to identify (1) the type of account involved, (2) whether the account is increased or decreased, and (3) whether the account needs to be debited or credited. You should always do this analysis before preparing a journal entry. It will help you understand the journal entries discussed in this chapter, as well as more complex journal entries in later chapters.

Transaction (1) →

Investment of cash by owner

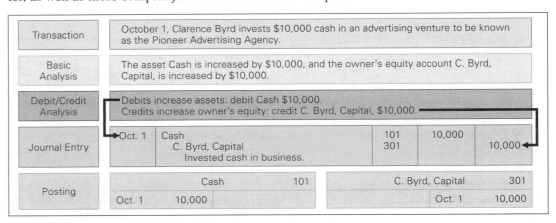

Transaction (2) →

Purchase of office equipment

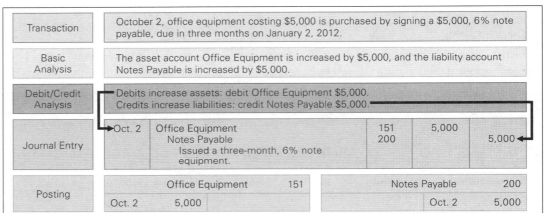

Transaction (3) →

Receipt of cash in advance from customer

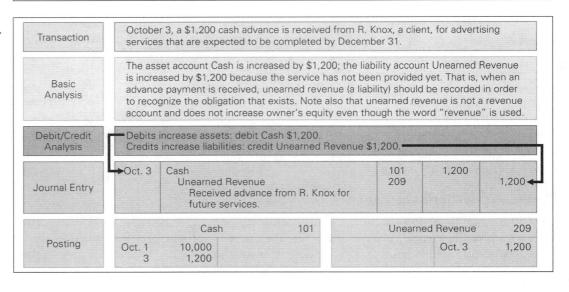

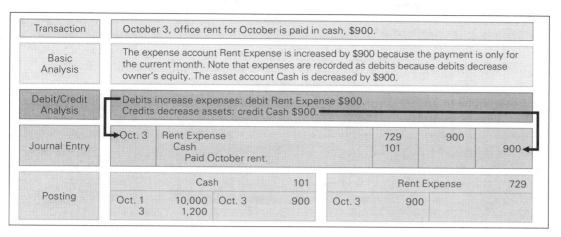

← Transaction (4)

Payment of monthly rent

	October 3, office rent for October is paid in cash, $900.
Transaction	
Basic Analysis	The expense account Rent Expense is increased by $900 because the payment is only for the current month. Note that expenses are recorded as debits because debits decrease owner's equity. The asset account Cash is decreased by $900.
Debit/Credit Analysis	Debits increase expenses: debit Rent Expense $900. Credits decrease assets: credit Cash $900.

Oct. 3 | Rent Expense | 729 | 900 |
| Cash | 101 | | 900 |
| Paid October rent. | | | |

Posting

Cash			101		Rent Expense		729
Oct. 1	10,000	Oct. 3	900	Oct. 3	900		
3	1,200						

← Transaction (5)

Payment of insurance

	October 3, $600 is paid for a one-year insurance policy, which will expire next year on September 30.
Transaction	
Basic Analysis	The asset account Prepaid Insurance is increased by $600 because the payment is for more than the current month. The asset account Cash is decreased by $600. Note that costs that will benefit more than one accounting period are identified as prepaid expenses or prepayments. When a prepayment is made, an asset account is debited in order to show the service or benefit that will be received in the future.
Debit/Credit Analysis	Debits increase assets: debit Prepaid Insurance $600. Credits decrease assets: credit Cash $600.

Oct. 3 | Prepaid Insurance | 130 | 600 |
| Cash | 101 | | 600 |
| Paid one-year policy, expiring on September 30, 2012. | | | |

Posting

Cash			101		Prepaid Insurance		130
Oct. 1	10,000	Oct. 3	900	Oct. 3	600		
3	1,200	3	600				

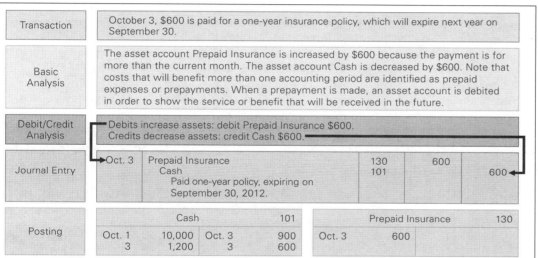

← Transaction (6)

Purchase of supplies on credit

	October 4, an estimated three-month supply of advertising materials is purchased on account from Aero Supply for $2,500.
Transaction	
Basic Analysis	The asset account Advertising Supplies is increased by $2,500. The liability account Accounts Payable is increased by $2,500.
Debit/Credit Analysis	Debits increase assets: debit Advertising Supplies $2,500. Credits increase liabilities: credit Accounts Payable $2,500.

Oct. 4 | Advertising Supplies | 129 | 2,500 |
| Accounts Payable | 201 | | 2,500 |
| Purchased supplies on account from Aero Supply. | | | |

Posting

Advertising Supplies		129		Accounts Payable		201
Oct. 4	2,500				Oct. 4	2,500

← Transaction (7)

Hiring of employees

	October 6, four employees are hired to begin work on October 10. Each employee is to receive a weekly salary of $500 for a five-day workweek (Monday–Friday), payable every two weeks. The first payment will be on October 21.
Transaction	
Basic Analysis	An accounting transaction has not occurred. There is only an agreement between the employer and the employees to enter into a business transaction beginning on October 10. Thus, a debit/credit analysis is not needed because there is no accounting entry. (See October 21 transaction for first entry.)

Transaction (8) ➡

Withdrawal of cash by owner

Transaction	October 20, Clarence Byrd withdraws $500 cash for personal use.
Basic Analysis	The owner's equity account C. Byrd, Drawings is increased by $500. Note that drawings are recorded as debits because debits reduce owner's equity. The asset account Cash is decreased by $500.
Debit/Credit Analysis	Debits increase drawings: debit C. Byrd, Drawings, $500. Credits decrease assets: credit Cash $500.

Journal Entry	Oct. 20	C. Byrd, Drawings	306	500	
		Cash	101		500
		Withdrew cash for personal use.			

Posting	Cash			101		C. Byrd, Drawings		306
	Oct. 1	10,000	Oct. 3	900	Oct. 20	500	
	3	1,200	3	600			
			20	500			

Transaction (9) ➡

Service performed on account

Transaction	October 21, a customer, Copa Company, is billed $10,000 for advertising services performed to date.
Basic Analysis	The asset account Accounts Receivable is increased by $10,000. The revenue account Service Revenue is increased by $10,000. Note that revenue is recorded when the service is performed, regardless of when the cash is received. Accounts Receivable is an asset because Pioneer Advertising expects a future benefit—the cash payment by Copa Company.
Debit/Credit Analysis	Debits increase assets: debit Accounts Receivable $10,000. Credits increase revenues: credit Service Revenue $10,000.

Journal Entry	Oct. 21	Accounts Receivable	112	10,000	
		Service Revenue	400		10,000
		Performed services on account for Copa Company.			

Posting	Accounts Receivable		112		Service Revenue		400
	Oct. 21	10,000				Oct. 21	10,000

Transaction (10) ➡

Payment of salaries

Transaction	October 21, employee salaries of $4,000 (4 × $500 × 2) are owed and paid. (See October 6 transaction.)
Basic Analysis	The expense account Salaries Expense is increased by $4,000. The asset account Cash is decreased by $4,000.
Debit/Credit Analysis	Debits increase expenses: debit Salaries Expense $4,000. Credits decrease assets: credit Cash $4,000.

Journal Entry	Oct. 21	Salaries Expense	726	4,000	
		Cash	101		4,000
		Paid biweekly salaries.			

Posting	Cash			101		Salaries Expense		726
	Oct. 1	10,000	Oct. 3	900	Oct. 21	4,000	
	3	1,200	3	600			
			20	500			
			21	4,000			

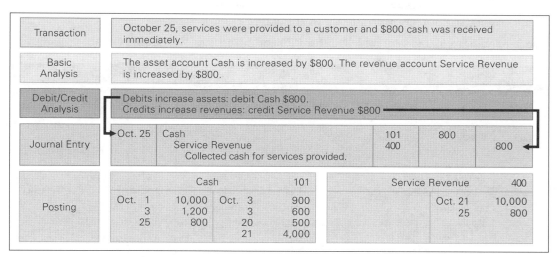

← **Transaction (11)**

Receipt of cash for services provided

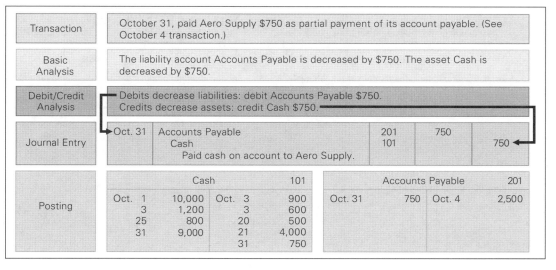

← **Transaction (12)**

Receipt of cash from collecting part of an account receivable

Transaction	October 31, received $9,000 cash from Copa Company in payment of part of its account. (See October 21 transaction.)
Basic Analysis	The asset account Cash is increased by $9,000. The asset account Accounts Receivable is decreased by $9,000. Note that service revenue is not recorded here; it was recorded on October 21 when the service was performed.
Debit/Credit Analysis	Debits increase assets: debit Cash $9,000. Credits decrease assets: credit Accounts Receivable $9,000.

← **Transaction (13)**

Partial payment of account payable

Transaction	October 31, paid Aero Supply $750 as partial payment of its account payable. (See October 4 transaction.)
Basic Analysis	The liability account Accounts Payable is decreased by $750. The asset Cash is decreased by $750.
Debit/Credit Analysis	Debits decrease liabilities: debit Accounts Payable $750. Credits decrease assets: credit Cash $750.

Journal Entry

Oct. 31	Accounts Payable	201	750	
	Cash	101		750
	Paid cash on account to Aero Supply.			

Posting

	Cash		101			Accounts Payable		201
Oct. 1	10,000	Oct. 3	900		Oct. 31	750	Oct. 4	2,500
3	1,200	3	600					
25	800	20	500					
31	9,000	21	4,000					
		31	750					

Summary Illustration of Journalizing and Posting

The general journal and general ledger for Pioneer Advertising Agency for October follow:

	GENERAL JOURNAL			J1
Date	Account Titles and Explanation	Ref.	Debit	Credit
2011 Oct. 1	Cash	101	10,000	
	C. Byrd, Capital	301		10,000
	Invested cash in business.			
2	Office Equipment	151	5,000	
	Notes Payable	200		5,000
	Issued three-month, 6% note for office equipment.			
3	Cash	101	1,200	
	Unearned Revenue	209		1,200
	Received advance from R. Knox for future services.			
3	Rent Expense	729	900	
	Cash	101		900
	Paid October rent.			
3	Prepaid Insurance	130	600	
	Cash	101		600
	Paid one-year policy, expiring on September 30, 2012.			
4	Advertising Supplies	129	2,500	
	Accounts Payable	201		2,500
	Purchased supplies on account from Aero Supply.			
20	C. Byrd, Drawings	306	500	
	Cash	101		500
	Withdrew cash for personal use.			
21	Accounts Receivable	112	10,000	
	Service Revenue	400		10,000
	Performed services on account for Copa Company.			
21	Salaries Expense	726	4,000	
	Cash	101		4,000
	Paid biweekly salaries.			
25	Cash	101	800	
	Service Revenue	400		800
	Collected cash for services provided.			
31	Cash	101	9,000	
	Accounts Receivable	112		9,000
	Received cash on account from Copa Company.			
31	Accounts Payable	201	750	
	Cash	101		750
	Paid cash on account to Aero Supply.			

GENERAL LEDGER							

| Cash | | | | 101 | Accounts payable | | | 201 |

		Cash		101		Accounts payable		201
Oct. 1	10,000	Oct. 3	900		Oct. 31	750	Oct. 4	2,500
3	1,200	3	600				Bal.	1,750
25	800	20	500					
31	9,000	21	4,000			Unearned Revenue		209
		31	750				Oct. 3	1,200
Bal.	14,250						Bal.	1,200

	Accounts Receivable		112		C. Byrd, Capital		301
Oct. 21	10,000	Oct. 31	9,000			Oct. 1	10,000
Bal.	1,000					Bal.	10,000

	Advertising Supplies		129		C. Byrd, Drawings		306
Oct. 4	2,500			Oct. 20	500		
Bal.	2,500			Bal.	500		

	Prepaid Insurance		130		Service Revenue		400
Oct. 3	600					Oct. 21	10,000
Bal.	600					25	800
						Bal.	10,800

	Office Equipment		151		Salaries Expense		726
Oct. 2	5,000			Oct. 21	4,000		
Bal.	5,000			Bal.	4,000		

	Notes Payable		200		Rent Expense		729
		Oct. 2	5,000	Oct. 3	900		
		Bal.	5,000	Bal.	900		

BEFORE YOU GO ON . . .

➜ Review It

1. What is the difference between journalizing and posting?
2. What is the purpose of (a) the ledger, and (b) a chart of accounts?

➜ Do It

The following events occurred during the second week of business of Hair It Is, a beauty salon owned by Eszter Schwenke.

May 13 Paid $92 for utilities.
   14 Performed $1,280 of hairstyling services ($1,000 was collected in cash and $280 was on account).
   15 Paid $500 in wages to the stylist hired on May 7.

The opening balance in the Cash account was $20,000.

(a) Record these transactions in the general journal.
(b) Post the journal entries to the general ledger.

Action Plan

- Analyze the transactions. Determine the accounts affected and whether the transaction increases or decreases the account.
- Record the transaction in the general journal using debits and credits. Remember that the name of the account to be credited is indented and the amount is recorded in the right-hand column.
- Posting involves transferring the journalized debits and credits to specific accounts in the ledger.
- Determine the ending balances by netting (calculating the difference between) the total debits and credits.

Solution

(a)

May 13	Utilities Expense		92	
	Cash			92
	Paid utilities.			
14	Cash		1,000	
	Accounts Receivable		280	
	Hairstyling Service Revenue			1,280
	Performed services for cash and on account.			
15	Wages Expense		500	
	Cash			500
	Paid employee.			

(b)

Cash		Accounts Receivable	Hairstyling Service Revenue	Wages Expense	Utilities Expense
20,000	92	280 |	| 1,280	500 |	92 |
1,000	500				
20,408					

The Navigator

Related exercise material: BE2–11, BE2–12, E2–7, and E2–8.

The Trial Balance

A **trial balance** is a list of accounts and their balances at a specific time. The preparation of the trial balance is the fourth step in the accounting cycle, as shown in Illustration 2-3. It is prepared monthly if the company is preparing monthly financial statements. Since companies must prepare annual financial statements, the trial balance must be prepared at least once a year.

In the trial balance, the accounts are listed in the same order as they are in the ledger, with debit balances in the left column and credit balances in the right column. The totals of the two columns must be equal.

The main purpose of a trial balance is to prove (check) that the debits equal the credits after posting. That is, the sum of the debit account balances must equal the sum of the credit account balances. If the totals are not the same, this means an error was made in journalizing or posting the transactions. For example, the trial balance will not balance if an incorrect amount is posted in the ledger. If the trial balance does not balance, then the error must be located and corrected before proceeding.

A trial balance is also useful in preparing financial statements, as will be explained in the next two chapters. The procedure for preparing a trial balance is as follows:

1. List the account titles and their balances in the same order as the chart of accounts. Debit balances are entered in the debit column and credit balances are entered in the credit column.
2. Total the debit and credit columns.
3. Ensure that the totals of the two columns are equal.

Illustration 2-7 is the trial balance prepared from the ledger of Pioneer Advertising Agency shown earlier in the chapter. Note that the total of the debit accounts, $28,750, is equal to the total of the credit accounts, $28,750. If any accounts have a zero balance, they can be omitted from the trial balance.

◄ Illustration 2-7

Pioneer Advertising Agency trial balance

PIONEER ADVERTISING AGENCY Trial Balance October 31, 2011		
	Debit	Credit
Cash	$14,250	
Accounts receivable	1,000	
Advertising supplies	2,500	
Prepaid insurance	600	
Office equipment	5,000	
Notes payable		$ 5,000
Accounts payable		1,750
Unearned revenue		1,200
C. Byrd, capital		10,000
C. Byrd, drawings	500	
Service revenue		10,800
Salaries expense	4,000	
Rent expense	900	
Totals	$28,750	$28,750

Limitations of a Trial Balance

Although a trial balance can reveal many types of bookkeeping errors, it does not prove that all transactions have been recorded or that the ledger is correct. There can be many errors even when the trial balance columns agree. For example, the trial balance may balance in the following cases: (1) a transaction is not journalized, (2) a correct journal entry is not posted, (3) a journal entry is posted twice, (4) incorrect accounts are used in journalizing or posting, or (5) offsetting errors (errors that hide each other) are made in recording the amount of a transaction. In other words, as long as equal debits and credits are posted, even to the wrong account or in the wrong amount, the total debits will equal the total credits when the trial balance is prepared.

Locating Errors

The procedure for preparing a trial balance is quite simple. However, if the trial balance does not balance, locating an error in a manual accounting system can be time-consuming, tiring, and frustrating. Errors generally result from mathematical mistakes, incorrect postings, or simply recopying data incorrectly. In a computerized system, the trial balance is usually balanced because most computerized systems will not let you enter an unbalanced journal entry, and because there are rarely software errors in posting or the preparation of the trial balance.

What do you do if you have a manual trial balance that does not balance? First determine the amount of the difference between the two columns of the trial balance. After you know this amount, try the following steps:

1. If the error is an amount such as $1, $100, or $1,000, re-add the trial balance columns. Recalculate the account balances.
2. If the error can be evenly divided by two, scan the trial balance to see if a balance equal to half the error has been entered in the wrong column.
3. If the error can be evenly divided by nine, retrace the account balances on the trial balance to see whether they are incorrectly copied from the ledger. For example, if a balance was $12 but was listed as $21, a $9 error has been made. Reversing the order of numbers is called a transposition error.

4. If the error cannot be evenly divided by two or nine, scan the ledger to see whether an account balance in the amount of the error has been omitted from the trial balance. Scan the journal to see whether a posting in the amount of the error has been omitted. Check your additions.

Of course, if there is more than one error, these steps may not work.

 ACCOUNTING IN ACTION: ALL ABOUT YOU

The double-entry accounting system used by many businesses today is in fact more than 500 years old. An Italian friar, Luca Pacioli, is considered to be the "Father of Accounting." His book, *Summa de Arithmetica, Geometria, Proportioni et Proportionalita (Everything about Arithmetic, Geometry, and Proportions)*, published in 1494, included a section on accounting. However, Pacioli didn't invent double-entry accounting; he simply described a method that Venetian merchants used during the Italian Renaissance. Pacioli's chapters on accounting, entitled "De Computis et Scripturis" (Of Reckonings and Writings), included most of the accounting cycle known today. They described journals and ledgers, assets (including receivables and inventories), liabilities, capital, revenue, and expense accounts. The book demonstrated year-end closing entries and proposed using a trial balance to prove a balanced ledger. The details of the bookkeeping method Pacioli presented have been followed in accounting texts and the profession for centuries.

Source: L. Murphy Smith, "Luca Pacioli: The Father of Accounting" (revised October 1, 2008), <http://acct.tamu.edu/smith/ethics/pacioli.htm> (accessed February 9, 2009).

Pacioli also wrote "a person should not go to sleep at night until the debits equalled the credits." Is this still good advice over 500 years later?

Some Simplistic Assumptions

To keep things simple, we have made some assumptions in the material in this textbook. These include not using cents and sales taxes in the transaction data.

Use of Dollars and Cents

We have not included cents in the amounts we record in journal entries, general ledger accounts, and trial balances. Excluding cents from entries will save you time and effort and you will still understand the accounting process. In reality, it is important to remember that cents are used in the formal accounting records.

Dollar signs are not used in the journals or ledgers. Dollar signs are used only in the trial balance and the financial statements. Generally, a dollar sign is shown only for the first item in the column, and for the total of that column. A single line is placed under the column of figures to be added or subtracted. The total amount is double-underlined to indicate the final sum.

Sales Taxes

Sales taxes in Canada include the Goods and Services Tax (GST) and the Provincial Sales Tax (PST). In British Columbia, Ontario, New Brunswick, Nova Scotia, and Newfoundland and Labrador, GST and PST have been combined into one tax, called the Harmonized Sales Tax (HST).

In general, a company pays sales taxes on the goods and services it purchases, and collects sales taxes on the goods that it sells and the services it provides. The company then remits the sales taxes, or portions of them, to the government. However, accounting for sales taxes is complicated and there are many exceptions. For example, not only do provincial sales tax rates vary across the country, but the method of calculating this tax can also vary. In addition, not all companies and their goods are taxable.

Although sales taxes are an important part of business, accounting transactions are presented in this textbook without the added complexity of these taxes. If you would like to learn more about this topic, sales taxes are discussed in more detail in Appendix B at the end of this textbook.

BEFORE YOU GO ON . . .

→ Review It

1. What is a trial balance, and what is its main purpose?
2. How is a trial balance prepared?
3. What are the limitations of a trial balance?

→ Do It

Koizumi Kollections has the following alphabetical list of accounts and balances at July 31, 2011:

Account	Amount	Account	Amount
Accounts payable	$33,700	Land	$ 51,000
Accounts receivable	71,200	Machinery and equipment	35,700
Building	86,500	Notes payable	49,500
Cash	3,200	Operating expenses	105,100
J. Koizumi, capital	99,400	Service revenue	171,100
J. Koizumi, drawings	4,000	Unearned service revenue	3,000

Each of the above accounts has a normal balance. Prepare a trial balance with the accounts in the same order as they would be in the ledger (in other words, in financial statement order).

Action Plan

- Reorder the accounts as they would normally be in the general ledger: balance sheet accounts are listed first (assets, liabilities, and equity) followed by income statement accounts (revenues and expenses).
- Determine whether each account has a normal debit or credit balance.
- List the amounts in the appropriate debit or credit column.
- Total the trial balance columns. Total debits must equal total credits or a mistake has been made.

Solution

KOIZUMI KOLLECTIONS Trial Balance July 31, 2011	Debit	Credit
Cash	$ 3,200	
Accounts receivable	71,200	
Land	51,000	
Building	86,500	
Machinery and equipment	35,700	
Accounts payable		$ 33,700
Unearned service revenue		3,000
Notes payable		49,500
J. Koizumi, capital		99,400
J. Koizumi, drawings	4,000	
Service revenue		171,100
Operating expenses	105,100	
Totals	$356,700	$356,700

Related exercise material: BE2–13, BE2–14, E2–1, E2–9, E2–10, E2–11, E2–12, and E2–13.

The Navigator

Demonstration Problem

Nge Aung opened the Campus Laundromat on September 1, 2011. During the first month of operations, the following transactions occurred:

Sept. 1 Invested $15,000 cash and laundry equipment worth $5,000 in the business.

      2 Paid $1,000 cash for store rent for the month of September.

      3 Borrowed $15,000 cash from the bank and signed a $15,000, 6-month, 5% note payable.

      3 Purchased washers and dryers for $20,000 cash.

      6 Paid $1,200 for a one-year insurance policy.

    10 Received a bill from *The Daily News* for advertising the opening of the laundromat, $300.

    15 Billed a nearby restaurant $500 for laundry services performed on account.

    20 Withdrew $700 cash for personal use.

    25 Received $300 cash from the restaurant billed on September 15. The balance of the account will be collected in October.

    29 Received $400 cash advance from the college residence for services to be performed in October.

    30 Cash receipts for laundry services performed for the month were $6,200.

    30 Paid employee salaries of $1,600.

    30 Paid *The Daily News* $200 of the amount owed from the bill received September 10.

The chart of accounts for the company is the same as the one for Pioneer Advertising Agency in Illustration 2-6 except for the following: No. 153 Laundry Equipment and No. 610 Advertising Expense.

Instructions

(a) Journalize the September transactions.

(b) Open ledger accounts and post the September transactions.

(c) Prepare a trial balance at September 30, 2011.

(d) Prepare an income statement, statement of owner's equity, and balance sheet for Campus Laundromat.

Solution to Demonstration Problem

(a)

GENERAL JOURNAL				J1
Date	Account Titles and Explanation	Ref.	Debit	Credit
2011				
Sept. 1	Cash	101	15,000	
	Laundry Equipment	153	5,000	
	N. Aung, Capital	301		20,000
	Invested cash and equipment in business.			
2	Rent Expense	729	1,000	
	Cash	101		1,000
	Paid September rent.			
3	Cash	101	15,000	
	Notes Payable	200		15,000
	Borrowed from bank and signed a 6-month, 5% note payable.			
3	Laundry Equipment	153	20,000	
	Cash	101		20,000
	Purchased laundry equipment for cash.			
6	Prepaid Insurance	130	1,200	
	Cash	101		1,200
	Paid one-year insurance policy.			

Action Plan

- Determine if the transaction should be recorded or not.
- In journalizing, use specific account titles taken from the chart of accounts.
- In journalizing, use the debit and credit rules and make sure debits equal credits.
- Give an appropriate description of each journal entry.
- Arrange the ledger in statement order, beginning with the balance sheet accounts.
- Post in chronological order.
- Put account numbers in the reference column to indicate the amount has been posted.
- Ensure the trial balance lists accounts in the same order as in the ledger.
- List debit balances in the left column of the trial balance and credit balances in the right column.

10	Advertising Expense	610	300	
	Accounts Payable	201		300
	Received bill from *The Daily News* for advertising.			
15	Accounts Receivable	112	500	
	Service Revenue	400		500
	Performed laundry services on account.			
20	N. Aung, Drawings	306	700	
	Cash	101		700
	Withdrew cash for personal use.			
25	Cash	101	300	
	Accounts Receivable	112		300
	Received cash on account.			
29	Cash	101	400	
	Unearned Revenue	209		400
	Received cash in advance from customer.			
30	Cash	101	6,200	
	Service Revenue	400		6,200
	Received cash for laundry services.			
30	Salaries Expense	726	1,600	
	Cash	101		1,600
	Paid employee salaries.			
30	Accounts Payable	201	200	
	Cash	101		200
	Made a partial payment to *The Daily News*.			

(b)

GENERAL LEDGER

		Cash		101			Unearned Revenue		209
Sept.	1	15,000	Sept. 2	1,000			Sept. 29		400
	3	15,000	3	20,000			Bal.		400
	25	300	6	1,200					
	29	400	20	700			N. Aung, Capital		301
	30	6,200	30	1,600			Sept. 1		20,000
			30	200			Bal.		20,000
Bal.		12,200							

	Accounts Receivable		112			N. Aung, Drawings		306
Sept. 15	500	Sept. 25	300		Sept. 20	700		
Bal.	200				Bal.	700		

	Prepaid Insurance		130			Service Revenue		400
Sept. 6	1,200					Sept. 15		500
Bal.	1,200					30		6,200
						Bal.		6,700

	Laundry Equipment		153			Advertising Expense		610
Sept. 1	5,000							
3	20,000				Sept. 10	300		
Bal.	25,000				Bal.	300		

	Notes Payable		200			Salaries Expense		726
		Sept. 3	15,000		Sept. 30	1,600		
		Bal.	15,000		Bal.	1,600		

	Accounts Payable		201			Rent Expense		729
Sept. 30	200	Sept. 10	300		Sept. 2	1,000		
		Bal.	100		Bal.	1,000		

(c)

CAMPUS LAUNDROMAT
Trial Balance
September 30, 2011

	Debit	Credit
Cash	$12,200	
Accounts receivable	200	
Prepaid insurance	1,200	
Laundry equipment	25,000	
Notes payable		$15,000
Accounts payable		100
Unearned revenue		400
N. Aung, capital		20,000
N. Aung, drawings	700	
Service revenue		6,700
Advertising expense	300	
Salaries expense	1,600	
Rent expense	1,000	
Totals	$42,200	$42,200

(d)

CAMPUS LAUNDROMAT
Income Statement
Month Ended September 30, 2011

Revenues		
Service revenue		$6,700
Expenses		
Advertising expense	$ 300	
Salaries expense	1,600	
Rent expense	1,000	2,900
Profit		$3,800

CAMPUS LAUNDROMAT
Statement of Owner's Equity
Month Ended September 30, 2011

N. Aung, capital, September 1		$ 0
Add: Investments	$20,000	
Profit	3,800	23,800
Less: Drawings		700
N. Aung, capital, September 30		$23,100

CAMPUS LAUNDROMAT
Balance Sheet
September 30, 2011

Assets		
Cash		$12,200
Accounts receivable		200
Prepaid insurance		1,200
Laundry equipment		25,000
Total assets		$38,600
Liabilities and Owner's Equity		
Liabilities		
Notes payable	$15,000	
Accounts payable	100	
Unearned service revenue	400	$15,500
Owner's equity		
N. Aung, capital		23,100
Total liabilities and owner's equity		$38,600

The Navigator

Summary of Study Objectives

1. Define debits and credits and illustrate how they are used to record transactions. Debit means left and credit means right. The normal balance of an asset is a debit because assets are on the left side of the accounting equation. Assets are increased by debits and decreased by credits. The normal balance of liabilities and owner's capital is a credit because they are on the right side of the accounting equation. Liabilities and owner's capital are increased by credits and decreased by debits. Revenues are recorded as credits because credits increase owner's equity. Credits increase revenues and debits decrease revenues. Expenses and drawings are recorded as debits because debits decrease owner's equity. Expenses and drawings are increased by debits and decreased by credits.

2. Describe the accounting cycle and the steps in the recording process. The accounting cycle is a series of steps followed by accountants in preparing financial statements. The steps in the recording process are the first three steps in the accounting cycle. These steps: (a) analyze each transaction for its effect on the accounts, (b) record the transaction in a journal, and (c) transfer the journal information to the correct accounts in the ledger.

3. Explain what a journal is, and journalize transactions. A journal (a) discloses the complete effect of a transaction in one place, (b) provides a chronological record of transactions, (c) helps to prevent and locate errors because the debit and credit amounts for each entry can be easily compared, and (d) explains the transaction and, if there is one, identifies the source document.

4. Explain what a ledger is, and post journal entries. The entire group of accounts maintained by a company is called the ledger. The ledger keeps in one place all the information about changes in each of the specific account balances. Posting is the procedure of transferring journal entries to the ledger accounts. This part of the recording process brings together in each account the effects of journalized transactions.

5. Explain the purpose of a trial balance, and prepare one. A trial balance is a list of accounts and their balances at a specific time. Its main purpose is to prove that debits and credits are equal after posting. A trial balance uncovers certain types of errors in journalizing and posting, and is useful in preparing financial statements. Preparing a trial balance is the fourth step in the accounting cycle.

The Navigator

Glossary

WILEY
PLUS Glossary
Key Term Matching Activity

Account A record of increases and decreases in a specific asset, liability, or owner's equity item. (p. 58)

Accounting cycle A series of steps followed by accountants in preparing financial statements. (p. 63)

Chart of accounts A list of accounts and the account numbers that identify where the accounts are in the ledger. (p. 68)

Compound entry An entry that affects three or more accounts. (p. 65)

Credit The right side of an account. (p. 58)

Debit The left side of an account. (p. 58)

Double-entry system A system that records the dual (two-sided) effect of each transaction in appropriate accounts. (p. 59)

General journal The book of original entry in which transactions are recorded when they are not recorded in other specialized journals. (p. 64)

General ledger A ledger that contains accounts for all assets, liabilities, equities, revenues, and expenses. (p. 67)

Journal An accounting record where transactions are recorded in chronological (date) order. (p. 64)

Journalizing The entering of transaction data in the journal. (p. 64)

Ledger A record that contains all of a company's accounts. (p. 67)

Posting The procedure of transferring journal entries to the ledger accounts. (p. 67)

T account A form of account that looks like the letter T. It has the title above the horizontal line. Debits are shown to the left of the vertical line, credits to the right. (p. 58)

Trial balance A list of accounts and their balances at a specific time, usually at the end of the accounting period. (p. 76)

Self-Study Questions

Answers are at the end of the chapter.

(SO 1) K 1. Which of the following statements about an account is true?
    (a) The left side of an account is the credit or decrease side.
    (b) An account is an individual accounting record of increases and decreases in specific asset, liability, and owner's equity items.
    (c) There are separate accounts for specific assets and liabilities but only one account for owner's equity items.
    (d) The right side of an account is the debit or increase side.

(SO 1) K 2. Debits:
    (a) increase both assets and liabilities.
    (b) decrease both assets and liabilities.
    (c) increase assets and decrease liabilities.
    (d) decrease assets and increase liabilities.

(SO 1) K 3. A revenue account:
    (a) is increased by debits.
    (b) is decreased by credits.
    (c) has a normal balance of a debit.
    (d) is increased by credits.

(SO 1) K 4. Accounts that normally have debit balances are:
    (a) assets, expenses, and revenues.
    (b) assets, expenses, and owner's capital.
    (c) assets, liabilities, and drawings.
    (d) assets, drawings, and expenses.

(SO 2) K 5. What is the correct sequence of steps in the recording process?
    (a) Analyzing transactions; preparing a trial balance
    (b) Analyzing transactions; entering transactions in a journal; posting transactions
    (c) Entering transactions in a journal; posting transactions; preparing a trial balance
    (d) Entering transactions in a journal; posting transactions; analyzing transactions

(SO 3) K 6. Which of these statements about a journal is false?
    (a) It is not a book of original entry.
    (b) It provides a chronological record of transactions.
    (c) It helps to locate errors because the debit and credit amounts for each entry can be easily compared.
    (d) It shows in one place the complete effect of a transaction.

(SO 4) K 7. A ledger:
    (a) contains only asset and liability accounts.
    (b) should show accounts in alphabetical order.
    (c) is a collection of the entire group of accounts maintained by a company.
    (d) is a book of original entry.

(SO 4) K 8. Posting:
    (a) is normally done before journalizing.
    (b) transfers ledger transaction data to the journal.
    (c) is an optional step in the recording process.
    (d) transfers journal entries to ledger accounts.

(SO 5) K 9. A trial balance:
    (a) is a list of accounts with their balances at a specific time.
    (b) proves that journalized transactions are accurate.
    (c) will not balance if a correct journal entry is posted twice.
    (d) proves that all transactions have been recorded.

(SO 5) AP 10. A trial balance will not balance if:
    (a) the collection of an account receivable is posted twice.
    (b) the purchase of supplies on account is debited to Supplies and credited to Cash.
    (c) a $100 cash drawing by the owner is debited to Drawings for $1,000 and credited to Cash for $100.
    (d) a $450 payment on account is debited to Accounts Payable for $45 and credited to Cash for $45.

The Navigator

Questions

(SO 1) C 1. What is an account? Will a company need more than one account? Explain.

(SO 1) K 2. What is debiting an account? What is crediting an account?

(SO 1) C 3. Jos Arcelus, a fellow student, says that the double-entry system means each transaction is recorded in two places: the journal and the ledger. Is Jos correct? Explain.

(SO 1) K 4. Explain the relationship between the normal balance in each type of account and the basic accounting equation.

(SO 1) K 5. Identify the normal balance for (a) asset accounts, (b) liability accounts, and (c) owner's equity accounts: (1) capital, (2) drawings, (3) revenue, and (4) expense. State the effect of debits and credits on each of these.

(SO 1) C 6. Kim Nguyen, a beginning accounting student, believes credit balances are favourable and debit balances are unfavourable. Is Kim correct? Discuss.

(SO 1) C 7. Why are increases to drawings and expenses recorded as debits?

(SO 1) C 8. Indicate whether the following accounts generally will have (a) debit entries only, (b) credit entries only, or (c) both debit and credit entries:
(a) Accounts Payable
(b) Accounts Receivable
(c) Cash
(d) Drawings
(e) Rent Expense
(f) Service Revenue

(SO 2) K 9. What is the accounting cycle? Describe the first three steps.

(SO 2) K 10. Jessica Gillies doesn't understand how to decide if a transaction should be recorded or not. Explain.

(SO 2) K 11. Give two examples of business documents that are analyzed when journal entries are being prepared.

(SO 2) K 12. Ben Benoit, a fellow student, is unclear about similarities and differences between using a manual system or a computerized system in the recording process. Briefly explain, including the benefit of a computerized system.

(SO 3) C 13. What is the difference between a simple and a compound journal entry? What rule must be followed when recording a compound entry so the accounting equation remains balanced?

(SO 3) C 14. A company receives cash from a customer. List three different accounts that could be credited and the circumstances under which each of these accounts are credited.

15. Amber Rose believes that accounting would be (SO 3, 4) AP
more efficient if transactions were recorded directly in the ledger accounts. Explain to Amber the advantages of first recording transactions in the journal, and then posting them to the ledger.

16. Explain the differences between the format of a T (SO 4) AP
account and the standard form of accounts. In your explanation, include the benefits of each format, and when each format is typically used.

17. What are the differences between a ledger and a (SO 4) AP
chart of accounts?

18. What is a trial balance? What are its purposes? (SO 5) AP

19. Kap Shin is confused about how accounting information moves through the accounting system. He (SO 3, 4, 5) AP
believes the flow of information is as follows:
(a) Debits and credits are posted to the ledger.
(b) The business transaction occurs.
(c) Information is entered in the journal.
(d) Financial statements are prepared.
(e) A trial balance is prepared.

Show Kap the correct flow of information.

20. Two students are discussing the use of a trial balance. They wonder if the following errors in different (SO 5) AN
companies would prevent a trial balance from balancing. For each error, what would you tell the students?
(a) The bookkeeper debited Supplies for $750 and debited Accounts Payable for $750 for the purchase of supplies on account.
(b) Cash collected on account was debited to Cash for $1,000 and credited to Service Revenue for $1,000.
(c) A journal entry recording the payment of rent expense was posted to the general ledger as a $650 debit to rent expense and a $560 credit to Cash.

21. Jamal Nazari is doing the accounting for a company (SO 5) C
that has a December 31 year end. He is wondering if the heading on its trial balance should read "Year Ended December 31" or just "December 31." Which one is correct? Explain why.

Brief Exercises

Calculate account balances.
(SO 1) AP

BE2–1 For the two accounts that follow, calculate the balance and indicate whether it is a debit or credit balance:

Accounts Receivable		Accounts Payable	
8,000	5,210	220	390
6,340	2,750	560	710
	2,390	175	850
		355	

Indicate type of account, financial statement classification and normal balance.
(SO 1) K

BE2–2 For each the following accounts, indicate (a) if the account is an asset, liability, or owner's equity account; (b) on which financial statement the account appears (balance sheet, income statement, or statement of owner's equity); and (c) whether the account would have a normal debit or credit balance.

1. Accounts Receivable
2. Accounts Payable
3. Equipment
4. Rent Expense
5. B. Damji, Drawings
6. Supplies
7. Unearned Revenue
8. Cash
9. Service Revenue
10. Prepaid Insurance

Indicate debit and credit effects and normal balance.
(SO 1) K

BE2–3 For each of the following accounts, indicate (a) the effect of a debit on the account, (b) the effect of a credit on the account, and (c) the normal balance:

1. Accounts Payable
2. Accounts Receivable
3. Cash
4. Office Equipment
5. J. Takamoto, Capital
6. J. Takamoto, Drawings
7. Notes Payable
8. Prepaid Rent
9. Insurance Expense
10. Salaries Expense
11. Service Revenue
12. Unearned Revenue

Indicate when to use debits and credits.
(SO 1) K

BE2–4 Indicate whether you would use a debit or credit to record the following changes:

1. Decrease in Accounts Receivable
2. Increase in Cash
3. Increase in Notes Payable
4. Increase in Salaries Expense
5. Increase in Drawings
6. Decrease in Equipment
7. Decrease in Accounts Payable
8. Increase in Service Revenue

Identify accounts to be debited and credited.
(SO 1) C

BE2–5 The following is a list of transactions. (a) Indicate the account debited and the account credited. (b) For each account, identify whether it is an asset, liability, or owner's equity account. For owner's equity accounts, state whether it is capital, drawings, revenue, or an expense.

1. Equipment is purchased on account.
2. Cash is received for services to be provided in the next month.
3. The current month's utility bill is paid in cash.
4. Cash is paid for office supplies.
5. Cash is received for services provided that day.
6. Customer is billed for services provided that day.
7. Joan Parker, the company's owner withdraws cash from the company's bank account for personal use.
8. Cash is paid to employees for the current month's wages.

Identify accounts to be debited and credited.
(SO 1) C

BE2–6 Ing Welding Company had the following transactions for June. Identify the accounts to be debited and credited for each transaction.

June   1   D. Ing invests $5,500 cash in a small welding business.

      2   Buys equipment on account for $3,000.

      3   Pays $500 to a landlord for June rent.

      4   Pays $800 for a one-year insurance policy.

    12   Bills T. Sargeant $350 for welding work done.

    22   Receives $350 cash from T. Sargeant for worked billed on June 12.

    25   Hires an employee to start work on July 2.

    29   Pays for equipment purchased on June 2.

BE2–7   Fischer's Financial Consulting has the following transactions during August.   *Identify accounts and basic debit/credit analysis.*

Aug.   1   Received $17,000 cash from the company's owner, Jim Fischer.   *(SO 1) C*

     4   Paid rent in advance for three months, $3,600.

     5   Purchased $440 of office supplies on account.

     6   Received $950 from clients for services provided.

   17   Billed clients $1,500 for services provided.

   27   Paid secretary $750 salary.

   29   Paid the company's owner, Jim Fischer, $500 cash for personal use.

For each transaction, indicate (a) the basic type of account to be debited and credited (asset, liability, owner's equity); (b) the specific accounts to debit and credit (for example, Cash, Service Revenue, Accounts Payable); and (c) whether each account is increased (+) or decreased (−), and by what amount. Use the following format, in which the first one has been done for you as an example:

	Account Debited			Account Credited		
	(a)	(b)	(c)	(a)	(b)	(c)
Transaction	Basic Type	Specific Account	Effect	Basic Type	Specific Account	Effect
Aug. 1	Asset	Cash	+ $17,000	Owner's Equity	J. Fischer, Capital	+ $17,000

BE2–8   Princess Printing Company had the following transactions with a customer during   *Analyze transactions.* January: (1) performed services, such as printing flyers, and billed the customer; (2) collected   *(SO 2) AP* cash on account from the customer; and (3) sent a statement at the end of the month, showing the balance owing, to the customer. Analyze each of these transactions and determine if they should be recorded or not. Explain why or why not for each transaction.

BE2–9   Using the data in BE2–6 for Ing Welding Company, journalize the transactions.   *Record transactions.* *(SO 3) AP*

BE2–10   Using the data in BE2–7 for Fischer's Financial Consulting, journalize the transactions.   *Record transactions.* *(SO 3) AP*

BE2–11   Using T accounts, post the journal entries from BE2–10 to the general ledger.   *Post journal entries.* *(SO 4) AP*

BE2–12   Using T accounts, post the following journal entries to the general ledger.   *Post journal entries.* *(SO 4) AP*

GENERAL JOURNAL			
Date	Account title and explanation	Debit	Credit
Sept. 2	Cash	875	
	Service Revenue		875
4	Furniture	750	
	Accounts Payable		750
10	Accounts Receivable	1,200	
	Service Revenue		1,200
15	Salaries Expense	250	
	Cash		250
28	Cash	300	
	Accounts Receivable		300
30	Accounts Payable	550	
	Cash		550

Prepare trial balance.
(SO 5) AP

BE2–13   Use the ledger balances that follow to prepare a trial balance for the Pettipas Company at April 30, 2011. All account balances are normal.

Accounts payable	$ 3,900	Prepaid insurance	$1,500
Accounts receivable	3,000	Rent expense	800
C. Pettipas, capital	22,000	Salaries expense	4,000
C. Pettipas, drawings	1,200	Service revenue	8,100
Cash	8,400	Supplies	650
Equipment	14,600	Unearned revenue	150

Identify errors in trial balance.
(SO 5) AP

BE2–14   There are two errors in the following trial balance: (1) one account has been placed in the wrong column, and (2) there is a transposition error. Identify the two errors.

BOURQUE COMPANY
Trial Balance
December 31, 2010

	Debit	Credit
Cash	$15,000	
Accounts receivable	1,800	
Prepaid insurance		$3,500
Accounts payable		2,000
Unearned revenue		2,200
L. Bourque, capital		15,400
L. Bourque, drawings	4,900	
Service revenue		27,500
Salaries expense	18,600	
Rent expense	2,400	
Totals	$42,700	$50,600

Exercises

Match concepts with descriptions.
(SO 1, 2, 3, 4, 5) K

E2–1   Here are some of the concepts discussed in the chapter:

1. Account	6. Journal
2. Analyzing transactions	7. Journalizing
3. Chart of accounts	8. Ledger
4. Credit	9. Posting
5. Debit	10. Trial balance

Instructions

Match each concept with the best description below. Each concept may be used more than once, or may not be used at all.

(a) ___ The normal balance for liabilities
(b) ___ The first step in the recording process
(c) ___ The procedure of transferring journal entries to the ledger accounts
(d) ___ A record of increases and decreases in a specific asset, liability, or owner's equity item
(e) ___ The left side of an account
(f) ___ The entering of transaction data in the journal
(g) ___ A list of accounts and their balances at a specific time
(h) ___ Used to decrease the balance in an asset account
(i) ___ A list of all of a company's accounts
(j) ___ An accounting record where transactions are recorded in chronological (date) order

E2-2 Kobayashi Company has the following accounts:

Identify type of account, financial statement, and normal balance.

(SO 1) K

Account	(a) Type of Account	(b) Financial Statement	(c) Normal Balance
1. Cash	Asset	Balance sheet	Debit
2. M. Kobayashi, Capital			
3. Accounts Payable			
4. Building			
5. Consulting Fee Revenue			
6. Insurance Expense			
7. Interest Earned			
8. Notes Receivable			
9. Prepaid Insurance			
10. Rent Expense			
11. Supplies			

Instructions

Complete the table. Identify (a) the type of account (e.g., asset, liability, owner's capital, drawings, revenue, expense); (b) what financial statement it is presented on; and (c) the normal balance of the account. The first one is done for you as an example.

E2-3 In the first month of business, Visser Interior Design Company had the following transactions:

Identify accounts and basic debit/credit analysis.

(SO 1) C

Mar. 3 The owner, Lynne Visser, invested $10,000 cash in the business.
   6 Purchased a used car for $6,500 cash, for use in the business.
   7 Purchased supplies on account for $500.
   12 Billed customers $2,100 for services performed.
   21 Paid $225 cash for advertising the launch of the business.
   25 Received $1,200 cash from customers billed on March 12.
   28 Paid for the supplies purchased on March 7.
   30 Received $750 cash from a customer for services to be performed in April.
   31 Paid Lynne Visser $600 cash for her personal use.

Instructions

For each transaction indicate:
  (a) The basic type of account debited and credited (asset, liability, owner's equity)
  (b) The specific account debited and credited (Cash, Rent Expense, Service Revenue, etc.)
  (c) Whether each account is increased (+) or decreased (−), and by what amount
Use the following format, in which the first transaction is given as an example:

	Account Debited			Account Credited		
Transaction	(a) Basic Type	(b) Specific Account	(c) Effect	(a) Basic Type	(b) Specific Account	(c) Effect
Mar. 3	Asset	Cash	+$10,000	Owner's Equity	L. Visser, Capital	+$10,000

E2-4 Data for Visser Interior Design are presented in E2-3.

Record transactions.
(SO 3) AP

Instructions

Journalize the transactions.

Record transactions.
(SO 3) AP

E2–5   Selected transactions for Gardiner Real Estate Agency during its first month of business follow:

Oct. 1 Samuel Gardiner opens Gardiner Real Estate Agency with an investment of $14,000 cash and $3,000 of office equipment.
      2 Hired an administrative assistant at an annual salary of $24,000.
      3 Purchased additional office equipment for $4,450, paying $850 cash and signing a note payable for the balance.
     10 Received $350 cash as a fee for renting an apartment.
     16 Sold a house and lot to B. Rollins. The commission due from Rollins is $7,500 (it is not paid by Rollins at this time).
     27 Paid $700 for advertising costs during October.
     29 Received a $95 bill for telephone service during the month of October (the bill is paid in November).
     30 Paid the administrative assistant $2,000 in salary for October.
     31 Received $7,500 cash from B. Rollins for the October 16 transaction.

Instructions

Journalize the transactions.

Record revenue and expense transactions.
(SO 3) AP

E2–6   Selected transactions for Chaloux Group Company are presented below:

1. Shelly Chaloux, the owner, invested $7,500 cash in the company.
2. Provided services to a client and billed the client $1,600.
3. Collected $1,600 from the client billed in transaction 2.
4. Provided services to a client and received $875 cash.
5. Received $15,000 cash from the bank and signed a one-year, 5% note payable.
6. Received $500 cash from a client for services to be provided next year.
7. Paid $625 for the current month's rent.
8. Purchased $440 of office supplies on account.
9. Paid $1,640 for a one-year insurance policy.
10. Purchased $5,000 office equipment for cash.
11. Paid $800 cash for legal services to be received the following year.
12. Paid for the office supplies purchased on account in transaction 8.
13. Shelly Chaloux, the owner, withdrew $900 cash for personal use.
14. Paid the current month's telephone bill, $220.

Instructions

(a) Identify the transactions that created revenue for the Chaloux Group and journalize those transactions.
(b) Identify the transactions that created expenses for the Chaloux Group and journalize those transactions.
(c) Explain why the other transactions did not create either revenues or expenses.

Post journal entries.
(SO 4) AP

E2–7   Journal entries for Gardiner Real Estate Agency's transactions were prepared in E2–5.

Instructions

Post the journal entries to the general ledger, using T accounts.

E2–8 Csilla Revesz has prepared the following list of statements about the general ledger.

Correct statements about the ledger.
(SO 4) K

1. The general ledger contains all the asset and liability accounts, but no owner's equity accounts.
2. The general ledger is sometimes referred to as simply the ledger.
3. The accounts in the general ledger are arranged in alphabetical order.
4. Each account in the general ledger must be numbered.
5. The general ledger is a book of original entry.
6. The ledger shows all of the increases and decreases to each account.

Instructions

Identify each statement as true or false. If false, correct the statement.

E2–9 Fortin Co.'s ledger is as follows:

Record transactions and prepare trial balance.
(SO 3, 5) AP

	Cash				
Oct. 1	1,200	Oct. 3	400		
10	650	12	500		
15	3,000	30	600		
20	800	31	250		
25	2,000	31	500		

	A. Fortin, Capital	
	Oct. 1	1,200
	25	2,000

	Accounts Receivable		
Oct. 6	1,000	Oct. 20	800
20	940		

	A. Fortin, Drawings	
Oct. 30	600	

	Service Revenue	
	Oct. 6	1,000
	10	650
	15	3,000
	20	940

	Supplies	
Oct. 4	800	

	Equipment	
Oct. 3	5,400	

	Advertising Expense	
Oct. 28	400	

	Notes Payable	
	Oct. 3	5,000

	Rent Expense	
Oct. 31	250	

	Store Expense	
Oct. 31	500	

	Accounts Payable		
Oct. 12	500	Oct. 4	800
		28	400

Instructions

(a) Journalize the October transactions, and give explanations for each entry.
(b) Determine the October 31, 2011, balance for each account. Prepare a trial balance at October 31, 2011.

E2–10 On July 31, 2011, Lee Meche, MD, had the following balances in the ledger for his medical practice: Cash $8,800; Accounts Receivable $2,750; Supplies $585; Equipment $15,550; Notes Payable $10,000; Accounts Payable $850; L. Meche, Capital $15,000; L. Meche, Drawings $5,125; Medical Fee Revenue $10,410; Rent Expense $1,200; and Salaries Expense $2,250. Selected transactions during August 2011 follow:

Post journal entries and prepare trial balance.
(SO 4, 5) AP

GENERAL JOURNAL				
Date	Account Titles and Explanation	Ref.	Debit	Credit
2011				
Aug. 1	Rent Expense		1,200	
	Cash			1,200
10	Accounts Payable		420	
	Cash			420
12	Cash		2,400	
	Accounts Receivable			2,400
25	Salaries Expense		2,250	
	Cash			2,250
30	Notes Payable		500	
	Interest Expense		40	
	Cash			540
31	Cash		5,910	
	Accounts Receivable		2,550	
	Medical Fee Revenue			8,460
31	L. Meche, Drawings		4,770	
	Cash			4,770

Instructions

(a) Create T accounts and enter the July 31 balances.
(b) Post the transactions to the T accounts. Create new T accounts if needed.
(c) Prepare a trial balance at August 31.

Analyze errors and their effect on the trial balance.
(SO 5) AN

E2–11 The accountant for Smistad Guitar Repair Company made a number of errors in journalizing and posting, as described below:

1. A credit posting of $400 to Accounts Receivable was omitted.
2. A debit posting of $750 for Prepaid Insurance was debited to Insurance Expense.
3. A collection on account of $100 was journalized and posted as a $100 debit to Cash and a $100 credit to Service Revenue.
4. A credit posting of $500 to Salaries Payable was made twice.
5. A cash purchase of supplies for $250 was journalized and posted as a $25 debit to Supplies and a $25 credit to cash.
6. A debit of $475 to Advertising Expense was posted as $457.

Instructions

Considering each error separately, indicate the following using the format below where error number 1 is given as an example.
(a) Will the trial balance be in balance?
(b) What is the amount of the error if the trial balance will not balance?
(c) Which trial balance column will have the larger total?

	(a)	(b)	(c)
Error	In Balance	Difference	Larger Column
1.	No	$400	Debit

Prepare corrected trial balance.
(SO 5) AP

E2–12 Terry Zelinski, the owner of Royal Mountain Tours, prepared the following trial balance at March 31, 2011.

Cash	$12,800	
Accounts receivable	4,090	
Supplies	840	
Equipment	7,350	
Accounts payable		$ 2,500
T. Zelinski, capital		24,000
T. Zelinski, drawings		3,650

Service revenue		6,750
Advertising expense	3,700	
Salaries expense	400	
Totals	$29,180	$36,900

A review shows that Terry made the following errors in the accounting records:

1. A purchase of $400 of supplies on account was recorded as a credit to cash. The debit entry was correct.
2. A $100 credit to accounts receivable was posted as $1,000.
3. A journal entry to record service revenue of $620 earned on account was not prepared or posted.
4. A journal entry to record the payment of $240 for an advertising expense was correctly prepared but the credit to cash was posted as a debit. The debit to advertising expense was properly posted.

Instructions

Prepare the correct trial balance at March 31, 2011, using the format shown in the chapter. (*Hint*: You should also make sure that the account balances are recorded in the correct columns on the trial balance.)

E2–13 The trial balance of O'Callaghan's Counselling Services, at its year end July 31, 2011, is presented below with the accounts in alphabetical order.

Prepare financial statements. (SO 5) AP

Accounts	Debit	Credit
Accounts payable		$ 4,515
Accounts receivable	$ 3,670	
C. O'Callaghan, capital		34,670
C. O'Callaghan, drawings	28,990	
Cash	2,895	
Equipment	29,450	
Insurance expense	1,020	
Prepaid insurance	340	
Rent expense	5,440	
Salaries expense	22,770	
Service revenue		58,090
Supplies	395	
Supplies expense	2,980	
Unearned revenue		675
	$97,950	$97,950

Instructions

Prepare an income statement, statement of owner's equity, and balance sheet.

Problems: Set A

P2–1A Miranda Brock, Lawyer, has the following accounts:

Identify type of account, financial statement, normal balances, and debits and credits. (SO 1) K

Accounts Payable	Land	Rent Revenue
Accounts Receivable	Legal Fees Earned	Salaries Expense
Building	M. Brock, Capital	Salaries Payable
Cash	M. Brock, Drawings	Supplies
Equipment	Notes Receivable	Supplies Expense
Insurance Expense	Prepaid Insurance	Unearned Legal Fees
Interest Earned	Rent Expense	

Instructions

For each of these accounts, identify (a) the type of account (e.g., asset, liability, owner's capital, drawings, revenue, expense); (b) what financial statement it is presented on; (c) the normal balance of the account; (d) whether the account is increased by a debit or credit; and (e) whether the account is decreased by a debit or credit. Use the following format, in which the first one is done for you as an example.

Account	(a) Type of Account	(b) Financial Statement	(c) Normal Balance	(d) Increase	(e) Decrease
Accounts payable	Liability	Balance sheet	Credit	Credit	Debit

Taking It Further   Explain the relationship between the normal balance in each type of account and the basic accounting equation.

Perform transaction analysis
and journalize transactions.
(SO 1, 2, 3) AP

P2–2A   JB Paint Designs began operations on April 1, 2011. The company completed the following transactions in its first month:

Apr.   1   The owner, Jay Butterfield, invested $13,500 cash in the company.
2   Purchased a one-year insurance policy effective April 1, and paid the first month's premium of $115.
2   Purchased painting equipment for $3,000 cash.
3   Purchased $375 of supplies on account.
7   Paid cash for $870 of advertising expenses.
8   Finished a painting project for Maya Angelina and billed her $750.
10   Received a $1,500 contract from a customer, SUB Terrain Inc., to paint its new office space. SUB Terrain will pay when the project is complete.
25   Completed the contract with SUB Terrain Inc. from April 10 and collected the amount owing.
27   Collected the amount owing from April 8.
28   The owner, Jay Butterfield, withdrew $870 cash for his personal use.
30   Paid for the supplies purchased on account on April 3.

Instructions

(a) For each transaction, indicate: (1) the basic type of account debited and credited (asset, liability, or owner's equity); (2) the specific account debited and credited (Cash, Rent Expense, Service Revenue, etc.); and (3) whether each account is increased (+) or decreased (−), and by what amount. Use the following format, in which the first transaction is given as an example:

	Account Debited			Account Credited		
Transaction	(1) Basic Type	(2) Specific Account	(3) Effect	(1) Basic Type	(2) Specific Account	(3) Effect
Apr. 1	Asset	Cash	+$13,500	Owner's Equity	J. Butterfield, Capital	+$13,500

(b) Prepare a journal entry for each transaction.

Taking It Further   Jay doesn't understand why a debit increases the cash account and yet a credit to J. Butterfield, Capital increases that account. He reasons that debits and credits cannot both increase account balances. Explain to Jay why he is wrong.

P2–3A Bucket Club Miniature Golf and Driving Range was opened on May 1. The following events and transactions are for May:

Journalize transactions.
(SO 3) AP

May 1 Amin Mawani, the owner, invested $70,000 cash in the business.

3 Purchased Lee's Golf Land for $210,000. The price consists of land, $100,000; building, $70,000; and equipment, $40,000. Paid $60,000 cash and signed a note payable for the balance.

4 Purchased golf clubs and other equipment for $6,000 from Woods Company on account.

5 Advertised the opening of Bucket Club Miniature Golf and Driving Range, paying $1,800.

6 Paid $2,760 cash for a one-year insurance policy.

15 Collected $2,500 cash from customers for golf fees earned.

19 Paid Woods Company $5,000 for the items purchased on May 4.

20 Billed a customer, Deer Fern Inc., $500 for golf fees earned. Deer Fern Inc. agreed to pay the amount owing in 10 days.

30 Paid salaries of $2,445.

30 Received $500 from Deer Fern Inc. for the May 20 transaction.

31 Collected $4,000 cash from customers for golf fees earned.

31 Paid $750 of interest on the note payable.

31 Paid Amin Mawani $1,750 for his personal use.

The company's chart of accounts includes the following accounts: Cash; Accounts Receivable; Prepaid Insurance; Land; Buildings; Equipment; Accounts Payable; Notes Payable; A. Mawani, Capital; A. Mawani, Drawings; Golf Fees Earned; Advertising Expense; Salaries Expense; and Interest Expense.

Instructions

Journalize the May transactions.

Taking It Further After Amin has reviewed the journal entries, he complains that they don't seem to be very useful. Explain to Amin the purpose of the journal entries and the next step in the accounting cycle. Include in your answer whether or not Amin will find any useful information after the next step is completed.

P2–4A Francesca Virmani, a licensed architect, formed a company called Virmani Architects on April 1, 2011. The following events and transactions occurred in the first month:

Journalize transactions, post, and prepare trial balance.
(SO 3, 4, 5) AP

Apr. 1 Francesca invested $15,000 cash and $6,000 of office equipment in the company.

2 Hired a secretary-receptionist at a salary of $1,900 monthly.

3 Paid office rent for the month, $950.

3 Purchased architectural supplies on account from Halo Company, $1,750.

10 Completed blueprints on garage for Pro-Built Construction and billed them $975.

20 Received $1,200 cash for services performed for a client, P. Donahue.

21 Received $800 cash from Pro-Built Construction for work completed on April 10.

23 Received a $1,000 cash advance from R. Sherstabetoff for the design of a new home.

28 Paid $900 to Halo Company on account.

29 Paid secretary-receptionist for the month, $1,900.

29 Paid Francesca $1,500 for her personal use.

30 The telephone bill for April was $155. The company will pay it in May.

Virmani Architects uses the following chart of accounts: No. 101 Cash; No. 112 Accounts Receivable; No. 126 Supplies; No. 151 Office Equipment; No. 201 Accounts Payable; No. 209 Unearned Revenue; No. 301 F. Virmani, Capital; No. 306 F. Virmani , Drawings; No. 400 Service Revenue; No. 726 Rent Expense; No. 729 Salaries Expense; and No. 737 Telephone Expense.

Instructions

(a) Journalize the transactions.
(b) Post to the ledger accounts. Use the standard form of account.
(c) Prepare a trial balance as at April 30, 2011.

Taking It Further   Francesca asks how to decide whether a transaction should be recorded or not. Provide her with a general rule and include specific reference to the May 2 and May 30 transactions in your answer.

Journalize transactions, post, and prepare trial balance.
(SO 3, 4, 5) AP

P2–5A   Abramson Financial Services was formed on May 1, 2011. The following events and transactions are from its first month:

May   1   Jacob Abramson invested $40,000 cash and office equipment worth $10,000 in the company.

      1   Hired one employee to work in the office for a salary of $2,475 per month.

      2   Paid $3,300 cash for a one-year insurance policy.

      5   Signed a two-year rental agreement on an office and paid $4,800 cash. Half was for the May 2011 rent and the other half was for the final month's rent. (*Hint*: The portion for the final month is considered prepaid rent.)

      8   Purchased additional office equipment costing $17,000. A cash payment of $7,000 was made immediately. Signed a note payable for the balance.

      9   Purchased office supplies for $500 cash.

    15   Purchased more office supplies for $750 on account.

    17   Completed a contract for a client for $3,000 on account.

    22   Paid $250 for May's telephone bill.

    25   Completed services for a client and immediately collected $1,100.

    26   Paid Jacob Abramson $1,600 cash for his personal use.

    28   Collected $2,500 from the client billed on May 17.

    30   Paid for the office supplies purchased on account on May 15.

    30   Paid $50 interest expense on the note payable.

    31   Received a cash advance of $500 for services to be completed in June.

    31   Paid the employee's monthly salary, $2,475.

Instructions

(a) Prepare journal entries to record the transactions.
(b) Post the journal entries to ledger accounts. Use T accounts.
(c) Prepare a trial balance as at May 31, 2011.

Taking It Further   Jacob asks if the change in his cash account balance, from the beginning to the end of the month, is equal to his profit or loss for the month. Explain to Jacob whether or not this is true and why.

Journalize transactions, post, and prepare trial balance.
(SO 3, 4, 5) AP

P2–6A   Vista Theatre, owned by Nadiya Fedkovych, is unique as it only shows movies that are part of a theme with two or more sequels. As at May 31, 2011, the ledger of Vista Theatre showed the following: Cash, $15,000; Land, $85,000; Buildings, $70,000; Equipment, $20,000; Accounts Payable, $5,000; Mortgage Payable, $118,000; and N. Fedkovych, Capital, $67,000. In June, the following events and transactions occurred:

Jun.   2   Rented three *Batman* movies, to be shown in the first three weeks of June. The film rental was $22,000. Of that amount, $10,000 was paid in cash and the balance will be paid on June 10.

2   Hired M. Brewer to operate the concession stand. Brewer agreed to pay Vista Theatre 18% of gross concession receipts, on the last day of each month, for the right to operate the concession stand.

3   Ordered three *Shrek* movies, to be shown the last 10 days of June. The film rental will cost $900 per night.

9   Received $16,300 cash from customers for admissions.

10   Paid the balance due on the *Batman* rental.

10   Paid the accounts payable owing at the end of May.

11   Paid advertising expenses, $950.

20   Received $16,600 cash from admissions.

21   Received the *Shrek* movies and paid one half of the $9,000 ($900 × 10 nights) rental fee. The balance is to be paid on July 1.

29   Paid salaries of $4,200.

30   Received statement from Brewer showing gross receipts from concessions of $8,500 and the balance due to Vista Theatre of $1,530 ($8,500 × 18%) for March. Brewer paid one half the balance due and will pay the rest on July 5.

30   Received $18,400 cash from admissions.

30   Made a $1,725 mortgage payment. Of this amount, $1,250 is a principal payment, and $475 is interest on the mortgage.

In addition to the accounts identified above, Vista Theatre's ledger includes the following: Accounts Receivable; Admission Revenue; Concession Revenue; Advertising Expense; Film Rental Expense; Interest Expense; and Salaries Expense.

Instructions

(a) Journalize the June transactions.
(b) Enter the beginning balances in the ledger as at June 1. Use the standard form of account.
(c) Post the June journal entries to the ledger.
(d) Prepare a trial balance at the end of June.

Taking It Further   A friend of yours is considering buying Vista Theatre from the current owner. Using the information in the trial balance, comment on whether or not this may be a sound company for your friend to purchase.

P2–7A   Collegiate Laundry has a December 31 year end. The company's trial balance on November 30, 2011, is as follows:

Journalize transactions, post, and prepare trial balance.
(SO 3, 4, 5) AP

	COLLEGIATE LAUNDRY Trial Balance November 30, 2011	
	Debit	Credit
Cash	$ 2,800	
Accounts receivable	6,800	
Supplies	1,100	
Laundry equipment	21,000	
Accounts payable		$ 5,765
Unearned revenue		1,300
J. Cochrane, capital		19,500
J. Cochrane, drawings	33,000	
Laundry revenue		69,900
Insurance expense	4,015	
Rent expense	9,350	
Salaries expense	11,525	
Utilities expense	6,875	
	$96,465	$96,465

The December transactions were as follows:

Dec.   1   Borrowed $5,000 cash from the First Financial Bank and signed a note payable.
       2   Purchased a used pressing machine for $5,500 cash from another company. The machine was probably worth $7,000, but the other company needed the cash and was anxious to sell it.
       2   Paid December rent, $850.
       4   Received $5,550 cash from customers in payment of their accounts.
       7   Paid the $365 monthly insurance premium.
       9   Paid $2,900 to creditors on account.
      10   Performed $800 of services for customers who had paid in advance in November.
      11   Received $1,350 cash from customers for services provided.
      15   Purchased $400 of supplies on account.
      20   Billed customers $5,750 for services provided.
      22   Paid employee salaries of $1,450 (includes a year-end bonus of $300).
      24   Owner withdrew $3,000 for personal use.
      29   Received $425 cash from a customer for services to be provided in January.
      30   Paid the bank $525. Of this amount, $25 is interest and the remainder is a principal payment.
      31   The bill for December utilities was $615. The bill will be paid in January.

Instructions

(a) Journalize the December transactions.
(b) Enter the November 30 balances in ledger accounts. Use T accounts.
(c) Post the December journal entries to the T accounts. You may need to add new accounts for some of the transactions.
(d) Prepare a trial balance at December 31, 2011.

Taking It Further   Comment on the company's cash balance. What concerns or suggestions do you have for the company to consider in January?

Prepare financial statements. (SO 5) AP

P2–8A   Refer to the trial balance for Abramson Financial Services prepared in P2–5A part (c).

Instructions

(a) Prepare an income statement for May.
(b) Prepare a statement of owner's equity for May.
(c) Prepare a balance sheet at the end of May 2011.

Taking It Further   Discuss how well the company performed in its first month of operations.

Journalize transactions, post, and prepare trial balance. (SO 3, 4, 5) AP

P2–9A   Leo Mataruka owns and manages a computer repair service. It had the following trial balance on December 31, 2010 (its fiscal year end):

CYBERDYNE REPAIR SERVICE Trial Balance December 31, 2010		
	Debit	Credit
Cash	$ 2,000	
Accounts receivable	16,500	
Repair parts inventory	16,000	
Shop equipment	28,000	
Accounts payable		$23,000
Unearned revenue		2,000
L. Mataruka, capital		37,500
Totals	$62,500	$62,500

A summary of transactions for January 2011 follows:

Jan. 2 Leo went to his bank and got a personal loan of $6,000 by signing a note payable.

3 Leo transferred $5,000 from his personal bank account into Cyberdyne's bank account.

4 Purchased additional repair parts inventory on account, $5,200.

6 Miscellaneous expenses were paid in cash, $1,300.

10 Collected $7,200 cash from customers on account.

15 Cash was paid to creditors on account, $6,500.

19 Advertising costs were paid in cash, $600.

20 Purchased additional equipment for $4,800 cash.

29 Repair services done in January were for $5,000 cash and $15,000 on account.

30 Wages for January were paid in cash, $2,900.

30 Paid January and February's rent, for a total of $1,800.

31 Leo withdrew $500 cash. He used the cash to make a payment on his personal loan.

31 A total of $4,500 of the repair parts inventory was used in the month. (*Hint*: Debit this to Repair Parts Expense.)

Instructions

(a) Prepare journal entries to record each of Cyberdyne's January transactions.

(b) Open ledger accounts for each of the accounts listed in the trial balance, and enter the December 31, 2010, balances. Use T accounts.

(c) Post the journal entries to the accounts in the ledger.

(d) Prepare a trial balance as at January 31, 2011.

Taking It Further   Is the purchase of the repair parts inventory a debit to an asset or an expense? Explain.

P2–10A   Refer to the trial balance prepared in part (d) of P2–9A for Cyberdyne Repair Service.

Prepare financial statements. (SO 5) AP

Instructions

Use the trial balance to do the following:

(a) Prepare an income statement for Cyberdyne Repair Service.

(b) Prepare a statement of owner's equity.

(c) Prepare a balance sheet.

Taking It Further   Leo does not understand (1) why even though his business is profitable, he still has to invest additional cash; and (2) why he was able to withdraw only $500 cash. Based on your review of the financial statements, what explanations can you give him?

P2–11A   The ledger of Super Delivery Service has the following account balances at the company's year end, August 31, 2011:

Prepare trial balance and financial statements. (SO 5) AP

Accounts Payable	$ 3,235	Repair Expense	1,580
Accounts Receivable	4,275	Salaries Expense	5,665
Cash	?	Salaries Payable	925
Delivery Equipment	49,720	Service Revenue	37,780
Gas and Oil Expense	12,145	Supplies	265
Insurance Expense	2,020	Supplies Expense	2,650
Interest Expense	975	J. Rowe, Capital	48,750
Notes Payable	19,500	J. Rowe, Drawings	24,400
Prepaid Insurance	405	Unearned Revenue	675

Instructions

(a) Prepare a trial balance, with the accounts arranged in ledger (financial statement) order, as illustrated in the chapter, and determine the missing amount for Cash.

(b) Prepare an income statement, statement of owner's equity, and balance sheet.

Taking It Further   The owner, Jan Rowe, is not sure how much cash she can withdraw from the company each year. After reviewing the financial statements, comment on the amount she withdrew this year.

Analyze errors and effects on trial balance.
(SO 5) AN

P2–12A   A co-op student, working for Insidz Co., recorded the company's transactions for the month. At the end of the month, the owner of Insidz Co. reviewed the student's work and had some questions about the following transactions:

1. Insidz Co. received $255 cash from a customer on account, which was recorded as a debit to Cash of $255 and a credit to Accounts Receivable of $552.
2. A service provided for cash was posted as a debit to Cash of $2,000 and a credit to Accounts Receivable of $2,000.
3. A credit of $750 for interest earned was neither recorded nor posted. The debit was recorded and posted correctly.
4. The debit to record $1,000 of drawings was posted to the Salary Expense account. The credit was posted correctly.
5. Services of $325 were provided to a customer on account. The co-op student debited Accounts Receivable $325 and credited Service Revenue $325.
6. A purchase of supplies for $2,500 on account was recorded as a debit to Supplies and a debit to Accounts Payable.
7. Insidz Co. received a cash advance of $500 from a customer for work to be done next month. Cash was debited $500 but there was no credit because the co-op student was not sure what to credit.
8. A cash payment of $495 for salaries was recorded as a debit to Salaries Expense and a credit to Salaries Payable.
9. Insidz Co. purchased $2,600 of equipment on account and made a $6,200 debit to Equipment and a $6,200 credit to Accounts Payable.
10. A $650 utility bill for the month was received at the end of the month. It was not recorded because it had not been paid.

Instructions

(a) Indicate which transactions are correct and which are incorrect.

(b) For each error identified in (a), answer the following:

1. Will the trial balance be in balance?
2. Which account(s) will be incorrectly stated because of the error?
3. For each account you identified in (2) as being incorrect, is the account overstated or understated? By how much?
4. Is the debit column total of the trial balance stated correctly? If not, does correcting the errors increase or decrease the total and by how much?
5. Is the credit column total of the trial balance stated correctly? If not, does correcting the errors increase or decrease the total and by how much?

Taking It Further Your best friend thinks it is a waste of time to correct all of the above errors. Your friend reasons that as long as the trial balance is balanced, then there is no need to correct an error. Do you agree or disagree with your friend? Explain, using at least two of the above errors to make your points.

P2–13A The trial balance of Winter Co. does not balance:

Prepare correct trial balance.
(SO 4, 5) AN

	Debit	Credit
WINTER CO.		
Trial Balance		
June 30, 2011		
Cash		$ 2,635
Accounts receivable	$ 1,942	
Supplies	500	
Equipment	6,400	
Accounts payable		2,200
Unearned fees	1,765	
F. Winter, capital		11,231
F. Winter, drawings	800	
Fees earned		2,680
Salaries expense	3,000	
Office expense	1,010	
	$15,417	$18,746

Your review of the ledger reveals that each account has a normal balance. You also discover the following errors:

1. Cash received from a customer on account was debited to Cash for $750 and Accounts Receivable was credited for the same amount. The actual collection was $570.
2. The purchase of supplies on account for $360 was recorded as a debit to Equipment for $360 and a credit to Accounts Payable for $360.
3. Services of $890 were performed on account for a client. Accounts Receivable was debited for $89 and Fees Earned was credited for $890.
4. A debit posting to Office Expense of $700 was not done.
5. A payment on account for $205 was credited to Cash for $205 and debited to Accounts Payable for $502.
6. The withdrawal of $400 cash for Winter's personal use was debited to Salaries Expense for $400 and credited to Cash for $400.
7. A transposition error (reversal of digits) was made when copying the balance in the Fees Earned to the trial balance. The correct balance recorded in the account was $2,860.
8. The general ledger contained a Prepaid Insurance account with a debit balance of $565.

Instructions

Prepare a correct trial balance.

Taking It Further After the trial balance is corrected for the above errors, could there still be errors? Explain why or why not.

Problems: Set B

Identify type of account, financial statement, normal balances, and debits and credits.
(SO 1) K

P2–1B   Walter Isaacson, Medical Practice, has the following accounts:

Wages Payable	Office Equipment
Wages Expense	Notes Payable
W. Isaacson, Drawings	Medical Fees Earned
W. Isaacson, Capital	Interest Expense
Unearned Medical Fees	Insurance Expense
Rent Revenue	Furniture
Rent Expense	Computer
Prepaid Rent	Cash
Office Supplies Expense	Accounts Receivable
Office Supplies	Accounts Payable

Instructions

For each of these accounts, identify (a) the type of account (e.g., asset, liability, owner's capital, drawings, revenue, expense); (b) what financial statement it is presented on; (c) the normal balance of the account; (d) whether the account is increased by a debit or credit; and (e) whether the account is decreased by a debit or credit. Use the following format, in which the first one is done for you as an example.

	(a)	(b)	(c)	(d)	(e)
Account	Type of Account	Financial Statement	Normal Balance	Increase	Decrease
Wages payable	Liability	Balance sheet	Credit	Credit	Debit

Taking It Further   Explain the relationship between the normal balance in each type of account and the basic accounting equation.

Perform transaction analysis and journalize transactions.
(SO 1, 2, 3) AP

P2–2B   Battistella Couture & Design Co. began operations in 2009. During February 2011, the company had the following transactions:

Feb.   1   Paid February rent, $475.

2   Purchased sewing supplies for $250 on account.

6   Finished sewing a suit, delivered it to the customer, and collected $750 cash.

7   Received an order from another customer to design and sew a leather jacket for $885.

10   Agreed to sew a wedding dress for a customer. Received $250 cash from the customer as a down payment.

12   The owner of the company, Karen Battistella, withdrew $700 cash for personal use.

15   Finished sewing the leather jacket (see February 7 transaction) and billed the customer.

25   Paid for the supplies purchased on February 2.

27   The customer billed on February 15 paid the amount owing.

28   Borrowed $2,000 cash from the bank and signed a note payable for the amount owing.

28   Purchased a new sewing machine for $2,500 cash.

Instructions

(a) For each transaction, indicate: (1) the basic type of account debited and credited (asset, liability, or owner's equity); (2) the specific account debited and credited (Cash, Rent Expense, Service Revenue, etc.); and (3) whether each account is increased (+) or decreased (−), and by what amount. Use the following format, in which the first transaction is given as an example:

	Account Debited			Account Credited		
	Basic	Specific		Basic	Specific	
Transaction	Type	Account	Effect	Type	Account	Effect
Feb. 1	Owner's Equity	Rent Expense	+ $475	Asset	Cash	− $475

(b) Prepare a journal entry for each transaction.

Taking It Further   Karen is confused about why debits are used to record expenses and why credits are used to decrease cash. Explain.

P2–3B   Mountain Adventure Biking Park was started on April 1 by Dustin Tanner. The following events and transactions are for June:

*Journalize transactions.
(SO 3) AP*

Apr. 1 Tanner invested $50,000 cash in the business.
     3 Purchased an out-of-use ski hill for $320,000, paying $25,000 cash and signing a note payable for the balance. The $320,000 purchase price consisted of land, $175,000; building, $80,000; and equipment, $65,000.
    8 Incurred advertising expenses of $2,800 on account.
   13 Paid $5,500 cash for a one-year insurance policy.
   15 Received $2,700 cash from customers for admission fees.
   16 Paid salaries to employees, $1,800.
   20 Billed a customer, Celtic Fern Ltd., $1,500 for admission fees for exclusive use of the park that day. Celtic Fern Ltd. agreed to pay the amount owing within 10 days.
   22 Hired a park manager at a salary of $4,000 per month, effective May 1.
   29 Received $1,500 cash from Celtic Fern Ltd. for the April 20 transaction.
   30 Received $5,900 cash for admission fees.
   30 Paid $1,650 on account for advertising expenses incurred on April 8.
   30 Paid $1,250 interest expense on the note payable.
   30 Paid Dustin Tanner $600 cash for his personal use.

The company's chart of accounts includes the following accounts: Cash; Accounts Receivable; Prepaid Insurance; Land; Building; Equipment; Accounts Payable; Notes Payable; D. Tanner, Capital; D. Tanner, Drawings; Admissions Revenue; Advertising Expense; Salaries Expense; and Interest Expense.

Instructions

Journalize the April transactions.

Taking It Further   After Dustin has reviewed the journal entries, he complains that they don't seem to be very useful. Explain to Dustin the purpose of the journal entries and the next step in the accounting cycle. Include in your answer whether or not Dustin will find any useful information after the next step is completed.

Journalize transactions, post, and prepare trial balance.
(SO 3, 4, 5) AP

P2–4B Ghita Mancini, a CGA, opened an accounting practice, Mancini Accounting Services, on May 1, 2011. The following events and transactions occurred in the first month of operations.

May 1 Ghita invested $20,000 cash and office equipment worth $8,500 in the business.

1 Paid $950 for office rent for May.

2 Hired a secretary-receptionist at a salary of $2,400 per month.

3 Purchased $950 of office supplies on account from Read Supply Company.

11 Completed a tax assignment and billed Arnold Co. $2,275 for services rendered.

17 Completed accounting services and collected $1,350 cash from the client.

21 Received $1,200 cash from Arnold Co. for the May 11 transaction.

22 Received a $3,500 cash advance on a management consulting engagement with Arch Co.

23 Paid 60% of the balance due to Read Supply Company.

30 The May telephone bill was $215. It will be paid in June.

31 Paid the secretary-receptionist $2,400 salary for the month.

31 Paid Ghita $925 cash for her personal use.

Mancini Accounting Services uses the following chart of accounts: No. 101 Cash; No. 112 Accounts Receivable; No. 126 Office Supplies; No. 151 Office Equipment; No. 201 Accounts Payable; No. 209 Unearned Accounting Fees; No. 301 G. Mancini, Capital; No. 306 G. Mancini, Drawings; No. 400 Accounting Fees Earned; No. 726 Rent Expense; No. 729 Salaries Expense; and No. 737 Telephone Expense.

Instructions

(a) Journalize the transactions.
(b) Post to the ledger accounts. Use the standard form of account.
(c) Prepare a trial balance at May 31, 2011.

Taking It Further Ghita asks how to decide whether a transaction should be recorded or not. Provide her with a general rule and include specific reference to the May 2 and May 30 transactions in your answer.

Journalize transactions, post, and prepare trial balance.
(SO 3, 4, 5) AP

P2–5B Kiersted Financial Services was formed on November 1, 2011. During the month of November, the following events and transactions occurred:

Nov. 1 Haakon Kiersted, the owner, invested $35,000 cash and office equipment in the company. The equipment had originally cost Haakon $25,000 but was currently worth $12,000.

2 Hired one employee to work in the office for a monthly salary of $2,825.

3 Signed a three-year contract to lease office space for $2,140 per month. Paid the first and last month's rent in cash. (*Hint*: The payment for the final month's rent should be considered an asset and be recorded in Prepaid Rent.)

4 Purchased a one-year insurance policy for $4,740 to be paid in monthly instalments on the fourth day of each month. Paid the first month's premium.

5 Purchased additional office equipment for $18,000. Paid $6,000 cash and signed a note payable for the balance.

6 Purchased supplies for $1,550 on account.

7 Purchased additional supplies for $475 cash.

16 Completed services for a customer and immediately collected $990.

20 Completed services for two customers and billed them a total of $4,500.

26 Paid $1,000 for the office supplies purchased on account on November 6.

27 The telephone bill for November was $220. It will be paid in December.

27 Received a $750 cash advance from a customer for services to be provided in December.

29 Collected $2,800 from one of the customers billed on November 20.
30 Paid $60 interest on the note payable.
30 Paid the employee's monthly salary, $2,825.
30 Paid Haakon Kiersted $700 for his personal use.
30 Paid Sony Ltd. for a new sound system for Haakon's home, $1,150 cash.

Instructions

(a) Prepare journal entries to record the transactions.
(b) Post the journal entries to T accounts.
(c) Prepare a trial balance as at November 30, 2011.

Taking It Further   Haakon asks if the change in his cash account balance from the beginning to the end of the month is equal to his profit or loss for the month. Explain to Haakon whether or not this is true and why.

P2–6B   Highland Theatre is owned by Finnean Ferguson. At June 30, 2011, the ledger showed the following: Cash $6,000; Land $90,000; Buildings $80,000; Equipment $25,000; Accounts Payable $5,000; Mortgage Payable $125,000; and F. Ferguson, Capital $71,000. During July, the following events and transactions occurred:

Journalize transactions, post,
and prepare trial balance.
(SO 3, 4, 5) AP

July   2   Paid film rental of $800 on first movie to run in July.
2   Paid advertising expenses, $625.
3   Ordered two additional films at $750 each.
5   Highland Theatre contracted with Seibert Company to operate a concession stand. Seibert agrees to pay Highland Theatre 20% of gross concession receipts, payable monthly, for the right to operate the concession stand.
10   Received $1,950 cash from admissions.
11   Made $2,000 principal payment on mortgage. Also paid $500 interest on the mortgage.
12   Paid $350 cash to have the projection equipment repaired.
15   Received one of the films ordered on July 3 and was billed $750. The film will be shown in July.
25   Received $5,500 cash from customers for admissions.
26   Paid $3,200 of the accounts payable.
28   Prepaid a $700 rental on a special film to be shown in August.
30   Paid Finnean Ferguson $1,200 for his personal use.
31   Received a statement from Seibert: it shows gross concession receipts of $2,600 and a balance due to Highland Theatre of $520 ($2,600 × 20%) for July. Seibert paid one half of the balance due and will pay the rest on August 5.
31   Paid salaries, $1,900.

In addition to the accounts identified above, Highland Theatre's ledger includes the following: Accounts Receivable; Prepaid Rentals; F. Ferguson, Drawings; Admission Revenue; Concession Revenue; Advertising Expense; Film Rental Expense; Repairs Expense; Salaries Expense; and Interest Expense.

Instructions

(a) Journalize the July transactions.
(b) Enter the beginning balances in the ledger as at June 30. Use the standard form of account.
(c) Post the July journal entries to the ledger.
(d) Prepare a trial balance at the end of July 2011.

Taking It Further   A friend of yours is considering buying Highland Theatre from the current owner. Using the information in the trial balance, comment on whether or not this may be a sound company for your friend to purchase.

Journalize transactions, post, and prepare trial balance.
(SO 3, 4, 5) AP

P2–7B Brisebois Dry Cleaners has a July 31 year end. The company's trial balance on June 30, 2011, is as follows:

BRISEBOIS DRY CLEANERS
Trial Balance
June 30, 2011

	Debit	Credit
Cash	$ 11,660	
Note receivable	5,000	
Accounts receivable	5,845	
Supplies	3,975	
Equipment	31,480	
Accounts payable		$ 13,090
Unearned revenue		1,920
E. Brisebois, capital		55,920
E. Brisebois, drawings	37,050	
Dry cleaning revenue		109,455
Salaries expense	57,750	
Rent expense	11,385	
Repair expense	1,720	
Utilities expense	14,520	
Totals	$180,385	$180,385

The July transactions were as follows:

July 2 Paid July rent, $1,035.
3 Purchased new equipment with a suggested manufacturer's price of $5,500. After much negotiating, paid $1,500 cash and signed a note payable for $3,600.
5 Collected $3,285 cash on the June 30 accounts receivable.
10 Performed $1,920 of services for customers who paid in advance in June.
11 Received $4,730 cash from customers for services performed.
13 Paid $9,742 to creditors on account.
14 Purchased supplies for $495 on account.
24 Billed customers $5,950 for services performed.
25 Collected the $5,000 note receivable plus interest of $200.
26 Signed a contract with a nursing home to provide laundry services at a rate of $1,650 per month starting in August. The first payment will be collected on August 1.
27 Received $650 cash from a customer for services to be provided in August.
28 The utility bill for July is $1,320. This bill will be paid in August.
29 Paid employee salaries of $5,250.
31 Paid the owner, E. Brisebois, $3,370 cash for personal use.
31 Paid $300 of the note payable plus $20 interest.

Instructions

(a) Journalize the transactions.
(b) Enter the June 30 balances in T accounts.
(c) Post the July journal entries to the T accounts. You may need to add new accounts for some of the transactions.
(d) Prepare a trial balance at July 31, 2011.

Prepare financial statements.
(SO 5) AP

Taking It Further Comment on the company's cash balance. What concerns and suggestions do you have for the company to consider in August?

P2–8B Refer to the trial balance prepared for Kiersted Financial Services in P2–5B part (c).

Instructions

(a) Prepare an income statement.
(b) Prepare a statement of owner's equity.
(c) Prepare a balance sheet.

Taking It Further   Discuss how well the company did in its first month of operations.

P2–9B   Gary Hobson owns and manages Soft-Q Repair Service, which fixes computers. Soft-Q had the following trial balance at March 31, 2011 (its year end):

Journalize transactions, post, and prepare trial balance.
(SO 3, 4, 5) AP

SOFT-Q REPAIR SERVICE		
Trial Balance		
March 31, 2011		
	Debit	Credit
Cash	$ 2,600	
Accounts receivable	14,400	
Repair parts inventory	17,400	
Shop equipment	30,100	
Accounts payable		$23,750
G. Hobson, capital		40,750
Totals	$64,500	$64,500

A summary of Soft-Q's transactions for April 2011 follows:

Apr.   1   Borrowed $12,000 cash from the bank, signing a note payable.
       2   Paid $11,000 to creditors on account.
       3   Purchased additional repair parts inventory on account, $4,700.
      10   Gary invested $3,000 of his own cash in the business.
      11   Miscellaneous expenses were paid in cash, $2,050.
      13   Advertising costs were paid in cash, $750.
      16   Cash was collected from customers on account, $6,000.
      29   Repair services provided in April were for $3,000 cash and $7,000 on account.
      30   Wages for April were paid in cash, $4,450.
      30   Gary withdrew $1,000 cash for personal use.
      30   Paid the bank $555 on the note payable, of which $55 is interest and $500 is a partial payment of the note.
      30   Paid April's rent, $1,650.
      30   A total of $3,705 of repair parts were used in the month. (*Hint*: Debit this to Repair Parts Expense.)

Instructions

(a) Prepare journal entries to record each of the April transactions.
(b) Open ledger accounts for each of the accounts listed in the trial balance, and enter the March 31, 2011, balances. Use T accounts.
(c) Post the journal entries to the accounts in the ledger.
(d) Prepare a trial balance as at the end of April.

Taking It Further   Is the purchase of the repair parts inventory a debit to an asset or an expense? Explain.

P2–10B   Refer to the trial balance prepared in part (d) of P2–9B for Soft-Q Repair Service.

Prepare financial statements.
(SO 5) AP

Instructions

Use the trial balance to do the following:
(a) Prepare an income statement.
(b) Prepare a statement of owner's equity.
(c) Prepare a balance sheet.

Taking It Further   Gary is considering selling the business. Based on your review of the financial statements, would you be interested in buying the business or do you have concerns? Discuss.

Prepare trial balance and financial statements.
(SO 5) AP

P2–11B   The ledger of Lazdowski Marketing Services has the following account balances at the company's year end, October 31, 2011:

Accounts payable	$ 4,430	Marketing fees earned	$?
Accounts receivable	6,010	Notes payable	48,850
Advertising expense	14,970	Office furniture	56,685
Cash	4,930	Office supplies	1,240
Computer equipment	25,970	Office supplies expense	5,000
D. Lazdowski, capital	57,410	Prepaid rent	975
D. Lazdowski, drawings	75,775	Rent expense	11,700
Insurance expense	2,020	Unearned marketing fees	3,555
Interest expense	2,445	Wages expense	20,545

Instructions

(a) Prepare a trial balance, with the accounts arranged in ledger (financial statement) order, as illustrated in the chapter, and determine the missing amount for Marketing fees earned.
(b) Prepare an income statement, statement of owner's equity, and balance sheet.

Taking It Further   The owner, Donna Lazdowski, is not sure how much cash she can withdraw from the company each year. After reviewing the financial statements, comment on the amount she withdrew this year.

Analyze errors and effects on trial balance.
(SO 5) AN

P2–12B   The bookkeeper for Shigeru's Dance Studio did the following in journalizing and posting:

1. A debit posting to Prepaid Insurance of $3,600 was not done.
2. A debit posting of $500 to Accounts Receivable was debited to Accounts Payable.
3. A purchase of supplies on account of $850 was debited to Supplies for $580 and credited to Accounts Payable for $580.
4. A credit to Wages Payable for $1,200 was posted as a credit to Cash.
5. A debit posting of $250 to Cash was posted twice.
6. A debit side of the entry to record the payment of $1,200 for drawings was posted to Wages Expense.
7. A credit to Service Revenue for $400 was posted as a credit to Unearned Service Revenue.
8. A debit to Accounts Payable of $250 was posted as a credit to Accounts Payable.
9. A purchase of equipment on account for $6,400 was posted as a $4,600 debit to Equipment and a $4,600 credit to Cash.
10. The provision of $950 of services on account was not recorded because the customer did not pay cash until the following month.

Instructions

(a) Indicate which of the above transactions are correct and which are incorrect.
(b) For each error identified in (a), answer the following:

1. Will the trial balance be in balance?
2. Which account(s) will be incorrectly stated because of the error?
3. For each account identified in (2) as being incorrect, is the account overstated or understated and by how much?
4. Is the debit column total of the trial balance stated correctly? If not, does correcting the errors increase or decrease the total and by how much?
5. Is the credit column total of the trial balance stated correctly? If not, does correcting the errors increase or decrease the total and by how much?

Taking It Further   Your best friend thinks it is a waste of time to correct all of the above errors. Your friend reasons that as long as the trial balance is balanced, then there is no need to correct an error. Do you agree or disagree with your friend? Explain using at least two of the above errors to make your points.

P2–13B   The trial balance that follows for Shawnee Slopes Company does not balance:

Prepare correct trial balance.
(SO 4, 5) AN

SHAWNEE SLOPES COMPANY Trial Balance June 30, 2011		
	Debit	Credit
Cash	$ 5,875	
Accounts receivable		$ 3,120
Prepaid insurance	500	
Equipment	14,200	
Accounts payable		5,140
Property taxes payable	500	
A. Shawnee, capital		17,900
Service revenue	6,847	
Advertising expense		1,132
Property tax expense	1,100	
Salaries expense	4,150	
Totals	$33,172	$27,292

Your review of the ledger reveals that each account has a normal balance. You also discover the following errors:

1. Prepaid Insurance and Property Tax Expense were each understated by $300.
2. A $410 credit to Service Revenue was incorrectly posted as a $140 credit.
3. A debit posting to Salaries Expense of $350 was not done.
4. A $750 cash withdrawal by the owner was debited to A. Shawnee, Capital, for $750 and credited to Cash for $750.
5. A $650 purchase of supplies on account was debited to Equipment for $650 and credited to Cash for $650.
6. A cash payment of $320 for advertising was debited to Advertising Expense for $230 and credited to Cash for $230.
7. A $275 collection from a customer was debited to Cash for $275 and debited to Accounts Receivable for $275.
8. A cash payment on account for $90 was recorded as a $90 credit to Cash and a $90 credit to Accounts Payable.
9. A $2,000 note payable was issued to purchase equipment. The transaction was neither journalized nor posted.

Instructions

Prepare a correct trial balance. (*Note*: You may need to add new accounts.)

Taking It Further   After the trial balance is corrected for the above errors, could there still be errors? Explain why or why not.

Continuing Cookie Chronicle

(*Note:* The Continuing Cookie began in Chapter 1 and will continue in each chapter.)

After researching the different forms of business organization, Natalie Koebel decides to operate "Cookie Creations" as a proprietorship. She then starts the process of getting the business running. In November 2010, the following activities take place:

Nov. 8   Natalie cashes her Canada Savings Bonds and receives $520, which she deposits in her personal bank account.

8   She opens a bank account under the name "Cookie Creations" and transfers $500 from her personal account to the new account.

10   Natalie pays $175 to have advertising brochures and posters printed. She plans to distribute these as opportunities arise.

12   She buys baking supplies, such as flour, sugar, butter, and chocolate chips, for $135 cash.

15   Natalie starts to gather some baking equipment to take with her when teaching the cookie classes. She has an excellent top-of-the-line food processor and mixer that originally cost her $750. Natalie decides to start using it only in her new business. She estimates that the equipment is currently worth $500.

16   Natalie realizes that her initial cash investment is not enough. Her grandmother lends her $2,000 cash, for which Natalie signs a one-year 3% note payable in the name of the business. Natalie deposits the money in the business bank account.

17   She buys more baking equipment for $900 cash.

20   She teaches her first class and collects $125 cash.

25   Natalie books a second class for December 4 for $125. She receives $25 cash in advance as a down payment.

26   Natalie teaches a group of Grade 2 students how to make sugar cookies. At the end of the class, Natalie leaves an invoice for $250 with the school principal. The principal says she will pass the invoice along to school board administration and the invoice will be paid sometime in December.

30   A $75 invoice is received for the use of Natalie's cell phone. The cell phone is used exclusively for Cookie Creations' business. The invoice is for services provided in November and is due on December 15, 2010.

Instructions

(a) Prepare journal entries to record the November transactions.
(b) Post the journal entries to ledger accounts.
(c) Prepare a trial balance at November 30, 2010.

Financial Reporting and Analysis

Financial Reporting Problem

BYP2–1 The financial statements of The Forzani Group for 2009 are shown in Appendix A at the back of this textbook. They contain the following selected accounts (in thousands):

Accounts payable and accrued liabilities	$277,820
Accounts receivable	84,455
Cash	3,474
Retail revenue	994,043
Inventory	291,497
Interest expense	5,175
Prepaid expenses	2,827

Instructions

(a) Answer the following questions:

1. What is the increase side (i.e., debit or credit) and decrease side for each of the above accounts?
2. What is the normal balance for each of these accounts?

(b) Identify the other account that is most commonly involved in the transaction, and the effect on that account, when:

1. Accounts receivable are decreased.
2. Accounts receivable are increased.
3. Retail revenue is increased.
4. Inventory is increased.
5. Interest expense is increased.
6. Prepaid expenses are increased.

Interpreting Financial Statements

BYP2–2 Viterra Inc. is one of Canada's leading agri-businesses. The following list of accounts and amounts was taken from Viterra Inc.'s 2008 financial statements:

VITERRA INC. List of Accounts October 31, 2008 (in thousands)	
Accounts payable and accrued liabilities	$ 928,596
Accounts receivable	773,830
Bank indebtedness and short-term debt	18,424
Cash	183,536
Cost of sales expense	5,750,735
Depreciation expense	106,832
Future income taxes—assets	61,875
Future income taxes—liabilities	166,476
Gain on disposal of assets	1,263

Goodwill and intangible assets	$ 322,254
Income tax expense	89,702
Interest expense	37,785
Inventories	837,943
Investments	7,645
Long-term debt	610,088
Operating, general, and administrative expenses	494,227
Other assets	69,238
Other expenses	11,266
Other liabilities	64,183
Prepaid expenses and deposits	91,183
Property, plant, and equipment	1,154,859
Sales and operating revenues	6,777,566
Shareholders' (owner's) equity, November 1, 2007	1,912,443
Short-term investments	486,129

Instructions

(a) Prepare a trial balance for Viterra Inc., with the accounts in financial statement order.
(b) Present the accounts and balances of Viterra Inc. in the form of the accounting equation: Assets = Liabilities + Shareholders' (Owner's) Equity.

Critical Thinking

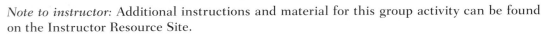

Collaborative Learning Activity

Note to instructor: Additional instructions and material for this group activity can be found on the Instructor Resource Site.

BYP2–3 In this group activity, you will work with a partner to complete five transactions using the handout from your teacher.

Working in Groups

Instructions

(a) Your instructor will divide the class into pairs.
(b) Each pair will complete the transactions on the paper handed out by the instructor.
(c) This exercise is followed by a brief quiz based on the above collaborative activity.

Communication Activity

Writing Handbook

BYP2–4 White Glove Company offers home cleaning services. Two common transactions for the company are billing customers for services performed and paying employee salaries. For example, on March 15, bills that totalled $6,000 were sent to customers, and $2,000 in salaries was paid to employees.

Instructions

Write a memo to your instructor that explains how these transactions are recorded in the double-entry system. Include in your memo (1) how the debit and credit rules are applied to these transactions, and (2) an explanation of what the normal balances are in the accounts affected by the transactions.

Ethics Case

WILEY PLUS
Ethics in Accounting

BYP2–5 Vu Hung is the assistant chief accountant at Lim Company, a manufacturer of computer chips and cellular phones. The company currently has total sales of $20 million. It is the end of the first quarter. Vu is hurriedly trying to prepare a general ledger trial balance so that quarterly financial statements can be prepared and released to management and regulatory agencies. The credits on the trial balance add up to $1,000 more than the debits.

In order to meet the 4:00 p.m. deadline, Vu decides to force the debits and credits into balance by adding the amount of the difference to the Equipment account. She chose Equipment because it is one of the larger account balances. Proportionally, it will be the least misstated. She believes that the difference will not affect anyone's decisions. She wishes that she had more time to find the error, but realizes that the financial statements are already late.

Instructions

(a) Who are the stakeholders in this situation?
(b) What are the ethical issues involved?
(c) What are Vu's alternatives?

"All About You" Activity

BYP2–6 The "All About You" feature indicates that Pacioli, who described the double-entry accounting system used over 500 years ago, wrote "a person should not go to sleep at night until the debits equalled the credits."

In the double-entry system, debits and credits are used to record the dual effect of each transaction in the appropriate accounts and to keep the basic accounting equation in balance. For each transaction, the debits must equal the credits; therefore, the total debits and credits for all of the accounts should be equal. If the total debits do not equal the credits, there is an error in the accounting records.

You are a first-year university student and very excited about moving away from home to go to university. Your parents have given you $4,000 and you have a $13,000 student loan. Your parents have told you that $4,000 is all you get for the school year and you are not to phone home for more money.

At September 1, you had $17,000 cash ($4,000 + $13,000), $1,000 worth of clothes, and a cell phone that cost $100. You have kept all of the receipts for all of your expenditures between September 1 and December 15. The following is a complete list of your receipts.

Receipts	Amount
Rent on furnished apartment	$1,600
Groceries	1,200
Tuition for September to December	2,800
Textbooks	600
Entertainment (movies, beverages, restaurants)	1,500
New clothes	1,500
Cell phone bill	200
Cable TV and Internet bill	250
Computer	1,000
Bus fare	175
Airfare to go home at Christmas	450

You are enrolled in an accounting course and you have set up an accounting system to track your expenditures. On December 15, you prepared the following trial balance from your accounting records:

Personal Trial Balance December 15, 2010		
Account	Debit	Credit
Cash	$ 6,175	
Clothes	2,500	
Cell phone	100	
Computer	100	
Student loan		13,000
Personal equity		5,100
Rent expense	1,600	
Groceries		1,200
Tuition for September to December	2,800	
Textbooks for September to December	600	
Entertainment	1,500	
Cell phone expense	200	
Cable TV and Internet expense	250	
Bus fare	175	
Airfare	540	
	$16,540	$19,300

On December 15, you checked the balance in your bank account and you only have $5,725 cash. You can't sleep, because you know there are some errors in your accounting records and that you will probably have to ask your parents for more money for the next semester.

Instructions

(a) Calculate your personal equity (deficit) at September 1, 2010.
(b) Prepare a corrected trial balance at December 15, 2010. For each error identified, describe the error.
(c) Calculate your personal equity (deficit) at December 15, 2010.
(d) Will it be necessary for you to ask you parents for more money for the next semester? Explain.

ANSWERS TO CHAPTER QUESTIONS

Answers to Accounting in Action Insight Questions

Business Insight, p. 66

Q: How can unrecorded accounts receivable transactions increase a loss on the income statement?

A: One possibility is that the problem was caused by company employees keeping payments from customers for themselves, and not recording the cash receipt transaction in the company's records. This would result in a larger accounts receivable balance than the amounts owed to the company by customers. When the problem is discovered, the company must reduce the accounts receivable balance to the correct amount. The other side of the journal entry is a debit to an expense on the income statement, and thus a smaller profit or larger loss.

Across the Organization, p. 69

Q: When deciding how to create a chart of accounts, whom should an accountant consult with?

A: When designing a chart of accounts, an accountant should consult with anyone who will need information from the accounting system. The more information required, the more complex the chart of accounts. For example, at Goodyear, there are different product lines and different regions so, a result, many accounts are required. The accountant (or accounting department) will need to consult with the different managers to determine what level of detail is required. They will then design the chart of accounts so the accounting system can provide the required level of detail.

At a small company like Beanz, typically only the manager or owner would be consulted to find out how much information they need. But if Beanz has bank loans, then the accountant may want to talk to the bank to ensure that the chart of accounts is designed to meet the lender's information needs.

All About You, p. 78

Q: Pacioli also wrote "a person should not go to sleep at night until the debits equalled the credits." Is this still good advice over 500 years later?

A: Perseverance can be a very useful attribute for an accounting student. Sometimes it can be difficult and time-consuming to find an error and correct it. Many students find this very frustrating and give up too soon and thus miss the opportunity to learn and increase their confidence. On the other hand, sleep is very important and can provide you with a fresh perspective the next day.

Answer to Forzani Review It Question 5, p. 62

Normal balances: Accounts Receivable (asset)—debit; Accounts Payable and Accrued Liabilities (liability)—credit; Retail Revenue (revenue)—credit; and Store Operating Expense (expense)—debit.

Answers to Self-Study Questions

1. b 2. c 3. d 4. d 5. b 6. a 7. c 8. d 9. a 10. c

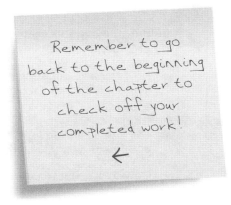

CHAPTER 10
CURRENT LIABILITIES AND PAYROLL

payroll.ca

✓ THE NAVIGATOR

- ☐ Understand *Concepts for Review*
- ☐ Read *Feature Story*
- ☐ Scan *Study Objectives*
- ☐ Read *Chapter Preview*
- ☐ Read text and answer *Before You Go On*
- ☐ Work *Demonstration Problem*
- ☐ Review *Summary of Study Objectives*
- ☐ Answer *Self-Study Questions*
- ☐ Complete assignments

CONCEPTS FOR REVIEW:

Before studying this chapter, you should understand or, if necessary, review:

a. How to make adjusting entries for unearned revenue (Ch. 3, p. 127) and accrued expenses. (Ch. 3, pp. 130–132)

b. The importance of liquidity in evaluating the financial position of a company. (Ch. 4, pp. 200–201)

c. How to account for sales discounts. (Ch. 5, p. 257)

d. Accounting for notes receivable. (Ch. 8, pp. 448–451)

Even Small Companies Have Big Payroll Obligations

A big portion of any organization's current liabilities is its payroll obligations: employees' salaries or wages, and any related deductions for things like the Canada Pension Plan, Employment Insurance, and income taxes. Then there are health care taxes, workers' compensation premiums, and any taxable benefits the employer offers. Depending on the size and reach of the business, there are up to 185 different pieces of legislation and regulations that a payroll person would have to keep up to date with, points out Steven Van Alstine, Vice President, Compliance Programs and Services, at the Canadian Payroll Association (CPA). This includes the federal *Income Tax Act* and *Employment Insurance Act*, provincial workers' compensation regulations, employment standards, health tax acts, and so on. "It is difficult, certainly if you're a new small business, being faced with myriad different requirements or legislation," he says. "It is a little daunting when you think, as a new business owner, 'What do I have to do?'"

No doubt, accounting for this liability can be a challenge for smaller businesses. Of the CPA's 14,000 members, 65% to 70% are organizations with 200 or fewer employees, says Van Alstine. But several resources are available to help them. For about one third of people working in payroll, payroll is their sole responsibility, he continues. But for the remaining two thirds, it's only a part of their responsibilities, which likely include such functions as human resources or accounts payable. The CPA is an information source for people who don't handle payroll on a full-time basis. "We are a support for those individuals who may be the sole payroll person within the organization," he says. Consultants are on hand to answer questions by phone and guide payroll staff through the process.

The CPA offers a certification program for payroll professionals. In addition, it offers "Learning Payroll" courses. The association also has a "Setting Up a New Payroll" checklist that lists various resources and forms an employer may need and where to locate them, including those specific to provinces.

The Canada Revenue Agency also has tools available to help employers with their payroll, including an on-line payroll deduction calculator, which many may think does the job for them. However, as Van Alstine points out, "The employer needs to know that those are the deductions for the employee."

Those lacking the necessary qualifications and skills to properly account for payroll may hire a CPA-certified professional, a bookkeeper, or an accounting firm to take over the paperwork. Or they may outsource the whole payroll function to a service provider like Ceridian or ADP. The benefits to employers include reduced costs, partly because they use the service provider's technology rather than setting up their own system. They also don't have to service the technology and update it, though they are still responsible for their day-to-day payroll administration.

Payroll is a liability that needs proper administration no matter what the size of the business is. After all, a company's employees are its greatest asset.

The Navigator

STUDY OBJECTIVES:

After studying this chapter, you should be able to:

1. Account for determinable or certain current liabilities.

2. Account for estimated liabilities.

3. Account for contingencies.

4. Determine payroll costs and record payroll transactions.

5. Prepare the current liabilities section of the balance sheet.

6. Calculate mandatory payroll deductions (Appendix 10A).

The Navigator

Whether it is a huge company such as one of Canada's chartered banks, or a small business such as your local convenience store, every company has current liabilities. As explained in Chapter 4, current liabilities are obligations that are expected to be settled within one year from the balance sheet date or in the company's normal operating cycle. Obligations that are expected to be paid after one year or longer are classified as long-term liabilities. We explain current liabilities in this chapter and long-term liabilities in Chapter 15. Payroll creates current liabilities and affects almost every company. It is also explained in this chapter.

The chapter is organized as follows:

Determinable (Certain) Current Liabilities

STUDY OBJECTIVE 1

Account for determinable or certain current liabilities.

In Chapter 1, we defined liabilities as present obligations, arising from past events, to make future payments of assets or services. A future commitment is not considered a liability unless an obligation also exists. For example, a company may have made a commitment to purchase an asset in the future, but the obligation normally arises only when the goods are delivered or if the company has entered into an irrevocable agreement. Thus, an essential characteristic of a liability is the existence of a *present* obligation.

Sometimes there is a great deal of uncertainty regarding whether or not a liability exists. Even if it is certain that the liability exists, then sometimes we are not certain as to whom we owe, how much we owe, or when we owe. We will discuss this type of liability in the sections on estimated liabilities and contingencies.

In this section of the chapter, we will discuss liabilities where there is no uncertainty about their existence, amount, or timing. Liabilities with a known amount, payee, and due date are often referred to as **determinable liabilities**.

Alternative terminology
Determinable liabilities are also referred to as *certain liabilities* or *known liabilities*.

Examples of determinable current liabilities include bank indebtedness from operating lines of credit, and notes payable, accounts payable, sales taxes payable, unearned revenue, and current maturities of long-term debt. This category also includes accrued liabilities such as property taxes, payroll, and interest.

The entries for many of these liabilities have been explained in previous chapters, including the entries for accounts payable and unearned revenues. We will discuss the accounting for other types of current liabilities in this section, including bank indebtedness from an operating line of credit, notes payable, sales taxes payable, property taxes payable, and current maturities of long-term debt. Payroll and employee benefits payable are also examples of determinable liabilities, but as the accounting for payroll is complex, we discuss it in a separate section of this chapter.

Operating Line of Credit and Bank Overdraft

Operating Line of Credit

Current assets (such as accounts receivable) do not always turn into cash at the exact time that current liabilities (such as accounts payable) must be paid. Consequently, most companies have an **operating line of credit** at their bank to help them manage temporary cash shortfalls. This means that the company has been pre-authorized by the bank to borrow money when it is needed, up to a pre-set limit.

Security, called **collateral**, is usually required by the bank as protection in case the company is unable to repay the loan. Collateral normally includes some, or all, of the company's current assets (e.g., accounts receivable or inventories); investments; or property, plant, and equipment. The Forzani Group Ltd. has a $250-million operating line of credit that is "collateralized by general security agreements against all existing and future acquired assets of the Company." Forzani refers to it as a "revolving credit facility" as opposed to an "operating line of credit."

Money borrowed through a line of credit is normally borrowed on a short-term basis, and is repayable immediately upon request—that is, on demand—by the bank. In reality, repayment is rarely demanded without notice. A line of credit makes it very easy for a company to borrow money. It does not have to make a call or visit its bank to actually arrange the transaction. The bank simply covers any cheques written in excess of the bank account balance, up to the approved credit limit.

Bank Overdraft

Some companies have a negative (credit), or overdrawn, cash balance at year end. This amount is usually called *bank indebtedness*, *bank overdraft*, or *bank advances*. No special entry or account is required to record the overdrawn amount. The Cash account has a credit balance because the dollar amount of cheques written exceeded the dollar amount of deposits. The credit balance in Cash is reported as a current liability with an appropriate note disclosure.

Interest is usually charged on the overdrawn amount at a floating rate, such as prime plus a specified percentage. The **prime rate** is the interest rate that banks charge their best customers. This rate is usually increased by a specified percentage according to the company's risk profile.

Short-Term Notes Payable

The line of credit described above is similar to a **note payable**. Notes payable are obligations in the form of written promissory notes. In Chapter 8, we discussed notes receivable and included an illustration of a promissory note. You will recall that the payee has a note receivable and the maker of the note has a note payable.

Notes payable may be used instead of accounts payable. This gives the lender proof of the obligation in case legal action is needed to collect the debt. Accounts and notes payable that result from purchase transactions (i.e., amounts owed to suppliers) are often called **trade payables**. Notes payable are also frequently issued to meet short-term financing needs.

> **Helpful hint** Notes payable are the opposite of notes receivable, and the accounting is similar.

Notes are issued for varying periods. If they are due for payment within one year of the balance sheet date, they are classified as current liabilities. Most notes are interest-bearing, with interest due monthly or at maturity.

To illustrate the accounting for notes payable, assume that Kok Co. borrows $100,000 from the local Caisse Populaire on March 1 for four months, at an interest rate of 6%. The note matures on July 1 and interest, along with the principal amount of the note, is payable at maturity.

Kok makes the following journal entry when it signs the note and receives the $100,000:

Mar. 1	Cash	100,000	
	Note Payable		100,000
	To record issue of four-month, 6% note to Caisse Populaire.		

A	=	L	+	OE
+100,000		+100,000		

 Cash flows: +100,000

Interest accrues over the life of the note; therefore, interest expense must be recorded in the period when the borrowed money is used. Also, at year end, all liabilities (all obligations) must be recorded. If Kok Co. has a March 31 year end, then the interest owing at the end of March must be recorded. An adjusting entry is made to recognize interest expense and interest payable of $500 ($100,000 × 6% × $\frac{1}{12}$) at March 31. Recall from Chapter 3 that interest is calculated by multiplying the principal amount by the annual interest rate by the fraction of the year in the accrual.

The adjusting entry is:

Cash flows: no effect

Mar. 31	Interest Expense	500	
	Interest Payable		500
	To accrue interest to March 31.		

In the March 31 financial statements, the current liabilities section of the balance sheet will show notes payable of $100,000 and interest payable of $500. In addition, interest expense of $500 will be reported as other expenses in the income statement. Interest payable is shown separately from the note payable.

At maturity (July 1), Kok Co. must pay the face value of the note ($100,000) plus $2,000 interest ($100,000 × 6% × $\frac{4}{12}$). One month ($500) of this interest has already been accrued. Interest must also be updated for $1,500 ($100,000 × 6% × $\frac{3}{12}$) for the three additional months—April through June—since interest was last recorded. This can be done in one compound entry or in separate journal entries as follows:

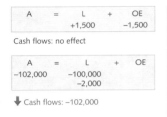

Cash flows: no effect

Cash flows: –102,000

July	1.	Interest Expense	1,500	
		Interest Payable		1,500
		To accrue interest for April, May, and June.		
	1	Note Payable	100,000	
		Interest Payable ($500 + $1,500)	2,000	
		Cash ($100,000 + $2,000)		102,000
		To record payment of Caisse Populaire note and accrued interest.		

Sales Taxes

As a consumer, you are well aware that you pay sales taxes on many of the products you buy at retail stores. For the retail store, sales taxes collected from customers are a liability because the company has an obligation to pay the amount collected to the appropriate government body.

Sales taxes are expressed as a percentage of the sales price. As discussed in earlier chapters and in Appendix B, sales taxes usually take the form of the federal Goods and Services Tax (GST) and Provincial Sales Tax (PST). In Quebec, the provincial sales tax is called the Quebec Sales Tax (QST). The GST is 5% across Canada. Provincial sales tax rates vary from 0% to 10% across the country.

At the time of writing, in British Columbia, Ontario, Newfoundland and Labrador, Nova Scotia, and New Brunswick, the PST and GST have been or were about to be combined into one 13% Harmonized Sales Tax (HST). It was also expected that Saskatchewan and Manitoba would decide to harmonize their sales taxes in the near future. Alberta, Yukon, Northwest Territories, and Nunavut do not have PST. Quebec and Prince Edward Island are the only two provinces with a separate provincial sales tax system, where there are currently no thoughts of harmonizing with the federal sales tax.

Whether GST, PST, or HST, the retailer collects the tax from the customer when the sale occurs. The retailer then pays (remits) the sales taxes collected to the designated federal and provincial collecting authorities. In the case of GST, HST, and QST, collections may be offset against payments. In such cases, only the net amount owing or recoverable must be paid or refunded. Depending on the size of the retailer, the sales taxes must be sent to the government monthly, quarterly or, for very small companies, annually.

The amount of the sale and the amount of the sales tax collected are usually rung up separately on the cash register. The cash register readings are then used to credit sales or services and the correct sales taxes payable accounts. For example, if the March 25 cash register reading for Comeau Company, in New Brunswick, shows sales of $10,000 and Harmonized Sales Tax of $1,300 ($10,000 × 13% HST rate), the entry is as follows:

Mar. 25	Cash	11,300	
	Sales		10,000
	HST Payable		1,300
	To record sales and sales taxes.		

A	=	L	+	OE
+11,300		+1,300		+10,000

↑ Cash flows: +11,300

Comeau Company does not report the sales taxes collected from customers as revenue; sales taxes collected from customers are a liability. Comeau Company serves only as a collection agent for the government. When Comeau Company remits (pays) these sales taxes to the appropriate government collecting authorities, the HST Payable account is debited and Cash is credited.

Some businesses include sales taxes in the selling price. They do not separate sales taxes from the price of the goods sold. In these businesses, however, sales taxes must still be recorded separately from sales revenues. To find the sales amount, the total receipts are divided by 100% plus the sales tax percentage.

To illustrate, assume that Comeau Company's total receipts of $11,300 include HST. The total receipts from the sale are equal to 100% of the sales amount plus 13% of sales, or 1.13 times the sales amount, which gives $11,300. We can use algebra to calculate the sales amount as follows: $11,300 ÷ 1.13 = $10,000. The HST of $1,300 can be found by multiplying the sales amount by the sales tax rate ($10,000 × 13% = $1,300).

Currently, in two provinces, the provincial sales tax is charged on the total selling price plus GST. For example, in Prince Edward Island a $100 sale is subject to $5 GST ($100 × 5%) and $10.50 PST [($100 + $5) × 10%]. The escalated sales tax rate is 15.5% [($5 + $10.50) ÷ $100] rather than 15% (5% GST + 10% PST). Quebec also charges QST on the selling price plus GST. It is important to be careful when getting sales tax amounts from total receipts because of the different rate combinations across Canada.

Helpful hint If sales taxes are included in the sales price, then the sales tax collected is equal to the selling price × the sales tax percentage *divided by 100% plus the sales tax percentage.*

Property Taxes

Businesses that own property pay property taxes. These taxes are charged by the municipal governments, and are calculated at a specified rate for every $100 of assessed value of property (i.e., land and building). Property taxes generally cover a full calendar year, although bills are not issued until the spring of each year.

To illustrate, assume that Tantramar Management owns land and a building in the city of Regina. Tantramar's year end is December 31 and it makes adjusting entries annually. It receives its property tax bill of $6,000 for the calendar year on March 1, which is due to be paid on May 31.

In March, when Tantramar receives the property tax bill for the calendar year, two months of that year have passed. The company records the property tax expense for the months of January and February and the liability owed at that point as follows:

Mar. 1	Property Tax Expense ($6,000 × 2/12)	1,000	
	Property Tax Payable		1,000
	To record property tax expense for January and February and		
	amount owing.		

A	=	L	+	OE
		+1,000		−1,000

Cash flows: no effect

On May 31, when Tantramar pays the property tax bill, the company records the payment of the liability recorded on March 1. It also records the expense incurred to date for the months of March, April, and May. As at May 31, five months have passed and should be recorded as property tax expense. The remaining seven months of the year are recorded as a prepayment, as shown in the following entry:

May 31	Property Tax Payable	1,000	
	Property Tax Expense ($6,000 × 3/12)	1,500	
	Prepaid Property Tax ($6,000 × 7/12)	3,500	
	Cash		6,000
	To record payment of property tax expense for March through		
	May, and amount prepaid for June through December.		

A	=	L	+	OE
+3,500		−1,000		−1,500
−6,000				

↓ Cash flows: −6,000

After the payment of the property tax, Tantramar has a zero balance in its liability account but still has a prepayment. Since Tantramar only makes adjusting entries annually, it would not adjust the prepaid property tax account until year end, December 31. At that time, it would make the following entry:

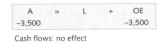

Cash flows: no effect

Dec. 31	Property Tax Expense	3,500	
	Prepaid Property Tax		3,500
	To record property tax expense for June through December.		

There are other acceptable ways to record and adjust property taxes. Some companies would debit Property Tax Expense when the bill is recorded on March 1 and avoid a later adjusting entry. In addition, companies may prepare monthly or quarterly adjusting entries. Whatever way is used, at year end the companies would have the same ending balances. In this case, the accounts Prepaid Property Tax and Property Tax Payable should each have a zero balance and Property Tax Expense should have a balance of $6,000.

Current Maturities of Long-Term Debt

Companies often have a portion of long-term debt that will be due in the current year. That amount is considered a current liability. Assume that on January 1, 2011, Cudini Construction issues a $25,000, five-year note payable. Each January 1, starting on January 1, 2012, $5,000 of the note will be repaid. When financial statements are prepared on December 31, 2011, $5,000 should be reported on the balance sheet as a current liability and the remaining $20,000 of the note should be reported as a long-term liability.

It is not necessary to prepare an adjusting entry to recognize the current maturity of long-term debt. The proper statement classification of each liability account is recognized when the balance sheet is prepared. Forzani reports $7,501 thousand as the "current portion of long-term debt" in the current liabilities section of its balance sheet.

BEFORE YOU GO ON . . .

➔ Review It

1. What is a determinable liability?
2. What are some examples of determinable current liabilities?
3. How is interest calculated on a note payable?
4. Why is sales tax not recorded as revenue to the company that collects it?

➔ Do It

Prepare the journal entries to record the following transactions. Round any calculations to the nearest dollar.

1. Accrue interest on January 31 (the company's year end) for a $10,000, 30-month, 8% note payable issued on December 1. Interest is payable the first of each month, beginning January 1.
2. The cash register total for sales on April 2 is $280,500. This total includes sales taxes. The HST tax rate is 13%. Record the sales and sales taxes.
3. A property tax bill of $12,000 for the calendar year is received on May 1 and is due on June 30. Record the entry on May 1, assuming the company has a January 31 year end.

Action Plan

• The formula for interest is as follows: principal (face) value × annual interest rate × time.
• Record sales separately from sales taxes. To calculate sales, divide the total proceeds by 100% plus the sales tax rates. Then calculate HST by multiplying sales by the appropriate rate.
• Record the property tax expense and the property tax payable for amounts incurred (owed) to date.

Solution

Jan. 31	Interest Expense ($10,000 × 8% × $\frac{1}{12}$)		67	
	Interest Payable			67
	To accrue interest on note payable.			
Apr. 2	Cash		282,500	
	Sales ($282,500 ÷ 113%)			250,000
	HST Payable ($250,000 × 13%)			32,500
	To record sales and sales taxes.			
May 1	Property Tax Expense ($12,000 × $\frac{3}{12}$)		3,000	
	Property Tax Payable			3,000
	To record property tax for February, March, and April.			

Related exercise material: BE10–1, BE10–2, BE10–3, BE10–4, E10–1, E10–2, E10–3, and E10–4.

The Navigator

Uncertain Liabilities

In the previous section, we discussed current liabilities where there was a high degree of certainty with regard to whom is owed, when it is owed, and how much is owed. There was no uncertainty about the liability's existence, amount, or timing. In this section, we will discuss liabilities that have a lower degree of certainty but are still likely to occur. We will then discuss situations where it is unlikely that an obligation exists, or where the existence of a liability depends on the outcome of a future event.

Estimated Liabilities

An **estimated liability** is a liability that is known to exist but whose amount and timing are uncertain. We know we owe someone, but are not necessarily sure how much and when. We may not even know whom we owe. There is a lower degree of certainty than in determinable liabilities, but as long as it is *likely* the company will have to settle the obligation, and the company can reasonably estimate the amount, the liability is recognized. Common estimated liabilities include product warranties, customer loyalty programs, and gift cards. We discuss these three examples in the following sections.

STUDY OBJECTIVE 2
Account for estimated liabilities.

Alternative terminology
Estimated liabilities are also known as *provisions*.

Product Warranties

Product warranties are promises made by the seller to a buyer to repair or replace the product if it is defective or does not perform as intended. Warranties (also known as guarantees) are usually issued by manufacturers. For a specified period of time after the item was sold, a manufacturer may promise to repair the item, replace it, or refund the buyer's money under certain conditions.

For example, Apple Computer Inc. offers a one-year warranty against "defects in materials and workmanship" on the sale of its iPod and iSight products. The company goes on to state that if a valid claim is received within the warranty period, it will either (1) repair the product at no charge, using new or refurbished replacement parts, (2) exchange the product with a product that is new or that has been manufactured from new or serviceable used parts and is at least functionally equivalent to the original product, or (3) refund the purchase price of the product. As a buyer, it is important to read all warranty contracts carefully because the promises they make can be quite different.

Warranties will lead to future costs for the manufacturer for the repair or replacement of defective units. At the time of the sale, it is not known which units will become defective, so it is not known in advance whom the company will have to pay. But the liability still exists even if the payee is unknown.

Also, the amount and the timing of the future warranty cost are not known, but these can be reasonably estimated. Based on their previous experience with a particular product, it is usually not that hard for companies such as Apple to estimate the future cost of servicing (honouring) the product's warranty. In addition, recording the estimated cost of product warranties as an expense and a liability in the period where the sale occurs also ensures that companies have recognized the full cost of the sale in the period the sale occurs. This is commonly known as matching expenses with revenues.

To illustrate the accounting for warranties, assume that Hermann Company sells 10,000 washers and dryers at an average price of $600 in the year ended December 31, 2011. The selling price includes a one-year warranty on parts. Based on past experience, it is expected that 500 units (5%) will be defective, and that warranty repair costs will average $100 per unit.

At December 31, it is necessary to accrue the estimated warranty costs for the 2011 sales. The calculation is as follows:

Number of units sold	10,000
Estimated rate of defective units	× 5%
Total estimated defective units	500
Average warranty repair cost	× $100
Estimated product warranty liability	$50,000

The adjusting entry is:

A	=	L	+	OE
		+50,000		−50,000

Cash flows: no effect

Dec. 31	Warranty Expense	50,000	
	Warranty Liability		50,000
	To accrue estimated warranty costs.		

In 2011, warranty contracts were honoured on 300 units at a total cost of $30,000. These costs are likely recorded when they are incurred, but for our illustration they are being recorded in one summary journal entry:

A	=	L	+	OE
−30,000		−30,000		

Cash flows: no effect

Dec. 31	Warranty Liability	30,000	
	Repair Parts Inventory (and/or Wages Payable)		30,000
	To record honouring of 300 warranty contracts on 2011 sales.		

At year end, a warranty expense of $50,000 is reported as an operating expense in the income statement. The estimated warranty liability of $20,000 ($50,000 − $30,000) is classified as a current liability on the balance sheet.

In 2012, all costs incurred to honour warranty contracts on 2011 sales should be debited to the Warranty Liability account, like what was shown above for the 2011 sales. The Warranty Liability account will be carried forward from year to year—increased by the current year's estimated expense and decreased by the actual warranty costs incurred. It is quite likely that the actual expenses will not exactly equal the estimated liability amount. Every year, as is done with accounts receivable and the allowance for doubtful accounts, the warranty liability should be reviewed and adjusted if necessary.

Customer Loyalty Programs

Alternative terminology
Customer loyalty programs are also called *promotions* or *incentive programs*.

To attract or keep customers, many companies offer **customer loyalty programs** that result in future savings for the customers on the merchandise or services the company sells. These customer loyalty programs take varying forms. For example, the program may require customers to collect points. A common example of that is airline frequent flyer programs. Or the programs may involve cash discounts on future sales.

The most successful loyalty program in Canadian retail history is Canadian Tire "money" (CTM), first introduced in 1958. The "money" resembles real currency (although the bills are considerably smaller than Bank of Canada notes) and is issued with no expiry date. CTM is given out by the cashiers for purchases paid for by cash, debit card, or Canadian Tire Options MasterCard credit card. Customers can use CTM to buy anything at a Canadian Tire store. In fact, some privately owned businesses in Canada also accept CTM as payment since the owners of many of these businesses shop at Canadian Tire.

Loyalty programs such as frequent flyer programs or CTM are designed to increase sales and are important for many businesses. In recent years, there has been a lot of debate about whether the cost of such programs should be recorded as an expense or as a decrease in revenue. While there are a few exceptions, accountants have decided that when a loyalty program results in a reduced selling price, it should be accounted for as a decrease in revenue and not as an expense.

Loyalty programs, similar to product warranties, result in an estimated liability because at the time of the sale it is not known if or when customers will redeem the reward. However, as long as some redemptions are likely and can be reasonably estimated based on past experience, the decrease in revenue and a related liability should be recorded in the period when the reward was issued to ensure that liabilities are correctly recognized.

To illustrate, assume that Greenville Co-op has a rewards program where Greenville Co-op Gas Bar customers get a redemption reward of 3 cents per litre of gasoline that can be used in Greenville Co-op Food Stores on the purchase of groceries. On January 31, the gas bar sells 9,600 litres of gasoline. Greenville Co-op will record the following for the redemption rewards issued:

Jan. 31	Sales Discount for Redemption Rewards Issued (9,600 × $0.03)	288	
	Redemption Rewards Liability		288
	To record redemption rewards issued on gasoline sales.		

A	=	L	+	OE
		+288		−288

Cash flows: no effect

The account Sales Discount for Redemption Rewards Issued is a contra sales account, and is deducted from sales to give net sales in the same way that sales returns and allowances are deducted from sales, as we learned in Chapter 5. The Redemption Rewards Liability is reported as a current liability on the balance sheet.

Helpful hint Reductions in revenue are recorded in the period the reward is issued, not when it is redeemed.

To illustrate what happens when the rewards are redeemed, assume that on February 1, customers redeem $100 of the rewards in the Greenville Co-op Food Store when purchasing $7,500 of groceries. Greenville Co-op makes the following entry that day (ignoring the cost of sales):

Feb. 1	Rewards Redemption Liability	100	
	Cash ($7,500 − $100)	7,400	
	Grocery Sales Revenue		7,500
	To record grocery sales and the redemption of rewards.		

A	=	L	+	OE
+7,400		−100		+7,500

⬆ Cash flows: +7,400

Note that when the rewards are redeemed, the amount of cash collected is less than the sales revenue recognized. The liability account is reduced by the difference between the sales revenue and cash collected, which is the amount of the redemption. As with warranties, the liability account should be reviewed periodically and adjusted based on the company's experience with redemption rates.

Accounting for loyalty rewards programs and other promotional items has many additional complexities that we have not seen here. Further details on this topic will be left to an intermediate accounting course.

ACCOUNTING IN ACTION: ACROSS THE ORGANIZATION

These days it seems that almost every retailer offers some kind of customer loyalty program, through club memberships, discount cards, or points programs. Shoppers Drug Mart has taken the trend a step further by having its Optimum Points program benefit others as well as customers. Shoppers Optimum Points® Donation Program allows Optimum card holders to donate some or all of their points to one of many registered charitable organizations. The organizations can then use the points to purchase products and supplies they need for their day-to-day activities and ongoing fundraising events. A wide variety of charitable organizations, both national and provincial, have signed up to receive the points.

A company's marketing department is responsible for designing customer loyalty programs. Why would Shoppers' marketing department add the option of donating points to charity?

Gift Cards

Gift cards or gift certificates have become an increasingly popular source of revenue for many companies. In general, they are similar to unearned revenues in that the company receives cash in advance of providing the goods or the services. Thus, when gift cards are issued, an unearned revenue account (liability) is recorded. When the gift card is redeemed (used), the company will then record the sales or service revenue and reduce or debit the Unearned Revenue account.

The difficulty with gift cards is that it is unknown when and even if the card will be redeemed. Many companies find that the longer a gift card is outstanding, the less likely it is to be redeemed for merchandise. Similarly, companies may find that gift cards that have been used but have relatively small remaining balances are less likely to be redeemed than newer, high-balance gift cards.

The main accounting problem is: At what point should a company write off the gift card liability if it expects the gift card will never be redeemed? Recent changes to Canadian laws have prohibited expiry dates on gift cards. Theoretically, if the gift card has no expiration date, the company should indefinitely report the unused portion on the balance sheet as a liability.

But if it is unlikely that the company will have to settle a portion of the liability, then an obligation no longer exists. As with warranties and customer loyalty programs, a company with a gift card program will need to estimate the appropriate balance for the liability. Currently, accounting standards do not give clear guidance on this issue and thus we leave further discussion of this topic to a more advanced accounting course.

Lawsuits

In some circumstances, lawsuits result in an estimated liability. If it is likely that the company will lose the lawsuit, and if the amount can be reliably estimated, then the company must record a liability for the same reasons warranty liabilities are recorded. But lawsuits can involve a much higher degree of uncertainty than warranties. In that case, the accounting for a lawsuit is different than accounting for an estimated liability. This is covered in the next section on contingencies.

BEFORE YOU GO ON . . .

→ Review It

1. Explain the difference between determinable liabilities and estimated liabilities.
2. When should warranty liabilities and expenses be recorded?
3. Why is the estimated cost of loyalty programs debited to a contra revenue account rather than an expense account?
4. In what respect are gift cards similar to unearned revenues?

→ Do It

Hockey Gear Company sells hockey skates with a two-year warranty against defects. The company expects that of the units sold each year, 5% will be returned in the first year after they are sold and 2% will be returned in the second year. The average cost to repair or replace a defective unit under warranty is $50. The company reported the following sales and warranty cost information:

	Units Sold	Actual Warranty Costs Incurred
2010	10,000	$20,000
2011	15,000	45,000

Calculate the balance in the Warranty Expense and Warranty Liability accounts at the end of 2011.

Action Plan

• Calculate the warranty expense by multiplying the number of units sold by the percentage that is expected to be returned and by the average warranty cost.
• Record warranty expenses in the period of the sale.
• The warranty liability is increased by the expense in each period and decreased by the actual costs of repairs and replacements.

Solution

2010: Total defective units = 5% + 2% = 7%

$\quad$ 10,000 × 7% = 700 × $50 = $35,000

Warranty Expense				Warranty Liability			
35,000			Actual	20,000	Estimate		35,000
					Bal. Dec. 31, 2010		15,000

2011: 15,000 × 7% = 1,050 × $50 = $52,500

Warranty Expense				Warranty Liability			
52,500			Actual	20,000	Estimate		35,000
					Bal. Dec. 31, 2010		15,000
			Actual	45,000	Estimate		52,500
					Bal. Dec. 31, 2010		22,500

Related exercise material: BE10–5, BE10–6, BE10–7, BE10–8, E10–6, E10–7, and E10–8.

The Navigator

Contingencies

STUDY OBJECTIVE 3

Account for contingencies.

Contingencies are events with uncertain outcomes. In these situations, it cannot be known with certainty if a gain (and a related asset) or loss (and a related liability) will result from the situation until one or more future events happen or do not happen. Although the topic of this chapter is liabilities, and contingent liabilities are far more common than contingent assets, we will discuss both contingent liabilities and contingent assets since there are some similarities in the accounting and disclosure requirements.

Contingent Liabilities

In the previous section, we have seen that liabilities are recorded even when estimations of the amount, timing, or even the payee are required. As long as it is considered *likely* that a present obligation exists, and the amount can be reliably estimated, the liability is recognized.

In other circumstances, there is a higher degree of uncertainty and one or more of the criteria for recognizing liabilities are not met. These circumstances include:

- a *possible* (but not likely) obligation exists but will be confirmed only by the occurrence or non-occurrence of an uncertain future event,
- a present obligation exists but it is not probable that the company will have to settle it, and
- a present obligation exists but the amount cannot be reliably measured.

Under International Financial Reporting Standards (IFRS), if any one of these circumstances exists, then it is called a **contingent liability**. Under IFRS, a company should not recognize a contingent liability in its balance sheet because it doesn't meet the definition of a liability. Contingent liabilities are disclosed only in the notes to the financial statements, unless the probability of occurrence is remote.

Under Canadian GAAP for Private Enterprises, contingent liabilities are viewed somewhat differently than under IFRS. Under this GAAP system a contingent liability is defined as a liability that is contingent on the occurrence or non-occurrence of some future event. The contingent liability would be recorded if **both** of the following conditions are met:

1. The contingency is likely (the chance of occurrence is high).
2. The amount of the contingency can be reasonably estimated.

Under IFRS, a liability would also be recorded if both those conditions existed, but such a liability would be considered an estimated liability, not a contingent liability. For example, in the previous section, we discussed how a lawsuit can be considered an estimated liability. Even though the existence of a liability is contingent on the outcome of the lawsuit, if it is likely the lawsuit will be lost, and the amount can be reliably estimated, it is considered an estimated liability.

Under IFRS, contingent liabilities are liabilities where there is too high a degree of uncertainty to record the liability. On the other hand, Canadian GAAP for Private Enterprises considers a liability to be a contingent liability as long as its ultimate existence depends on the outcome of a future event. Thus, a lawsuit would be considered a contingent liability under Canadian GAAP for Private Enterprises.

The differences between IFRS and Canadian GAAP for Private Enterprises are to a certain extent based on semantics because of the different definitions of contingent liabilities. But it is still important to understand the distinction, as private companies will have the choice to follow Canadian GAAP for Private Enterprises or IFRS, while public companies must follow IFRS. The IFRS rule of never recording contingent liabilities may sound less strict than Canadian GAAP for Private Enterprises where contingent liabilities are sometimes recorded. But in fact, IFRS is generally regarded as having a lower threshold for recognizing liabilities. Under IFRS, estimated liabilities are recognized for probable events, defined as being more likely than not. Under Canadian GAAP for Private Enterprises, only highly likely contingent liabilities are recognized.

Under Canadian GAAP for Private Enterprises, the existence of a contingent loss at the date of the financial statements should be disclosed in notes to the financial statements when:

- a contingent liability is likely but the amount of the loss cannot be reasonably estimated, or
- the existence of the contingent liability is not determinable.

Under Canadian GAAP for Private Enterprises, if a contingency is unlikely—the chance of occurrence is small—it should still be disclosed if the event could have a substantial negative effect on the company's financial position. Otherwise, it does not need to be disclosed. A loan guarantee for another company is an example of a contingency that should be disclosed even if the chance of having to pay the loan, because the other company defaulted on it, is small. Contingencies that can affect anyone who is operating a business, such as the general risk of a war, strike, or recession, are not reported in the notes to the financial statements.

Forzani's 2009 financial statements were prepared before Canadian public companies were required to use IFRS. At that time, Forzani followed rules similar to Canadian GAAP for Private Enterprises described above. It disclosed both guarantees and lawsuits in the notes to its financial statements. Here are two selected extracts from this note:

Illustration 10-1 ➡

Disclosure of contingent liabilities

THE FORZANI GROUP LTD.
Notes to the Consolidated Financial Statements
February 1, 2009

LE GROUPE FORZANI LTÉE | THE FORZANI GROUP LTD.

15. Contingencies and Guarantees

The Company has provided the following guarantees to third parties:

(a) The Company has provided guarantees to certain franchisees' banks pursuant to which it has agreed to buy back inventory from the franchisee in the event that the bank realizes on the related security... Historically, the Company has not had to repurchase significant inventory from franchisees pursuant to these guarantees. The Company has not recognized the guarantee in its financial statements.

(d) Claims and suits have been brought against the Company in the ordinary course of business. In the opinion of management, all such claims and suits are adequately covered by insurance, or if not so covered, the results are not expected to materially affect the Company's financial policies.

Contingent Assets

Like contingent liabilities, **contingent assets** arise from past events where the asset's existence will only be resolved when a future event occurs or does not occur. This event will confirm the existence of a future cash inflow or other economic benefits that will result in an asset. Examples of contingent assets include insurance claims or potential legal actions that could favour the company.

Contingent assets or gains are never recorded or accrued in the financial statements. They are disclosed in the notes only if it is likely that a gain will be realized. Under IFRS, if it is virtually certain that a gain will occur, the related asset is not considered a contingent asset. It is just considered to be an asset and is recognized in the financial statements as appropriate. Under Canadian GAAP for Private Enterprises, a contingent asset can only be recognized when the contingency is resolved and the asset is realized. Under both standards, it is not considered appropriate to disclose the existence of a contingent asset that in management's opinion is unlikely to occur.

ACCOUNTING IN ACTION: BUSINESS INSIGHT

There are many contingencies in the real world. Lawsuits are the most common type of contingency, followed by environmental contingencies. Environmental contingencies generally relate to liabilities that could be incurred in order to clean up environmental problems.

The Canadian National Railway Company discloses the following information in the notes to its financial statements: "A risk of environmental liability is inherent in railroad and related transportation operations…" The Company goes on to say, "The magnitude of such… liabilities and the costs of complying with future environmental laws and containing or remediating contamination cannot be reasonably estimated… There can thus be no assurance that liabilities or costs related to environmental matters will not be incurred in the future, or will not have a material adverse effect on the Company's financial position or results of operations in a particular quarter or fiscal year, or that the Company's liquidity will not be adversely impacted by such environmental liabilities or costs."

Environmental contingencies are generally considered to be harder to estimate than contingencies from lawsuits. What might be the reason for this difference?

BEFORE YOU GO ON . . .

→ Review It

1. Under IFRS, what is a contingent liability?
2. Under IFRS, when should a contingent liability be recorded? Disclosed?
3. Under Canadian GAAP for Private Enterprises, what is a contingent liability?
4. Under Canadian GAAP for Private Enterprises, when should a contingent liability be recorded? Disclosed?
5. When are contingent assets recorded? Disclosed?

→ Do It

A list of possible contingencies follows. Identify whether each of the following should be recorded, disclosed, or not reported:

1. A private company following Canadian GAAP risks being damaged by floods. The company is located on a flood plain but has never experienced any damage from flooding in the past.
2. The government may expropriate a private company's assets so that a new highway can be built. So far, there have been no discussions about how much the government might pay the company. Assume the company follows Canadian GAAP.
3. A public company is being sued for $1 million for unlawful termination of an employee.
4. A private company following Canadian GAAP has guaranteed other companies' loans but the guarantees are unlikely to result in any payments.
5. A reassessment of a public company's income tax will likely result in a refund.

Action Plan

- Remember that under IFRS, a contingent liability is a possible obligation or a present obligation where settlement is unlikely or the obligation cannot be measured. Contingent liabilities are never recorded; they are disclosed unless they are unlikely.
- Under Canadian GAAP for Private Enterprises, contingent liabilities are accrued when they are likely and estimable. Otherwise, they are only disclosed. They are not disclosed if they are unlikely.

- Remember that contingent assets are never recorded. They are only disclosed if they are likely.

Solution

1. No disclosure required.
2. Disclosure required.
3. If the company is likely to lose and the amount can be reasonably estimated, then this would be considered an estimated liability and it would be recorded; otherwise, just disclose.
4. Disclosure required.
5. Disclosure required.

The Navigator

Related exercise material: BE10–9, BE10–10, E10–9, and E10–10.

Payroll

STUDY OBJECTIVE 4

Determine payroll costs and record payroll transactions.

Payroll accounting involves more than just paying employee salaries and wages. In addition to paying salaries and wages, companies are required by law to have payroll records for each employee, to report and remit payroll deductions, and to respect provincial and federal laws on employee compensation. As mentioned in our feature story, there are up to 185 different pieces of legislation and regulations that employers have to consider when doing payroll. In this section, we will discuss some of the basic issues regarding payroll costs, journalizing payroll, and payroll records. In the appendix to this chapter, we explain calculating mandatory payroll deductions.

There are two types of payroll costs to a company: employee costs and employer costs. The first type, employee costs, involves the gross amount earned by employees. The second type, employer costs, involves amounts paid by the employer on behalf of the employee (employee benefits). We will explore employee and employer payroll costs in the following sections.

Employee Payroll Costs

Accounting for employee payroll costs involves calculating (1) gross pay, (2) payroll deductions, and (3) net pay.

Gross Pay

Gross pay, or earnings, is the total compensation earned by an employee. It consists of wages or salaries, plus any bonuses and commissions. The terms "salaries" and "wages" are often used interchangeably and the total amount of salaries or wages earned by the employee is called **gross pay**, or gross earnings.

Managerial, professional, administrative, and sales personnel are generally paid salaries. Salaries are usually based on a weekly, biweekly, monthly, or yearly rate. If the rate is a yearly one, it is pro-rated over the number of payroll periods (e.g., 26 or 52) that the company uses.

Part-time employees, store clerks, factory employees, and manual labourers are normally paid wages. Wages are based on a rate per hour or on piecework (an amount per unit of product). When wages are based on a rate per hour, total wages are determined by multiplying the hours worked by the hourly rate of pay.

In addition to the hourly pay rate, most companies are required by law to pay hourly workers for overtime work at the rate of at least one and one-half times the government-regulated minimum hourly wage. The number of hours that need to be worked before overtime becomes payable is based on a standard workweek. A 44-hour standard workweek is fairly common but this will vary by industry and occupation. Most employees in executive, managerial, and administrative positions do not earn overtime pay.

To illustrate gross pay for a wage earner, assume that Mark Jordan works for Academy Company as a shipping clerk. His authorized pay rate is $20 per hour. The calculation of Mark's gross pay (total wages) for the 48 hours shown on his time card for the weekly pay period ending June 20, 2009, is as follows:

Type of Pay	Hours	×	Rate	=	Gross Pay
Regular	44	×	$20	=	$ 880
Overtime	4	×	30	=	120
Total wages					$1,000

This calculation assumes that Mark receives one and one-half times his regular hourly rate ($20 × 1.5) for any hours worked in excess of 44 hours per week (overtime). Overtime rates can be as much as twice the regular rates.

Payroll Deductions

As anyone who has received a paycheque knows, gross pay is usually very different from the amount that is actually received. The difference is referred to as **payroll deductions**. Payroll deductions are also frequently called "withholdings" because these are the amounts that the employer withholds or holds back from the employee.

Payroll deductions may be mandatory or voluntary. Illustration 10-2 shows the types of payroll deductions that most companies usually make.

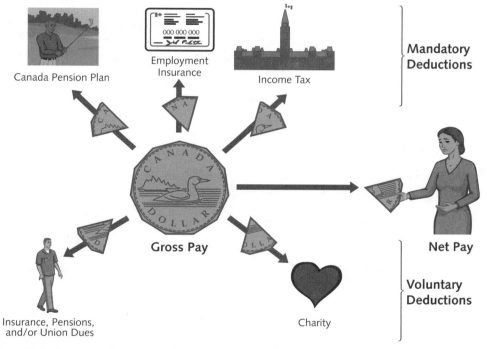

◄ Illustration 10-2

Employee payroll deductions

Payroll deductions do not result in an expense for the employer. The employer is only a collection agent. The mandatory deductions are later paid to the government (for deductions such as Canada Pension Plan, Employment Insurance, and income tax). The voluntary deductions are later paid to some other agency (such as a union, an insurance company, or the United Way). The designated collection agency for the federal government is the Canada Revenue Agency (CRA), which collects money on behalf of the Receiver General of Canada, the cabinet minister responsible for accepting payments to the Government of Canada.

Mandatory Payroll Deductions. Mandatory deductions are required by law and include Canada Pension Plan contributions, Employment Insurance premiums, and personal income tax. We will discuss these three deductions in the following sections.

Canada Pension Plan. All employees between the ages of 18 and 70, except those employed in the province of Quebec, must contribute to the **Canada Pension Plan (CPP)**. Quebec has its own similar program, the Quebec Pension Plan (QPP). These mandatory plans give disability, retirement, and death benefits to qualifying Canadians.

Contribution rates are set by the federal government and are adjusted every January if there are increases in the cost of living. We will show how to calculate CPP contributions in Appendix 10A. For now, assume that Mark Jordan's CPP contribution for the weekly pay period ending June 20, 2009, is $46.17.

Employment Insurance. The *Employment Insurance Act* requires all Canadian workers who are not self-employed to pay **Employment Insurance (EI)** premiums. Employment Insurance is designed to give income protection (in the form of payments representing a portion of one's earnings) for a limited period of time to employees who are temporarily laid off, who are on parental leave, or who lose their jobs. Starting January 2010, if you are self employed you also may choose to pay EI to qualify for special benefits such as maternity or parental benefits. But this will not qualify you for employment insurance if you are not able to work.

Each year, the federal government determines the contribution rate and the maximum amount of premiums for the year. We will show how to calculate EI premiums in Appendix 10A. For now, assume that Mark Jordan's EI premium for the weekly pay period ending June 20, 2009, is $17.30.

Personal Income Tax. Under the *Income Tax Act*, employers are required to withhold income tax from employees for each pay period. The amount to be withheld is determined by three variables: (1) the employee's gross pay, (2) the number of credits claimed by the employee, and (3) the length of the pay period. The amount of provincial income taxes also depends on the province in which the employee works. There is no limit on the amount of gross pay that is subject to income tax withholdings. The higher the pay or earnings, the higher the amount of taxes withheld.

The calculation of personal income tax withholdings is complicated and is best done using payroll deduction tables supplied by the CRA. We will show this in Appendix 10A. For now, assume that Mark Jordan's federal income tax is $124.70 and provincial income tax is $67.25, for a total income tax owed of $191.95 on his gross pay of $1,000 for the weekly pay period ending June 20, 2009.

Voluntary Payroll Deductions. Unlike mandatory payroll deductions, which are required by law, voluntary payroll deductions are chosen by the employee.

Employees may choose to authorize withholdings for charitable, retirement, and other purposes. All voluntary deductions from gross pay should be authorized in writing by the employee. The authorization may be made individually or as part of a group plan. Deductions for charitable organizations, such as the United Way, or for financial arrangements, such as Canada Savings Bonds and the repayment of loans from company credit unions, are determined by each employee. In contrast, deductions for union dues, extended health insurance, life insurance, and pension plans are often determined on a group basis. In the calculation of net pay in the next section, we assume that Mark Jordan has voluntary deductions of $10 for the United Way and $5 for union dues.

Net Pay

The difference between an employee's gross pay, or total earnings, less any employee payroll deductions withheld from the earnings is known as **net pay**. This is the amount that the employer must pay to the employee.

Net pay is determined by subtracting payroll deductions from gross pay. For Mark Jordan, net pay for the weekly pay period ending June 20, 2009, is $729.58, as shown in Illustration 10-3:

Illustration 10-3 ➡

Employee payroll deductions

Gross pay		$1,000.00
Payroll deductions:		
CPP	$ 46.17	
EI	17.30	
Income tax (federal and provincial)	191.95	
United Way	10.00	
Union dues	5.00	270.42
Net pay		$ 729.58

Before we learn how to record employee payroll costs and deductions, we will turn our attention to *employer* payroll costs. After this discussion, we will record the total employee and employer payroll costs for Academy Company, where Mark Jordan works.

Employer Payroll Costs

Employer payroll costs are amounts that the federal and provincial governments require employers to pay. The federal government requires CPP and EI contributions from employers. The provincial governments require employers to fund a workplace health, safety, and compensation plan. These contributions, plus such items as paid vacations and pensions, are referred to as **employee benefits**. Employer payroll costs are not debited to the Salaries and Wages Expense account, but rather to a separate Employee Benefits Expense account.

Canada Pension Plan

Employers must also contribute to the CPP. For each dollar withheld from the employee's gross pay, the employer must contribute an equal amount. The CPP Payable account is credited for both the employees' and employer's CPP contributions.

Employment Insurance

Employers are required to contribute 1.4 times an employee's EI premiums. The EI Payable account is credited for both the employees' and employer's EI premiums.

Workplace Health, Safety, and Compensation

Each provincial workplace health, safety, and compensation plan gives benefits to workers who are injured or disabled on the job. The cost of this program is paid entirely by the employer; employees do not make contributions to these plans. Employers are assessed a rate—usually between 0.25% and 10% of their gross payroll—based on the risk of injury to employees in their industry and past experience.

> **Helpful hint** CPP contributions and EI premiums are paid by both the employer and the employee. Workers' compensation premiums are paid entirely by the employer.

Additional Employee Benefits

In addition to the three employer payroll costs described above, employers have other employee benefit costs. Two of the most important are paid absences and post-employment benefits. We will describe these briefly here, but leave further details to an intermediate accounting course.

Paid Absences. Employees have the right to receive compensation for absences under certain conditions. The compensation may be for paid vacations, sick pay benefits, and paid statutory holidays. A liability should be estimated and accrued for future paid absences. Ordinarily, vacation pay is the only paid absence that is accrued. Other types of paid absences are disclosed only in notes to the statements.

Post-Employment Benefits. Post-employment benefits are payments by employers to retired or terminated employees. These payments are for (1) pensions, and (2) supplemental health care, dental care, and life insurance. Employers must use the accrual basis in accounting for post-employment benefits. It is important to match the cost of these benefits with the periods where the employer benefits from the services of the employee.

Recording the Payroll

Recording the payroll involves maintaining payroll records, recording payroll expenses and liabilities, paying the payroll, and filing and remitting payroll deductions.

Payroll Records

A separate record of an employee's gross pay, payroll deductions, and net pay for the calendar year is kept for each employee and updated after each pay period. It is called the **employee earnings record** and its cumulative payroll data are used by the employer to (1) determine when an employee has reached the maximum earnings subject to CPP and EI premiums, (2) file information returns with the CRA (as explained later in this section), and (3) give each employee a statement of gross pay and withholdings for the year.

An extract from Mark Jordan's employee earnings record for the month of June is shown in Illustration 10-4. This record includes the pay details shown in Illustration 10-3 for the week ending June 20, 2009, highlighted in red.

Illustration 10-4 ↓

Employee earnings record

ACADEMY COMPANY
Employee Earnings Record
Year Ending December 31, 2009

Name Mark Jordan	Address 162 Bowood Avenue
Social Insurance Number 113-114-496	Toronto
Date of Birth December 24, 1985	Ontario, M4N 1Y6
Date Employed September 1, 2007	Telephone 416-486-0669
Date Employment Ended	E-mail jordan@sympatico.ca
Job Title Shipping Clerk	Claim Code 1

2009 Period Ending	Total Hours	Gross Pay				Deductions						Payment	
		Regular	Overtime	Total	Cumulative	CPP	EI	Income Tax	United Way	Union Dues	Total	Net Amount	Cheque #
June 6	46	880.00	60.00	940.00	19,940.00	43.20	16.26	172.30	10.00	5.00	246.76	693.24	974
13	47	880.00	90.00	970.00	20,910.00	44.68	16.78	182.25	10.00	5.00	258.71	711.29	1028
20	48	880.00	120.00	1,000.00	21,910.00	46.17	17.30	191.95	10.00	5.00	270.42	729.58	1077
27	46	880.00	60.00	940.00	22,850.00	43.20	16.26	172.30	10.00	5.00	246.76	693.24	1133
June Total		3,520.00	330.00	3,850.00		177.25	66.60	718.80	40.00	20.00	1,022.65	2,827.35	

In addition to employee earnings records, many companies find it useful to prepare a **payroll register**. This record accumulates the gross pay, deductions, and net pay per employee for each pay period and becomes the documentation for preparing paycheques for each employee. Academy Company's payroll register for the week ended June 20, 2009, is presented in Illustration 10-5. It shows the data for Mark Jordan in the wages section, highlighted in red. In this example, Academy Company's total weekly payroll is $34,420, as shown in the gross pay column.

Illustration 10-5 ↓

Payroll register

ACADEMY COMPANY
Payroll Register
Week Ending June 20, 2009

Employee	Total Hours	Gross Pay			Deductions						Payment	
		Regular	Overtime	Gross	CPP	EI	Income Tax	United Way	Union Dues	Total	Net Pay	Cheque #
Office Salaries												
Aung, Ng	44	1,276.00		1,276.00	59.83	22.07	276.78	15.00		373.68	902.32	998
Canton, Mathew	44	1,298.00		1,298.00	60.92	22.46	283.89	20.00		387.27	910.73	999
Mueller, William	44	1,166.00		1,166.00	54.39	20.17	241.80	11.00		327.36	838.64	1024
Subtotal		10,400.00		10,400.00	452.40	179.92	2,231.21	180.00		3,043.53	7,356.47	
Wages												
Caron, Réjean	44	880.00	60.00	940.00	43.20	16.26	172.30	10.00	5.00	246.76	693.24	1025
Jordan, Mark	48	880.00	120.00	1,000.00	46.17	17.30	191.95	10.00	5.00	270.42	729.58	1077
Milroy, Lee	47	880.00	90.00	970.00	44.68	16.78	182.25	10.00	5.00	258.71	711.29	1078
Subtotal		22,000.00	2,020.00	24,020.00	1,044.88	415.55	4,491.65	300.00	150.00	6,402.08	17,617.92	
Total		32,400.00	2,020.00	34,420.00	1,497.28	595.47	6,722.86	480.00	150.00	9,445.61	24,974.39	

Note that this record is a listing of each employee's payroll data for the June 20, 2009, pay period. In some companies, the payroll register is a special journal. Postings are made directly to ledger accounts. In other companies, the payroll register is a supplementary record that gives the data for a general journal entry and later posting to the ledger accounts. At Academy Company, the second procedure is used.

Recording Payroll Expenses and Liabilities

Payroll expenses are equal to the employees' gross salaries and wages plus the employer's payroll costs. Typically, as shown in the following entry, employee payroll costs and employer's payroll costs are recorded in separate journal entries.

Employee Payroll Costs. A journal entry is made to record the employee portion of the payroll. For the week ending June 20, the entry for Academy Company, using total amounts from the company's payroll register for the period, as shown in Illustration 10-5, is as follows:

June 20	Salaries Expense	10,400.00	
	Wages Expense	24,020.00	
	CPP Payable		1,497.28
	EI Payable		595.47
	Income Tax Payable		6,722.86
	United Way Payable		480.00
	Union Dues Payable		150.00
	Salaries and Wages Payable		24,974.39
	To record payroll for week ending June 20.		

A	=	L	+	OE
+1,497.28				−10,400.00
+595.47				−24,020.00
+6,722.86				
+480.00				
+150.00				
+24,974.39				

Cash flows: no effect

The above journal entry records the gross pay of $34,420 in Academy Company's Salaries Expense and Wages Expense account. Separate expense accounts are used for gross pay because office workers are on salary and other employees are paid an hourly rate. The net pay of $24,974.39 that is owed to employees is recorded in the Salaries and Wages Payable account. This is equal to the sum of the individual cheques that the employees will receive when the payroll is paid. Academy Company uses separate liabilities accounts for the amounts that it owes for its employee payroll deductions to the government for CPP, EI, and income tax, and amounts owed to third parties like United Way and for union dues.

Employer Payroll Costs. Employer payroll costs are usually recorded when the payroll is journalized. The entire amount of gross pay is subject to four of the employer payroll costs mentioned earlier: CPP, EI, workers' compensation, and vacation pay. For the June 20 payroll, Academy Company's CPP is $1,497.28 ($1,497.28 × 1). Its EI premium is $833.66 ($595.47 × 1.4).

Assume that Academy Company is also assessed for workers' compensation at a rate of 1%. Its expense for the week would therefore be $344.20 [($10,400 + $24,020) × 1%]. For vacation pay, assume that Academy Company employees accrue vacation days at an average rate of 4% of the gross payroll (equivalent to two weeks of vacation). The accrual for vacation benefits in one pay period—one week—is therefore $1,376.80 [($10,400 + $24,020) × 4%].

Some provinces, including the Province of Ontario, require an additional employer payroll cost—an employer health tax to help fund health care. The maximum health tax in the Province of Ontario is 1.95% of payroll, but the tax rate varies by the amount of payroll, and the first $400,000 of remuneration is exempt from this tax. Academy's payroll for the year has not yet reached this level so it is exempt from this health tax.

Accordingly, the entry to record the employer payroll costs or employee benefits associated with the June 20 payroll is as follows:

June 20	Employee Benefits Expense	4,051.94	
	CPP Payable		1,497.28
	EI Payable		833.66
	Workers' Compensation Payable		344.20
	Vacation Pay Payable		1,376.80
	To record employer payroll costs on June 20 payroll.		

A	=	L	+	OE
		+1,497.28		−4,051.94
		+ 833.66		
		+ 344.20		
		+ 1,376.80		

Cash flows: no effect

Employer payroll costs are debited to a separate expense account, normally called Employee Benefits Expense, so the employer can keep track of these costs. It is combined with Salaries and Wages Expense on the income statement. The liability accounts are classified as current liabilities since they will be paid within the next year.

Recording Payment of the Payroll

Payment of the payroll by cheque or electronic funds transfer (EFT) is made from either the employer's regular bank account or a payroll bank account. Each paycheque or EFT is usually accompanied by a statement of earnings document. This shows the employee's gross pay, payroll deductions, and net pay for the period and for the year to date.

After the payroll has been paid, the cheque numbers are entered in the payroll register. The entry to record payment of the payroll for Academy Company follows:

A = L + OE
−24,974.39   −24,974.39
↓ Cash flows: −24,974.39

June 20	Salaries and Wages Payable	24,974.39	
	Cash		24,974.39
	To record payment of payroll.		

Note that Academy Company is only recording payments to its employees in this entry and not its payroll deductions. Employee and employer deductions will be remitted to government authorities or other third parties when they are due later in the month.

Many companies use a separate bank account for payroll. Only the total amount of each period's payroll is transferred, or deposited, into that account before it is distributed. This helps the company determine if there are any unclaimed amounts.

When companies report and remit their payroll deductions, they combine withholdings of CPP, EI, and income tax. Generally, the withholdings must be reported and remitted monthly on a Statement of Account for Current Source Deductions (known by the CRA as the PD7A remittance form), and no later than the 15th day of the month following the month's pay period. Depending on the size of the payroll deductions, however, the employer's payment deadline could be different. For example, large employers must remit more often than once a month, and small employers with perfect payroll deduction remittance records can remit quarterly.

Workplace health, safety, and compensation costs are remitted quarterly to the provincial workers' compensation commission or board. Remittances can be made by mail or through deposits at any Canadian financial institution. When payroll deductions are remitted, payroll liability accounts are debited and Cash is credited.

The entry to record the remittance of payroll deductions by Academy Company in the following month is as follows:

A = L + OE
−12,120.75   −2,994.56
             −1,429.13
             −6,722.86
               −480.00
               −150.00
               −344.20
↓ Cash flows: −12,120.75

July 13	CPP Payable ($1,497.28 + $1,497.28)	2,994.56	
	EI Payable ($595.47 + $833.66)	1,429.13	
	Income Tax Payable	6,722.86	
	United Way Payable	480.00	
	Union Dues Payable	150.00	
	Workers' Compensation Payable	344.20	
	Cash		12,120.75
	To record payment of payroll deductions for June 20 payroll.		

Note that the vacation pay liability recorded on June 20 is not debited or "paid" until the employees actually take their vacation.

Other payroll information returns or forms must be filed by the employer with the government by the last day of February each year. In addition, as noted previously, employers must give employees a Statement of Remuneration Paid (called a T4 slip by the CRA) by the same date.

ACCOUNTING IN ACTION: ALL ABOUT YOU

Employers are required by law each month to remit to the CRA mandatory payroll deductions as well as the employer's share of CPP and EI. Failure to do so can lead to interest and stiff penalties.

What happens if you are self-employed and providing consulting services to a company? If you are self employed, you are required to pay CPP equal to both the employee's and employer's share, and you are also responsible for paying income tax. Starting January 2010, if you are self-employed you can choose to pay EI to qualify for special benefits such as maternity or parental benefits. But this will not qualify you for employment insurance if you are not able to work. If you choose to pay EI, you will not be required to pay the employers' portion of the EI premium.

It may seem beneficial to some companies to hire consultants and avoid paying the employer's share of CPP and EI as well as other benefits. However, the CRA has strict guidelines as to whether an individual is considered an employee or a self-employed consultant. If a company inappropriately treats an individual as self-employed and fails to deduct CPP and EI, the company will be required to pay both the employer's and employee's share of CPP and EI as well as penalties and interest.

If you are providing services to a company, what are the advantages and disadvantages of being a self-employed consultant versus an employee of the company?

BEFORE YOU GO ON . . .

➔ Review It

1. What is the difference between gross pay and net pay?
2. What are the mandatory payroll deductions?
3. What is the difference between employee payroll deductions and employer payroll costs?

➔ Do It

Prepare the journal entries to record the following transactions. Round any calculations to the nearest dollar.

1. A company's gross wages amount to $10,000 for the week ended July 11. The following amounts are deducted from the employees' wages: CPP of $495; EI of $173; income tax of $3,965; and health insurance of $950. Assume employees are paid in cash on July 11.
2. The company accrues employer's payroll costs on the same day as it records payroll. Assume vacation days are accrued at an average rate of 4% of the gross payroll and that the health insurance is 100% funded by the employees.
3. Record the payment of the mandatory payroll deductions from the July 11 payroll on August 15.

Action Plan

- Record both the employees' portion of the payroll and the benefits owed by the employer.
- Employee deductions are not an expense to the employer.
- The vacation pay liability is not "paid" until the employees actually take their vacation.

Solution

July 11	Wages Expense	10,000	
	CPP Payable		495
	EI Payable		173
	Income Tax Payable		3,965
	Health Insurance Payable		950
	Cash		4,417
	To record payment of wages for week ending July 11.		

July	11	Employee Benefits Expense	1,137	
		CPP Payable		495
		EI Payable ($173 × 1.4)		242
		Vacation Pay Payable ($10,000 × 4%)		400
		To record employer's payroll costs on July 11 payroll.		
Aug.	15	CPP Payable ($495 + $495)	990	
		EI Payable ($173 + $242)	415	
		Income Tax Payable	3,965	
		Cash		5,370
		To record payment of mandatory payroll deductions.		

The Navigator

Related exercise material: BE10–11, BE10–12, BE10–13, E10–11, and E10–12.

Financial Statement Presentation

STUDY OBJECTIVE 5

Prepare the current liabilities section of the balance sheet.

Under Canadian GAAP, current liabilities are the first category reported in the liabilities section of the balance sheet. Each of the main types of current liabilities is listed separately. In addition, the terms of operating lines of credit and notes payable and other information about the individual items are disclosed in the notes to the financial statements.

Current liabilities are usually listed in order of liquidity, by maturity date. Sometimes it is difficult to determine which specific obligations should be listed in which order. A more common method of presenting current liabilities is to list them by order of size, with the largest ones first. Many companies show bank loans, notes payable, and accounts payable first, regardless of the amounts.

As discussed in Chapter 4, some companies reporting under IFRS may choose to order their current liability category on the lower section of the balance sheet, in order of reverse liquidity. Or they may choose to continue with the traditional placement as the first liability category on the balance sheet, in order of liquidity.

The following is an excerpt from Tim Hortons' balance sheet:

Illustration 10-6 ➜

Presentation of current liabilities

TIM HORTONS INC. Balance Sheet (partial) March 29, 2009 (in thousands)	
Current assets	$392,002
Current liabilities	
Accounts payable	$111,803
Accrued expenses	53,619
Gift certificate obligations	10,685
Cash card obligations	35,144
Advertising fund restricted liabilities	46,293
Current portion of long-term obligations	6,753
Total current liabilities	$264,297

Tim Hortons also discloses information about contingencies in the notes to its financial statements, as follows:

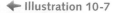

Illustration 10-7

Disclosure of contingent liabilities

| TIM HORTONS INC. |
| Notes to Consolidated Financial Statements (partial) |
| March 29, 2009 |

NOTE 7 COMMITMENTS AND CONTINGENCIES

The Company has guaranteed certain lease and debt payments, primarily related to franchisees, amounting to $0.7 million. In the event of default by a franchise owner, the Company generally retains the right to acquire possession of the related restaurants. The Company is also the guarantor on $11.5 million in letters of credit and surety bonds with various parties; however, management does not expect any material loss to result from these instruments because management does not believe performance will be required. The length of the lease, loan and other arrangements guaranteed by the Company or for which the Company is contingently liable varies, but generally does not exceed seven years. ...

On June 12, 2008, a claim was filed against the Company and certain of its affiliates in the Ontario Superior Court of Justice ("Court") by two of its franchisees, Fairview Donut Inc. and Brule Foods Ltd., alleging, generally, that the Company's Always Fresh baking system and expansion of lunch offerings have led to lower franchisee profitability. The claim, which seeks class action certification on behalf of Canadian franchisees, asserts damages of approximately $1.95 billion. The Company believes the claim is frivolous and completely without merit, and the Company intends to vigorously defend the action. However, there can be no assurance that the outcome of the claim will be favourable to the Company or that it will not have a material adverse impact on the Company's financial position or liquidity in the event that the determinations by the Court and/or appellate court are not in accordance with the Company's evaluation of this claim. Neither the probability of this claim's success nor the ultimate amount payable, if any, are determinable at this time, and, coupled with the Company's position that this claim is without merit, the Company has not recorded any provisions in the Condensed Consolidated Financial Statements related to this claim. ...

Companies must carefully monitor the relationship of current liabilities to current assets. This relationship is critical in evaluating a company's short-term ability to pay debt. There is usually concern when a company has more current liabilities than current assets, because it may not be able to make its payments when they become due.

In Tim Hortons' case, it has a positive current ratio. You will recall from Chapter 4 that the current ratio is calculated by dividing current assets by current liabilities. Tim Hortons' current ratio is 1.48:1 ($392,002 ÷ $264,297), which indicates that Tim Hortons has enough current assets to cover its current liabilities. In addition, Tim Hortons discloses in the notes to its financial statements that it has overdraft protection of $15 million and a $300-million operating line of credit that it can draw on for additional liquidity requirements.

Recall also that the current ratio should never be interpreted without also looking at the receivables and inventory turnover ratios to ensure that all of the current assets are indeed liquid. It is also important to look at the acid-test ratio. If we wanted to do a more complete analysis of Tim Hortons' liquidity, we would need additional information.

BEFORE YOU GO ON . . .

→ Review It

1. Describe the reporting and disclosure requirements for current liabilities.
2. What current liabilities does The Forzani Group report and in what order? The answer to this question is at the end of the chapter.

Related exercise material: BE10–14, BE10–15, E10–5, E10-13, and E10–14.

The Navigator

APPENDIX 10A ▶ PAYROLL DEDUCTIONS

Mandatory Payroll Deductions

As discussed in the chapter, payroll deductions may be mandatory or voluntary. Mandatory deductions are required by law and include Canada Pension Plan contributions, Employment Insurance premiums, and income tax. We discuss how to calculate these in the following sections.

Canada Pension Plan (CPP)

CPP contributions are based on a maximum ceiling or limit (called the maximum pensionable earnings) less a basic yearly exemption, and on the contribution rate set each year by the federal government. As of January 1, 2009, the following amounts were in effect:

Maximum pensionable earnings	$46,300
Basic yearly exemption	$3,500
CPP contribution rate	4.95%
Maximum annual employee CPP contribution	$2,118.60

Pensionable earnings are gross earnings less the basic yearly exemption.

Illustration 10A-1 shows the formulas and calculations used to determine Mark Jordan's CPP contribution on his gross pay of $1,000 for the weekly pay period ending June 20, 2009.

Illustration 10A-1 ➡

Formula for CPP contributions

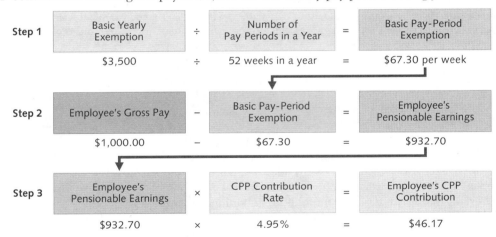

Note that the basic pay-period exemption of $67.30 is a per-week exemption and is used in this case because Academy Company pays its employees weekly. If a company pays its employees monthly, the basic pay-period exemption would be $291.67 ($3,500 ÷ 12).

An employer stops deducting CPP contributions if and when the employee's earnings are greater than the maximum pensionable earnings. In this way, the employee's CPP contributions will not be greater than the maximum annual CPP contribution. Self-employed individuals pay both the employee and employer share of CPP.

Employment Insurance (EI)

EI calculations are based on a maximum earnings ceiling (called the maximum annual insurable earnings) and the contribution rate set by the federal government each year. Different from CPP, there is no basic yearly exemption. For 2009, the following amounts were in effect:

Maximum insurable earnings	$42,300
EI contribution rate	1.73%
Maximum annual employee EI premium	$731.79

In most cases, **insurable earnings** are gross earnings.

The required EI premium is calculated by multiplying the employee's insurable earnings by the EI contribution rate. Illustration 10A-2 shows the formula and calculations to determine Mark Jordan's EI premium on his gross pay of $1,000 for the pay period ending June 20, 2009.

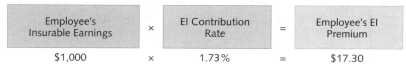

Employee's Insurable Earnings	×	EI Contribution Rate	=	Employee's EI Premium
$1,000	×	1.73%	=	$17.30

◄ Illustration 10A-2

Formula for EI premiums

An employer stops deducting EI premiums if and when the employee's earnings are greater than the maximum insurable earnings. In this way, the employee's EI premiums will not be greater than the maximum annual EI premium. Self-employed individuals who have chosen to pay EI pay only the employee's share of EI.

Personal Income Tax

Income tax deductions are based on income tax rates set by the federal and provincial governments. The federal government uses a progressive tax scheme when calculating income taxes. Basically, this means that the higher the pay or earnings, the higher the income tax percentage, and thus the higher the amount of taxes withheld. For example, effective April 1, 2009, the federal tax rates were:

- 15.5% **on the first** $41,200 of taxable income, plus
- 22% **on the next** $41,199 of taxable income (on the portion of taxable income between $41,200 and $82,399), plus
- 26% **on the next** $43,865 of taxable income (on the portion of taxable income between $82,399 and $126,264), plus
- 29% of taxable income **over** $126,264.

Taxable income is determined by the employee's gross pay and the amount of personal tax credits claimed by the employee. **Personal tax credits** are amounts deducted from an individual's income taxes and determine the amount of income taxes to be withheld. To indicate to the Canada Revenue Agency (CRA) which credits he or she wants to claim, the employee must complete a Personal Tax Credits Return (known as a TD1 form). In 2009, all individuals were entitled to a minimum personal credit (called the basic personal credit) of $10,375.

In addition, provincial income taxes must be calculated. All provinces, except Alberta, also use a progressive tax scheme. Each province has its own specific tax rates and calculations.

As you can see, the calculation of personal income tax deductions is very complicated. Consequently it is best done using one of the many payroll accounting programs that are available or by using the payroll deduction tools provided by the CRA. These tools include: (1) Payroll Deduction Tables, (2) Tables on Diskette, and (3) the Payroll Deductions Online Calculator. We will illustrate how to use the payroll deduction tables.

Using Payroll Deduction Tables

Payroll deduction tables are prepared by the CRA and can be easily downloaded from the CRA website at <http://www.cra-arc.gc.ca/tx/bsnss/tpcs/pyrll/menu-eng.html>. There are separate payroll deduction tables for determining federal tax deductions, provincial tax deductions, Canada Pension Plan contributions, and Employment Insurance premiums.

These tables are updated at least once a year on January 1 to reflect the new rates for that year. Income tax tables are also reissued during the year if the federal or provincial governments make changes to income tax rates during the year. It is important to make sure you have the tables that are in effect during the payroll period for which you are calculating deductions.

There are separate sections of the federal and provincial income tax and the CPP tables for weekly, biweekly, semi-monthly, and monthly pay periods. Thus, when determining these amounts, it is important to make sure you are using the table prepared for the company's pay period. The Academy Company would use the weekly tables.

Illustration 10A-3 →

Excerpts from CPP, EI, and Income Tax Deduction Tables prepared by the Canada Revenue Agency, effective April 1, 2009

Reproduced with permission of the Minister of Public Works and Government Services Canada, 2009.

Canada Pension Plan Contributions
Weekly (52 pay periods a year)

Cotisations au Régime de pensions du Canada
Hebdomadaire (52 périodes de paie par année)

Pay Rémunération From - De	To - À	CPP RPC	Pay Rémunération From - De	To - À	CPP RPC	Pay Rémunération From - De	To - À	CPP RPC	Pay Rémunération From - De	To - À	CPP RPC
910.44	920.43	41.98	1630.44	1640.43	77.62	2350.44	2360.43	113.26	3070.44	3080.43	148.90
920.44	930.43	42.48	1640.44	1650.43	78.12	2360.44	2370.43	113.76	3080.44	3090.43	149.40
930.44	940.43	42.97	1650.44	1660.43	78.61	2370.44	2380.43	114.25	3090.44	3100.43	149.89
940.44	950.43	43.47	1660.44	1670.43	79.11	2380.44	2390.43	114.75	3100.44	3110.43	150.39
950.44	960.43	43.96	1670.44	1680.43	79.60	2390.44	2400.43	115.24	3110.44	3120.43	150.88
960.44	970.43	44.46	1680.44	1690.43	80.10	2400.44	2410.43	115.74	3120.44	3130.43	151.38
970.44	980.43	44.95	1690.44	1700.43	80.59	2410.44	2420.43	116.23	3130.44	3140.43	151.87
980.44	990.43	45.45	1700.44	1710.43	81.09	2420.44	2430.43	116.73	3140.44	3150.43	152.37
990.44	1000.43	45.94	1710.44	1720.43	81.58	2430.44	2440.43	117.22	3150.44	3160.43	152.86
1000.44	1010.43	46.44	1720.44	1730.43	82.08	2440.44	2450.43	117.72	3160.44	3170.43	153.36
1010.44	1020.43	46.93	1730.44	1740.43	82.57	2450.44	2460.43	118.21	3170.44	3180.43	153.85
1020.44	1030.43	47.43	1740.44	1750.43	83.07	2460.44	2470.43	118.71	3180.44	3190.43	154.35
1030.44	1040.43	47.92	1750.44	1760.43	83.56	2470.44	2480.43	119.20	3190.44	3200.43	154.84
1040.44	1050.43	48.42	1760.44	1770.43	84.06	2480.44	2490.43	119.70	3200.44	3210.43	155.34
1050.44	1060.43	48.91	1770.44	1780.43	84.55	2490.44	2500.43	120.19	3210.44	3220.43	155.83
1060.44	1070.43	49.41	1780.44	1790.43	85.05	2500.44	2510.43	120.69	3220.44	3230.43	156.33
1070.44	1080.43	49.90	1790.44	1800.43	85.54	2510.44	2520.43	121.18	3230.44	3240.43	156.82
1080.44	1090.43	50.40	1800.44	1810.43	86.04	2520.44	2530.43	121.68	3240.44	3250.43	157.32

Employment Insurance Premiums

Cotisations à l'assurance-emploi

Insurable Earnings Rémunération assurable From - De	To - À	EI premium Cotisation d'AE	Insurable Earnings Rémunération assurable From - De	To - À	EI premium Cotisation d'AE	Insurable Earnings Rémunération assurable From - De	To - À	EI premium Cotisation d'AE	Insurable Earnings Rémunération assurable From - De	To - À	EI premium Cotisation d'AE
999.14	999.71	17.29	1040.76	1041.32	18.01	1082.37	1082.94	18.73	1123.99	1124.56	19.45
999.72	1000.28	17.30	1041.33	1041.90	18.02	1082.95	1083.52	18.74	1124.57	1125.14	19.46
1000.29	1000.86	17.31	1041.91	1042.48	18.03	1083.53	1084.10	18.75	1125.15	1125.72	19.47
1000.87	1001.44	17.32	1042.49	1043.06	18.04	1084.11	1084.68	18.76	1125.73	1126.30	19.48
1001.45	1002.02	17.33	1043.07	1043.64	18.05	1084.69	1085.26	18.77	1126.31	1126.87	19.49
1002.03	1002.60	17.34	1043.65	1044.21	18.06	1085.27	1085.83	18.78	1126.88	1127.45	19.50
1002.61	1003.17	17.35	1044.22	1044.79	18.07	1085.84	1086.41	18.79	1127.46	1128.03	19.51
1003.18	1003.75	17.36	1044.80	1045.37	18.08	1086.42	1086.99	18.80	1128.04	1128.61	19.52
1003.76	1004.33	17.37	1045.38	1045.95	18.09	1087.00	1087.57	18.81	1128.62	1129.19	19.53
1004.34	1004.91	17.38	1045.96	1046.53	18.10	1087.58	1088.15	18.82	1129.20	1129.76	19.54
1004.92	1005.49	17.39	1046.54	1047.10	18.11	1088.16	1088.72	18.83	1129.77	1130.34	19.55
1005.50	1006.06	17.40	1047.11	1047.68	18.12	1088.73	1089.30	18.84	1130.35	1130.92	19.56
1006.07	1006.64	17.41	1047.69	1048.26	18.13	1089.31	1089.88	18.85	1130.93	1131.50	19.57
1006.65	1007.22	17.42	1048.27	1048.84	18.14	1089.89	1090.46	18.86	1131.51	1132.08	19.58
1007.23	1007.80	17.43	1048.85	1049.42	18.15	1090.47	1091.04	18.87	1132.09	1132.65	19.59
1007.81	1008.38	17.44	1049.43	1049.99	18.16	1091.05	1091.61	18.88	1132.66	1133.23	19.60
1008.39	1008.95	17.45	1050.00	1050.57	18.17	1091.62	1092.19	18.89	1133.24	1133.81	19.61
1008.96	1009.53	17.46	1050.58	1051.15	18.18	1092.20	1092.77	18.90	1133.82	1134.39	19.62

Federal tax deductions
Effective April 1, 2009
Weekly (52 pay periods a year)
Also look up the tax deductions
in the provincial table

Retenues d'impôt fédéral
En vigueur le 1er avril 2009
Hebdomadaire (52 périodes de paie par année)
Cherchez aussi les retenues d'impôt
dans la table provinciale

Pay Rémunération From - De Less than Moins de	Federal claim codes/Codes de demande fédéraux										
	0	1	2	3	4	5	6	7	8	9	10
	Deduct from each pay / Retenez sur chaque paie										
920 - 928	136.60	106.65	103.80	98.10	92.45	86.75	81.05	75.35	69.70	64.00	58.30
928 - 936	138.35	108.40	105.55	99.90	94.20	88.50	82.80	77.15	71.45	65.75	60.05
936 - 944	140.10	110.20	107.35	101.65	95.95	90.25	84.60	78.90	73.20	67.50	61.80
944 - 952	141.85	111.95	109.10	103.40	97.70	92.05	86.35	80.65	74.95	69.25	63.60
952 - 960	143.60	113.70	110.85	105.15	99.50	93.80	88.10	82.40	76.70	71.05	65.35
960 - 968	145.40	115.45	112.60	106.90	101.25	95.55	89.85	84.15	78.50	72.80	67.10
968 - 976	147.15	117.20	114.35	108.70	103.00	97.30	91.60	85.95	80.25	74.55	68.85
976 - 984	148.90	119.00	116.15	110.45	104.75	99.05	93.40	87.70	82.00	76.30	70.60
984 - 992	150.65	120.75	117.90	112.20	106.50	100.85	95.15	89.45	83.75	78.05	72.40
992 - 1000	152.40	122.50	119.65	113.95	108.30	102.60	96.90	91.20	85.50	79.85	74.15
1000 - 1012	154.60	124.70	121.85	116.15	110.50	104.80	99.10	93.40	87.70	82.05	76.35
1012 - 1024	157.25	127.35	124.50	118.80	113.10	107.45	101.75	96.05	90.35	84.65	79.00
1024 - 1036	159.90	130.00	127.15	121.45	115.75	110.05	104.40	98.70	93.00	87.30	81.60
1036 - 1048	162.55	132.60	129.75	124.10	118.40	112.70	107.00	101.35	95.65	89.95	84.25
1048 - 1060	165.20	135.25	132.40	126.70	121.05	115.35	109.65	103.95	98.30	92.60	86.90
1060 - 1072	167.80	137.90	135.05	129.35	123.70	118.00	112.30	106.60	100.90	95.25	89.55
1072 - 1084	170.45	140.55	137.70	132.00	126.30	120.65	114.95	109.25	103.55	97.85	92.20
1084 - 1096	173.10	143.20	140.35	134.65	128.95	123.25	117.60	111.90	106.20	100.50	94.80
1096 - 1108	175.75	145.80	142.95	137.30	131.60	125.90	120.20	114.55	108.85	103.15	97.45
1108 - 1120	178.40	148.45	145.60	139.90	134.25	128.55	122.85	117.15	111.50	105.80	100.10
1120 - 1132	181.00	151.10	148.25	142.55	136.90	131.20	125.50	119.80	114.10	108.45	102.75
1132 - 1144	183.65	153.75	150.90	145.20	139.50	133.85	128.15	122.45	116.75	111.05	105.40
1144 - 1156	186.30	156.40	153.55	147.85	142.15	136.45	130.80	125.10	119.40	113.70	108.00
1156 - 1168	188.95	159.00	156.15	150.50	144.80	139.10	133.40	127.75	122.05	116.35	110.65
1168 - 1180	191.60	161.65	158.80	153.10	147.45	141.75	136.05	130.35	124.70	119.00	113.30

Ontario provincial tax deductions
Effective April 1, 2009
Weekly (52 pay periods a year)
**Also look up the tax deductions
in the federal table**

Retenues d'impôt provincial de l'Ontario
En vigueur le 1ᵉʳ avril 2009
Hebdomadaire (52 périodes de paie par année)
**Cherchez aussi les retenues d'impôt
dans la table fédérale**

Pay Rémunération		Provincial claim codes/Codes de demande provinciaux										
From De	Less than Moins de	0	1	2	3	4	5	6	7	8	9	10
		Deduct from each pay / Retenez sur chaque paie										
938	946	72.45	62.10	61.00	58.80	56.55	54.35	52.10	49.90	47.65	45.45	43.20
946	954	73.20	62.85	61.75	59.50	57.30	55.05	52.85	50.60	48.40	46.15	43.95
954	962	73.90	63.60	62.45	60.25	58.00	55.80	53.55	51.35	49.10	46.90	44.65
962	970	74.65	64.30	63.20	61.00	58.75	56.55	54.30	52.10	49.85	47.60	45.40
970	978	75.40	65.05	63.95	61.70	59.50	57.25	55.05	52.80	50.60	48.35	46.15
978	986	76.10	65.80	64.65	62.45	60.20	58.00	55.75	53.55	51.30	49.10	46.85
986	994	76.85	66.50	65.40	63.15	60.95	58.70	56.50	54.25	52.05	49.80	47.60
994	1002	77.60	67.25	66.15	63.90	61.70	59.45	57.25	55.00	52.80	50.55	48.35
1002	1010	78.30	68.00	66.85	64.65	62.40	60.20	57.95	55.75	53.50	51.30	49.05
1010	1018	79.05	68.70	67.60	65.35	63.15	60.90	58.70	56.45	54.25	52.00	49.80
1018	1030	79.95	69.60	68.50	66.30	64.05	61.85	59.60	57.40	55.15	52.95	50.70
1030	1042	81.05	70.70	69.60	67.40	65.15	62.95	60.70	58.50	56.25	54.05	51.80
1042	1054	82.15	71.80	70.70	68.50	66.25	64.05	61.80	59.60	57.35	55.15	52.90
1054	1066	83.25	72.90	71.80	69.60	67.35	65.15	62.90	60.70	58.45	56.25	54.00
1066	1078	84.35	74.00	72.90	70.70	68.45	66.25	64.00	61.75	59.55	57.30	55.10
1078	1090	85.45	75.10	74.00	71.80	69.55	67.30	65.10	62.85	60.65	58.40	56.20
1090	1102	86.55	76.20	75.10	72.85	70.65	68.40	66.20	63.95	61.75	59.50	57.30
1102	1114	87.65	77.30	76.20	73.95	71.75	69.50	67.30	65.05	62.85	60.60	58.40
1114	1126	88.75	78.40	77.30	75.05	72.85	70.60	68.40	66.15	63.95	61.70	59.50
1126	1138	89.85	79.50	78.40	76.15	73.95	71.70	69.50	67.25	65.05	62.80	60.60

Illustration 10A-3 shows excerpts from the CPP, EI, and federal and Ontario income tax tables effective April 1, 2009. You can use these tables to determine the appropriate deductions for Mark Jordan's gross pay of $1,000 during the pay period ended June 20, 2009.

In the CPP table, under the Pay column, find $1,000. The CPP deduction for the pay range $990.44 to $1,000.43 is $45.94. Earlier in the appendix we showed how to calculate Mark Jordan's CPP and determined it was $46.17. Why the difference? The amount shown in the table is calculated using the mid-point in the range. As the mid-point is not equal to $1,000, there is a difference between the two amounts. Both ways of determining the CPP contribution are correct—the table is just slightly less precise than the calculation. The Academy Company could have used either amount.

In the EI table, under the Insurable Earnings column, find $1,000. The EI deduction in the pay range $999.72 to $1,000.28 is $17.30. This is exactly the same amount we calculated earlier in the appendix because Mark Jordan's pay of $1,000 is the mid-point of this range. As with CPP, companies can either calculate the EI as shown earlier, or use the tables. Both amounts are correct—the table is just slightly less precise than the calculation.

In the Federal Tax Deduction table, first find $1,000 in the Pay column. Now follow across the table to the Federal Claim Code 1 column. The federal tax deduction in the "from" $1,000 to "less than" $1,012 range, claim code 1, is $124.70. The same process is used in the Ontario Tax Deduction table. In the "from" $994 to "less than" $1,002 range, Provincial claim code 1, the provincial tax deduction is $67.25. These amounts agree with the amounts given for Mark Jordan's income tax deduction earlier in the chapter.

Claim code 1 is used for individuals who qualify for only the basic personal credit on the TD1 form discussed earlier in the appendix. You will notice on the Federal and Provincial Tax Deduction tables that the higher the claim code, the lower the income tax deduction. These claim codes can be used for employees who will have more personal tax credits. We have assumed that Mark Jordan will qualify for only the basic personal credit.

As mentioned earlier, employers may also use the Tables on Diskette or the Payroll Deductions Online Calculator to determine payroll deductions. All three methods will provide correct deductions as long as the correct dates, gross pay, pay period, and claim codes are used.

BEFORE YOU GO ON . . .

→ **Do It**

Highland Company pays salaries on a weekly basis. The payroll for the week ended May 29, 2009, includes three employees as follows:

Employee Name	Weekly Earnings	Claim Code
Hudson, James	$ 975	4
Randell, Findley	$ 975	2
Jaegeun, Kim	$1,125	1

Determine the appropriate mandatory payroll deductions and net pay for each employee. Calculate the CPP and EI deductions using the formula provided in Appendix 10A. Use the tables in Illustration 10A-3 to determine federal and provincial income taxes.

Action Plan
- The CPP basic pay-period deduction is the annual basic deduction divided by number of pay periods in a year.
- CPP deductions are equal to an employee's pensionable earnings times the CPP contribution rate.
- EI premiums are equal to an employee's insurable earnings times the EI premium rate.
- The federal tax deduction is the amount in the correct Pay range and Claim Code column on the Federal Tax Deduction Table.
- The provincial tax deduction is the amount in the correct Pay range and Claim Code column on the Provincial Tax Deduction Table.

Solution

Employee	Gross Pay	Deductions					Net Pay
		CPP	EI	Federal Income Tax	Provincial Income Tax	Total	
Hudson, James	$ 975.00	44.93[1]	16.87[3]	103.00	59.50	224.30	750.70
Randell, Findley	975.00	44.93	16.87	114.35	63.95	240.10	734.90
Jaegeun, Kim	1,125.00	52.36[2]	19.46[4]	151.10	78.40	301.32	823.68

Calculations:
Note: CPP basic pay period deduction = $3,500 ÷ 52 = $67.30
[1] ($975.00 − $67.30) × 4.95% = $44.93
[2] ($1,125.00 − $67.30) × 4.95% = $52.36
[3] $975.00 × 1.73% = $16.87
[4] $1,125.00 × 1.73% = $19.46

Related exercise material: *BE10–16, *BE10–17, *BE10–18, *E10–15, and *E10–16.

The Navigator

Demonstration Problem

Benoit Company has the following selected transactions:

Feb. 1 Signed a $50,000, six-month, 7% note payable to the CIBC, receiving $50,000 in cash. Interest is payable at maturity.

10 Cash register receipts totalled $37,565, plus 13% HST.

28 The payroll for the month is salaries of $50,000. CPP contributions and EI premiums withheld are $2,475 and $865, respectively. A total of $15,000 in income taxes is withheld. The salaries are paid on March 1.

The following adjustment data are noted at the end of the month:

1. Interest expense should be accrued on the note.
2. Employer payroll costs are recorded. In addition to mandatory costs, the company also pays $800 a month for a dental plan for all its employees.
3. Some sales were made under warranty. Of the units sold under warranty this month, 350 are expected to become defective. Repair costs are estimated to be $40 per defective unit.

Instructions

(a) Record the February transactions. Round your calculations to the nearest dollar.
(b) Record the adjusting entries at February 28.

Solution to Demonstration Problem

(a)

Date		Account	Debit	Credit
Feb.	1	Cash	50,000	
		Notes Payable		50,000
		Issued six-month, 7% note to CIBC.		
	10	Cash	42,448	
		Sales		37,565
		HST Payable ($37,565 × 13%)		4,883
		To record sales and sales tax payable.		
	28	Salaries Expense	50,000	
		Income Taxes Payable		15,000
		CPP Payable		2,475
		EI Payable		865
		Salaries Payable		31,660
		To record February salaries.		

(b)

Date		Account	Debit	Credit
Feb.	28	Interest Expense ($50,000 × 7% × $\frac{1}{12}$)	292	
		Interest Payable		292
		To record accrued interest for February.		
	28	Employee Benefits Expense	4,486	
		CPP Payable ($2,475 × 1)		2,475
		EI Payable ($865 × 1.4)		1,211
		Dental Plan Payable		800
		To record employee benefit costs for February.		
	28	Warranty Expense (350 × $40)	14,000	
		Warranty Liability		14,000
		To record estimated product warranty liability.		

WILEY PLUS

Demonstration Problems

Action Plan

- Remember that interest rates are annual rates and must be adjusted for periods of time less than one year.
- Remember that sales taxes collected must be sent to the government and are not part of sales revenue.
- Remember that employee deductions for CPP, EI, and income tax reduce the salaries payable.
- Employer contributions to CPP, EI, and the dental plan create an additional expense.
- Warranty costs are expensed in the period when the sales occur.

The Navigator

Summary of Study Objectives

1. *Account for determinable or certain current liabilities.* Liabilities are present obligations arising from past events, to make future payments of assets or services. Determinable liabilities have certainty about their existence, amount, and timing—in other words, they have a known amount, payee, and due date. Examples of determinable current liabilities include operating lines of credit, notes payable, accounts payable, sales taxes, unearned revenue, current maturities of long-term debt, and accrued liabilities such as property taxes, payroll, and interest.

2. *Account for estimated liabilities.* Estimated liabilities exist, but their amount or timing is uncertain. As long as it is *likely* the company will have to settle the obligation, and the company can reasonably estimate the amount, the liability is recognized. Product warranties, customer loyalty programs, and gift cards result in liabilities that must be estimated. They are recorded either as an expense (for warranties) or as a decrease in revenue (for customer loyalty programs) and a liability in the period when the sales occur. These liabilities are reduced when repairs under warranty or redemptions occur. Gift cards are similar to unearned revenues and result in a liability until the gift card is redeemed. As some cards are never redeemed, it is necessary to make adjustments to the liability.

3. *Account for contingencies.* A contingency depends on a future event to confirm its existence (and possibly the amount and timing). Under IFRS, a contingent liability is a possible obligation or a present obligation where settlement is unlikely or the obligation cannot be measured. Contingent liabilities are never recorded; they are disclosed unless they are unlikely. Under Canadian GAAP for Private Enterprises, contingent liabilities are accrued when they are likely and estimable. Otherwise, they are only disclosed. They are not disclosed if they are unlikely. Contingent assets are not recorded. They are only disclosed if they are likely.

4. *Determine payroll costs and record payroll transactions.* Payroll costs consist of employee and employer payroll costs. In recording employee costs, Salaries and Wages Expense is debited for the gross pay, individual liability accounts are credited for payroll deductions, and Salaries and Wages Payable is credited for net pay. In recording employer payroll costs, Employee Benefits Expense is debited for the employer's share of CPP, EI, workers' compensation, vacation pay, and any other deductions or benefits provided. Each benefit is credited to its specific current liability account.

5. *Prepare the current liabilities section of the balance sheet.* The nature and amount of each current liability and contingency should be reported in the balance sheet or in the notes accompanying the financial statements. Under Canadian GAAP, current liabilities are reported first and in order of liquidity. Under IFRS, there is the option to report current liabilities on the lower section of the balance sheet and in reverse order of liquidity.

6. *Calculate mandatory payroll deductions (Appendix 10A).* Mandatory payroll deductions include CPP, EI, and income taxes. CPP is calculated by multiplying pensionable earnings (gross pay minus the pay period exemption) by the CPP contribution rate. EI is calculated by multiplying insurable earnings by the EI contribution rate. Federal and provincial income taxes are calculated using a progressive tax scheme and are based on taxable earnings and personal tax credits. The calculations are very complex and it is best to use one of the CRA income tax calculation tools such as payroll deduction tables.

The Navigator

Glossary

WILEY PLUS   Glossary
Key Term Matching Activity

Canada Pension Plan (CPP) A mandatory federal plan that gives disability, retirement, and death benefits to qualifying Canadians. (p. 571)

Collateral Property pledged as security for a loan. (p. 559)

Contingency Events with uncertain outcomes. (p. 567)

Contingent asset A possible asset that arises from past events and whose existence will be resolved only when a future event occurs or does not occur. (p. 568)

Contingent liability A possible obligation whose existence will be confirmed only by the occurrence or non-occurrence of a future event or a present obligation where it is not likely it will have to be settled or the amount cannot be reasonably determined. (p. 567)

Customer loyalty programs Programs that result in future savings for the customers on the merchandise or services the company sells. (p. 564)

Determinable liability A liability whose existence, amount, and timing are known with certainty. (p. 558)

Employee benefits Payments made by an employer, in addition to wages and salaries, to give pension, insurance, medical, or other benefits to its employees. (p. 573)

Employee earnings record A separate record of an employee's gross pay, payroll deductions, and net pay for the calendar year. (p. 574)

Employment Insurance (EI) A federal mandatory insurance program designed to give income protection for a limited period of time to employees who are temporarily laid off, who are on parental leave, or who lose their jobs. (p. 572)

Estimated liability A liability that is known to exist but whose amount or timing is uncertain. (p. 563)

Gross pay Total compensation earned by an employee. Also known as gross earnings. (p. 570)

Insurable earnings Gross earnings used to calculate EI deductions. There is a maximum amount of insurable earnings set each year by the government. (p. 581)

Net pay Gross pay less payroll deductions. (p. 572)

Notes payable Obligations in the form of written promissory notes. (p. 559)

Operating line of credit Pre-authorized approval to borrow money at a bank when it is needed, up to a preset limit. (p. 559)

Payroll deductions Deductions from gross pay to determine the amount of a paycheque. (p. 571)

Payroll register A record that accumulates the gross pay, deductions, and net pay per employee for each pay period and becomes the documentation for preparing a paycheque for each employee. (p. 574)

Pensionable earnings Gross earnings less the basic yearly exemption. There is a maximum amount of pensionable earnings set each year by the government. (p. 580)

Personal tax credits Amounts deducted from an individual's income taxes that determine the amount of income taxes to be withheld. (p. 581)

Prime rate The interest rate banks charge their best customers. (p. 559)

Product warranties Promises made by the seller to a buyer to repair or replace a product if it is defective or does not perform as intended. (p. 563)

Trade payables Accounts and notes payable that result from purchase transactions with suppliers. (p. 559)

Note: All questions, exercises, and problems below with an asterisk (*) relate to material in Appendix 10A

Self-Study Questions

WILEY **PLUS** Quizzes

Answers are at the end of the chapter.

(SO 1) AP 1. Gilbert Company borrows $88,500 on July 1, 2011, from the Bank of Nova Scotia by signing an eight-month, 6% note. Interest is payable at maturity. What is the accrued interest at December 31, 2011?
   (a) $5,310
   (b) $3,540
   (c) $3,982
   (d) $2,655

(SO 1) AP 2. RedEarth Company, located in Ontario, has $5,007 of sales, which included 13% HST. What is the amount (rounded to the nearest dollar) that should be credited to HST Payable?
   (a) $651
   (b) $354
   (c) $576
   (d) $401

(SO 1) AP 3. On March 1, Swift Current Company receives its property tax assessment of $13,200 for the 2011 calendar year. The property tax bill is due May 1. If Swift Current prepares quarterly financial statements, how much property tax expense should the company report for the quarter ended March 31, 2011?
   (a) $3,300

   (b) $4,400
   (c) $1,100
   (d) $13,200

4. Big Al's Appliance Store offers a two-year warranty on (SO 2) AP all appliances sold. The company estimates that 5% of all appliances sold need to be serviced at an average cost of $100 each. At December 31, 2010, the Warranty Liability account had a balance of $20,000. During 2011, the store spends $14,500 repairing 145 appliances. An additional 4,500 appliances are sold in 2011. On the 2011 income statement, warranty expense will be:
   (a) $28,000.
   (b) $22,500.
   (c) $14,500.
   (d) $20,000.

5. Friendly Department Store has a customer loyalty (SO 2) K program in which customers receive points when they make a purchase. The points can be redeemed on future purchases. The value of the points issued should be recorded as:
   (a) a contra revenue when the points are issued.
   (b) an expense when the points are issued.
   (c) a contra revenue when the points are redeemed.
   (d) an expense when the points are redeemed.

(SO 3) K 6. Under IFRS, a contingent liability is defined as:
(a) a *possible* obligation whose existence will be confirmed only by the occurrence or non-occurrence of uncertain future events.
(b) a present obligation that is not recognized because it is not probable the company will have to settle the obligation.
(c) a present obligation that is not recognized because the amount of the obligation cannot be reliably measured.
(d) any of the above.

(SO 3) K 7. Under Canadian GAAP for Private Enterprises, if a contingent asset is reasonably estimable and it is likely that the contingency will occur, the contingent asset should:
(a) be accrued in the accounts.
(b) be disclosed in the notes accompanying the financial statements.
(c) not be recorded or disclosed until the contingency actually happens.
(d) be collected immediately.

(SO 4) AP 8. In a recent pay period, Blue Company employees have gross salaries of $17,250. Total deductions are: CPP $866, EI $298, and income taxes $4,312.

What is Blue Company's total payroll expense for this pay period? Ignore vacation benefits and workers' compensation.
(a) $17,250
(b) $18,533
(c) $11,774
(d) $18,414

9. Under IFRS, current liabilities: (SO 5) K
(a) must be presented in reverse order of liquidity.
(b) must be presented after long-term liabilities in the balance sheet.
(c) are combined with long-term liabilities.
(d) may be presented before or after long-term liabilities in the balance sheet.

*10. During the first week of May 2009, Emily Marquette worked 42 hours at an hourly wage of $25 per hour for an employer in Ontario. Using the payroll deduction tables in Appendix 10A, what was her net pay, assuming her only personal tax credit is the basic personal amount? (SO 4, 6) AP
(a) $1,050.00
(b) $776.36
(c) $842.95
(d) $736.06

The Navigator

Questions

(SO 1) K 1. Why is a present commitment to purchase an asset in the future not recorded as a liability?

(SO 1) K 2. How is a note payable similar to, and different from, (a) an account payable, and (b) an operating line of credit?

(SO 1) K 3. What is the difference between an operating line of credit and a bank overdraft?

(SO 1) C 4. Your roommate says, "Sales taxes are reported as revenues in the income statement." Do you agree? Explain.

(SO 1) C 5. Explain how property taxes should be recorded when the bill arrives sometime in the spring but covers the entire calendar year.

(SO 1) C 6. Laurel Hyatt believes that if a company has a long-term liability, the entire amount should be classified as long-term liabilities. Is Laurel correct? Explain.

(SO 2) C 7. The accountant for Amiable Appliances feels that warranty expense should not be recorded unless an appliance is returned for repair. "Otherwise, how do you know if the appliance will be returned, and if so, how much it will cost to fix?" he says. Do you agree? Explain.

8. Explain what happens if the estimated warranty liability does not agree with the actual warranty costs incurred. (SO 2) C

9. A restaurant recently started a customer loyalty program. For all bills in excess of $100, the customer receives a 2-for-1 voucher for an appetizer for future meals. How should the restaurant account for the vouchers? (SO 2) C

10. Why is the cost of product warranties recorded as an expense but the cost of rewards issued in a customer loyalty program is recorded as a decrease in revenue? (SO 2) C

11. In what respects are gift cards similar to unearned revenues and why are they classified as a liability? How is a gift card different than an airline's unearned passenger revenue for flights paid in advance? (SO 2) C

12. What are the differences between determinable, estimated, and contingent liabilities? (SO 1, 2, 3) K

13. What are the differences between the definitions of a contingent liability under IFRS and under Canadian GAAP for Private Enterprises? (SO 3) C

(SO 3) C 14. Under what circumstances is a contingent liability recorded in the accounts? Under what circumstances is a contingent liability disclosed only in the notes to the financial statements?

(SO 3) C 15. What is a debt guarantee? Why is a debt guarantee an example of a contingent liability?

(SO 3) C 16. What is the difference between a contingent liability and a contingent asset? Give an example of each.

(SO 3) C 17. What is the accounting treatment for (a) contingent liabilities and (b) contingent assets? Why is it not the same?

(SO 4) C 18. What is the difference between salaries and wages?

(SO 4) C 19. What is the difference between gross pay and net pay? Which amount (gross or net) should a company record as salaries and wages expense?

(SO 4) C 20. Explain the different types of employee and employer payroll deductions, and give examples of each.

(SO 4) K 21. What are an employee earnings record and a payroll register?

(SO 4) C 22. To whom, and how often, are payroll deductions remitted?

(SO 4) K 23. What are some additional employee benefits paid by employers? How are they accounted for?

(SO 5) K 24. In what order should current liabilities be listed on the balance sheet?

(SO 5) K 25. How is an operating line of credit reported or disclosed in the financial statements?

(SO 5) K 26. Where in the financial statements should a company report employee payroll deductions? Employer payroll costs?

(SO 5) K 27. How can a company determine if its current liabilities are too high?

(SO 6) K *28. Explain how CPP and EI are each calculated.

(SO 6) K *29. How is the amount deducted from an employee's wages for income tax determined?

Brief Exercises

BE10–1 Bourque Company borrows $60,000 from First Bank on July 1, 2010, signing a nine-month, 6% note payable. Interest is payable the first of each month, starting August 1. Prepare journal entries for Bourque Company to record: (a) the receipt of the proceeds of the note on July 1, 2010; (b) the first interest payment on August 1, 2010; (c) the accrual of interest at Bourque's year end, December 31, 2010; and (d) the payment of the note at maturity, April 1, 2011.

Record note payable.
(SO 1) AP

BE10–2 Auto Supply Company reports cash sales of $11,526 on March 16. All sales are subject to 13% HST. Record the sales assuming the sales amount of $11,526 (a) does not include the HST, and (b) does include the HST.

Calculate and record HST.
(SO 1) AP

BE10–3 Summertime Productions Company in Prince Edward Island reports cash sales of $8,200 on July 23. All sales are subject to 5% GST and 10% PST. Calculate the (a) sales taxes collected, (b) total amount collected, and (c) combined sales tax rate in effect in Prince Edward Island.

Calculate PST and GST.
(SO 1) AP

BE10–4 Dresner Company has a December 31 fiscal year end. It receives a $7,620 property tax bill for the 2011 calendar year on February 28, 2011. The bill is payable on May 31. Prepare entries for February 28, May 31, and December 31, assuming the company adjusts its accounts annually.

Record property tax.
(SO 1) AP

BE10–5 On December 1, Ng Company introduces a new product that includes a two-year warranty on parts. In December, 1,000 units are sold. Management believes that 6% of the units will be defective and that the average warranty cost will be $70 per unit. (a) Prepare the adjusting entry at December 31 to accrue the estimated warranty cost. (b) The following year, the cost of defective parts replaced under the warranty was $3,800. Prepare an entry to record the replacement of the parts.

Record warranty.
(SO 2) AP

Record loyalty rewards issued and redeemed.
(SO 2) AP

BE10-6 One-Stop Department Store has a loyalty program where customers are given One-Stop "Money" for cash or debit card purchases. The amount they receive is equal to 2% of the pre-tax sales total. Customers can use the One-Stop Money to pay for part or all of their next purchase at One-Stop Department Store. On July 3, 2011, Judy Wishloff purchases merchandise for $150. She uses $20 of One-Stop Money that she has from earlier purchases, and pays for the rest of the purchase with cash. What entry or entries will One-Stop Department Store record for this transaction? Ignore taxes.

Record estimated liability for cash rebate program.
(SO 2) AP

BE10-7 In September, Mega-Big Motion Picture Company sells 100,000 copies of a recently released DVD of a popular movie. Each DVD contains a $4 rebate if the consumer sends in proof of purchase with the completed rebate form. Mega-Big estimates that 15% of the purchasers will claim the rebate. Prepare an adjusting entry at September 30 to accrue the estimated rebate liability. Assume in October that 2,000 rebate forms are received and processed. Prepare one journal entry to record processing the rebate forms.

Record gift cards issued and redeemed.
(SO 2) AP

BE10-8 Rikard's Menswear sells $4,200 of gift cards for cash in December 2010. Rikard's has a December 31 fiscal year end and uses a perpetual inventory system. In January 2011, $2,950 of the gift cards are redeemed for merchandise, with a cost of $1,325. Prepare journal entries for Rikard's for December 2010 and January 2011.

Account for contingencies.
(SO 3) C

BE10-9 For each of the following independent situations, indicate whether it should be (1) recorded, (2) disclosed, or (3) neither recorded nor disclosed. Explain your reasoning and indicate if the accounting treatment would be the same or different under IFRS and Canadian GAAP for Private Enterprises.

(a) A customer has sued a company for $1 million. Currently the company is unable to determine if it will win or lose the lawsuit.
(b) A customer has sued a company for $1 million. The company will likely lose the lawsuit.
(c) A company has appealed an income tax assessment by the CRA. If the company's appeal is successful, it will recover $100,000 of income tax. The company's accountant has advised management that the company has a good chance of winning the appeal.
(d) A company has guaranteed a $300,000 loan for one of its key suppliers. The supplier has a good credit rating and is not expected to default on the loan.

Discuss contingent liability.
(SO 3) AP

BE10-10 Athabasca Toil & Oil Company, a public company, is a defendant in a lawsuit for improper discharge of pollutants and waste into the Athabasca River. Athabasca's lawyers have advised that the company will likely lose this lawsuit and that it could settle out of court for $50,000. How should Athabasca record this current liability? What are the arguments for and against recording this contingent liability?

Calculate gross, net pay, and employer costs.
(SO 4) AP

BE10-11 Becky Sherrick's regular hourly wage rate is $16, and she receives an hourly rate of $24 for work over 40 hours per week. In the pay period ended January 5, Becky worked 43 hours. Becky's CPP deductions total $31.91, EI deductions total $12.32, and her income tax withholdings are $104.65. (a) Calculate Becky's gross and net pay for the pay period. (b) What are Becky's employer's costs for CPP, EI, and income tax?

Record payroll.
(SO 4) AP

BE10-12 Data for Becky Sherrick are given in BE10-11. Prepare the journal entries to record Becky's pay for the period, including employer costs, assuming she was paid on January 5.

Record payroll.
(SO 4) AP

BE10-13 Bri Company's gross pay for the week ended August 22 totalled $70,000, from which $3,330 was deducted for CPP, $1,211 for EI, and $19,360 for income tax. Prepare the entries to record (a) the employee payroll costs, assuming salaries were paid August 22, and (b) the employer payroll costs, assuming these will not be paid until September.

BE10–14 Identify which of the following items should be classified as a current liability. For those that are not current liabilities, identify where they should be classified.

Identify current liabilities. (SO 1, 2, 3, 4, 5) K

1. A product warranty
2. Cash received in advance for airline tickets
3. HST collected on sales
4. Bank indebtedness
5. Interest owing on an overdue account payable
6. Interest due on an overdue account receivable
7. A lawsuit pending against a company. The company is not sure of the likely outcome.
8. Amounts withheld from the employees' weekly pay
9. Prepaid property tax
10. A $75,000 mortgage payable, of which $5,000 is due in the next year

BE10–15 Suncor Energy Inc. reported the following current assets and current liabilities (in millions) at December 31, 2008:

Prepare current liabilities section and calculate ratios. (SO 5) AP

Accounts payable and accrued liabilities	$3,229
Accounts receivable	1,580
Cash	660
Income taxes payable	192
Income taxes recoverable	88
Inventories	909
Sales taxes payable	97
Short-term debt	11

(a) Prepare the current liabilities section of the balance sheet.
(b) Calculate the current and the acid-test ratios.

*BE10–16 Cecilia Hernandez earned $55,200 in 2009 and was paid on a monthly basis. She worked for HillSide Tours for all of 2009. What were her CPP and EI deductions in (a) January 2009 and (b) December 2009?

Calculate CPP and EI deductions. (SO 6) AP

*BE10–17 In 2009, Viktor Petska was paid a gross salary of $1,090 on a weekly basis. For the week ended May 8, 2009: (a) calculate his CPP and EI deductions and (b) use the excerpts in Illustration 10A-3 to determine his income tax deductions assuming his TD1 claim code is 1.

Calculate payroll deductions. (SO 6) AP

*BE10–18 Augustus Jackson earns $720 for a 40-hour week and is paid time and a half for hours above 40. During the week ended April 24, 2009, he worked 50 hours. (a) Calculate his gross pay for the week. (b) Calculate his CPP and EI deductions. (c) Use the excerpts in Illustration 10A-3 to determine his income tax deductions assuming his TD1 claim code is 3. (d) Calculate his net pay.

Calculate gross pay, payroll deductions, and net pay. (SO 4, 6) AP

Exercises

E10–1 Briffet Construction borrows $200,000 from TD Bank on October 1, 2010. It signs a 10-month, 6% note payable. Interest is payable the first of each month, starting November 1.

Record note payable and note receivable; interest paid monthly. (SO 1) AP

Instructions

(a) Record for Briffet Construction (1) the transaction on October 1, 2010; (2) the first interest payment on November 1, 2010; and (3) the payment of the note on August 1, 2011.
(b) Record for TD Bank (1) the transaction on October 1, 2010; (2) the first interest receipt on November 1, 2010; and (3) the collection of the note on August 1, 2011.

Record note payable and note receivable; interest paid at maturity.
(SO 1) AP

E10–2 On March 1, 2011, Tundra Trees Company purchased equipment from Edworthy Equipment Dealership for $20,000, terms n/30. On March 31, Tundra was unable to pay its account. Edworthy agreed to accept a seven-month, 8% note payable to settle the account. Interest is due at maturity. Tundra Trees has a July 31 fiscal year end. Edworthy has a May 31 fiscal year end. Both companies adjust their accounts annually. Tundra honours the note at maturity.

Instructions

(a) For Tundra Trees, record: (1) the transactions on March 1 and March 31, 2011; (2) the adjusting entry on July 31, 2011; and (3) the payment of the note on October 31, 2011.
(b) For Edworthy Equipment, record: (1) the transactions on March 1 and March 31, 2011 (assume the equipment had cost Edworthy $12,000); (2) the adjusting entry on May 31, 2011; and (3) the collection of the note on October 31, 2011.

Record sales taxes.
(SO 1) AP

E10–3 In providing accounting services to small businesses, you encounter the following independent situations:

1. Sainsbury Company rang up $26,500 of sales, plus HST of 13%, on its cash register on April 10.
2. Hockenstein Company prices its merchandise with sales taxes included. Its register total for April 15 is $33,674, which includes 13% HST.
3. Montgomery Company rang up $30,000 of sales, before sales taxes, on its cash register on April 21. The company charges 5% GST and 10% PST on all sales. PST is charged on sales plus GST.

Instructions

Record the sales transactions and related taxes for each client.

Record unearned subscription revenue.
(SO 1) AP

E10–4 Westwood Company publishes a monthly skateboard magazine, *Adventure Time*. Subscriptions to the magazine cost $48 per year. In October 2010, Westwood sells 6,000 subscriptions, which begin with the November issue. Westwood prepares financial statements quarterly and recognizes subscription revenue earned at the end of each quarter. Westwood's year end is December 31.

Instructions

(a) Prepare the entry in October for the receipt of the subscriptions.
(b) Prepare the adjusting entry at December 31, 2010, to record subscription revenue earned by the end of December.
(c) Prepare the adjusting entry at March 31, 2011, to record subscription revenue earned in the first quarter of 2011.

Record property tax; determine financial statement impact.
(SO 1, 5) AP

E10–5 Seaboard Company receives its annual property tax bill of $18,660 for the 2011 calendar year on May 31, 2011, and it is payable on July 31, 2011. Seaboard has a December 31 fiscal year end.

Instructions

(a) Prepare the journal entries for Seaboard on May 31, July 31, and December 31, 2011, assuming that the company makes monthly adjusting entries. (Assume property tax expense in 2010 was $1,475 per month.)
(b) What is recorded on Seaboard's December 31, 2011, balance sheet and income statement for the year ended December 31, 2011, in regard to property taxes?

Record warranty costs.
(SO 2) AP

E10–6 Sinclair Company sells popcorn makers under a 90-day warranty for defective merchandise. Based on past experience, Sinclair estimates that 3% of the units sold will become defective in the warranty period. Management estimates that the average cost of replacing or repairing a defective unit is $15. The units sold and actual units defective in the last two months of 2011 are as follows:

Month	Units Sold	Units Defective
November	45,000	450
December	48,000	930
	93,000	1,380

Instructions

(a) Calculate the estimated warranty liability at December 31 for the units sold in November and December.

(b) Prepare the journal entries to record (1) the estimated liability for warranties, and (2) the costs incurred in honouring the 1,380 warranty claims as at December 31 (assume an actual cost of $20,700).

E10–7 The CopyCat Company manufactures and sells photocopiers, with a two-year service warranty. The company estimates that on average it will make 10 service calls a year for each unit sold over the two-year warranty period, at an average cost of $60 per service call.

Calculate warranty costs for multiple years. (SO 2) AP

The company reports the following sales and service call information:

	2009	**2010**	**2011**
Sales (units)	2,000	2,200	2,400
Actual service calls	20,000	40,000	50,000

Instructions

(a) Calculate the warranty expense for each year.
(b) Calculate the warranty liability at the end of each year.

E10–8 Steig's Sports Store has a customer loyalty program in which it issues points to customers for every cash purchase that can be applied to future purchases. For every dollar spent, a customer receives five points. Each point is worth one cent. There is no expiry date on the points. Steig's estimates that 15% of the points issued will eventually be redeemed. Steig's has a December 31 year end.

Calculate customer loyalty program liability. (SO 2) AP

The program was started in 2010. During 2010, 600,000 points were issued. In 2011, 800,000 points were issued. Redemptions total 50,000 points in 2010 and 80,000 in 2011.

Instructions

(a) What amount should be recorded as contra revenue (sales discounts for redemption rewards issued) in 2010? In 2011?
(b) What was the value of the points redeemed in 2010? In 2011?
(c) What is the redemption rewards liability that should be reported at December 31, 2010? At December 31, 2011?
(d) When the points are redeemed, how is this accounted for? What is the impact of the point redemptions on profit?

E10–9 A list of possible liabilities follows:

Identify type of liability. (SO 1, 2, 3) C

1. An automobile company recalled a particular car model because of a possible problem with the brakes. The company will pay to replace the brakes.
2. A large retail store has a policy of refunding purchases to dissatisfied customers under a widely advertised "money-back, no questions asked" guarantee.
3. A manufacturer offers a three-year warranty at the time of sale.
4. To promote sales, a company offers prizes (e.g., a chance to win a trip) in return for a specific type of bottle cap.
5. A local community has filed suit against a chemical company for contamination of drinking water. The community is demanding compensation, and the amount is uncertain. The company is vigorously defending itself.

Instructions

(a) State whether you believe each of the above liabilities is determinable, estimable, or contingent, and explain why.

(b) If you identify the liability as contingent in part (a), state what factors should be considered in determining if it should be recorded, disclosed, or neither recorded nor disclosed in the financial statements.

Analyze contingent liability.
(SO 3) AP

E10–10   Sleep-a-Bye Baby Company, a public company, is the defendant in a lawsuit alleging that its portable baby cribs are unsafe. The company has offered to replace the cribs free of charge for any concerned parent. Nonetheless, it has been sued for damages and distress amounting to $1.5 million. The company plans to vigorously defend its product safety record in court.

Instructions

(a) What should the company record or report in its financial statements for this situation? Explain why.

(b) What if Sleep-a-Bye Baby Company's lawyers advise that it is likely the company will have to pay damages of $100,000? Does this change what should be recorded or reported in the financial statements? Explain.

(c) How would your answers to (a) and (b) change if Sleep-a-Bye Baby Company were a private company that had chosen to follow Canadian GAAP?

Record payroll.
(SO 4) AP

E10–11   Hidden Dragon Restaurant's gross payroll for August is $41,500. The company deducted $1,860 for CPP, $718 for EI, and $8,025 for income taxes from the employees' cheques. Employees are paid monthly at the end of each month.

Instructions

(a) Prepare a journal entry for Hidden Dragon on August 31 to record the payment of the August payroll to employees.

(b) Prepare a journal entry on August 31 to accrue Hidden Dragon's employer payroll costs. Assume that Hidden Dragon is assessed workers' compensation premiums at a rate of 1% per month and accrues for vacation pay at a rate of 4% per month.

(c) On September 15, Hidden Dragon pays the government the correct amounts for August's payroll. Prepare a journal entry to record this remittance.

Calculate gross pay, prepare payroll register, and record payroll.
(SO 4) AP

E10–12   Ahmad Company has the following data for the weekly payroll ending May 31:

Employee	M	Tu	W	Th	F	S	Hourly Rate	CPP Deduction	Income Tax Withheld	Health Insurance
A. Kassam	8	8	9	8	10	3	$11	$23.35	$81	$10
H. Faas	8	8	8	8	8	2	13	24.34	87	15
G. Labute	9	10	8	10	8	0	14	29.59	107	15

Employees are paid 1.5 times the regular hourly rate for all hours worked over 40 hours per week. Ahmad Company must make payments to the workers' compensation plan equal to 2% of the gross payroll. In addition, Ahmad matches the employees' health insurance contributions and accrues vacation pay at a rate of 4%.

Instructions

(a) Prepare the payroll register for the weekly payroll. Calculate each employee's EI deduction at a rate of 1.73% of gross pay.

(b) Record the payroll and Ahmad Company's employee benefits.

Determine financial statement impact of transactions.
(SO 1, 2, 3, 4) AP

E10–13   Here is a list of transactions:

1. Purchased inventory (perpetual system) on account.

2. Extended the payment terms of the account payable in item 1 above by issuing a nine-month, 5% note payable.

3. Recorded accrued interest on the note payable from item 2 above.

4. Recorded cash sales of $8,000, plus HST of 13%.

5. Recorded wage expense of $35,000. Paid employees $25,000; the difference was for various payroll deductions withheld.

6. Recorded employer's share of employee benefits.

7. Accrued property taxes payable when bill received.

8. Disclosed a contingent liability on a lawsuit whose outcome the company cannot determine.

9. Recorded the estimated liability for product warranties outstanding.

10. Paid product warranty claims that were accrued in item 9 above.

Instructions

Set up a table using the format shown below. Indicate the effect ("+" for increase, "–" for decrease, and "NE" for no effect) of each of the above transactions on the financial statement categories indicated. The first one has been done for you as an example.

	Assets	Liabilities	Owner's Equity	Revenues	Expenses	Profit
1.	+	+	NE	NE	NE	NE

E10–14 Larkin Company has the following liability accounts at August 31, 2011, after posting adjusting entries:

Prepare current liabilities section of balance sheet. Calculate current and acid-test ratios.
(SO 5) AP

Accounts payable	$ 72,000
Bank indebtedness	50,000
CPP payable	6,000
Customer loyalty liability	4,000
EI payable	3,000
HST payable	12,000
Income tax payable	28,000
Interest payable	8,000
Mortgage payable	120,000
Note payable	80,000
Property taxes payable	8,000
Unearned revenue	24,000
Warranty liability	18,000
Workers' compensation payable	1,000

Additional information:

1. Bank indebtedness is from an operating line of credit that is due on demand.

2. On August 31, 2011, the unused operating line of credit is $25,000.

3. Customer loyalty and warranty costs are expected to be incurred within one year.

4. Of the mortgage, $10,000 is due each year.

5. The note payable matures in three years.

6. On August 31, 2011, the company had current assets composed of accounts receivable of $145,000; inventory of $220,000; and prepaid assets of $10,000.

Instructions

(a) Prepare the current liabilities section of the balance sheet.

(b) Calculate Larkin's current ratio and acid-test ratio.

(c) Explain why the company did not report any cash as part of its current assets.

*E10–15** Kate Gough's regular hourly wage rate is $20.50, and she receives a wage of 1.5 times the regular hourly rate for work over 40 hours per week. In a September weekly pay period, Kate worked 44 hours. Kate lives in Ontario and has a claim code of 1 for tax deductions.

Calculate gross pay and payroll deductions; record payroll.
(SO 4, 6) AP

Instructions

(a) Calculate Kate's gross pay and her payroll deductions. Use Illustration 10A-3 to determine her income tax deductions.
(b) Record Kate's salary on September 16, assuming it was also paid on this date.
(c) Record the employer's related payroll costs on September 16, assuming they were not paid on this date.

Calculate gross pay and
payroll deductions.
(SO 6) AP

*E10–16   In 2009, Donald Green worked for the Green Red Company and earned a gross salary of $48,000 for the year ($4,000 per month). He is paid once a month at the end of each month.

Instructions

Calculate Donald's CPP and EI deductions for the following:

(a) September 2009
(b) October 2009
(c) November 2009
(d) December 2009
(e) In total for 2009

Problems: Set A

Identify liabilities.
(SO 1, 2, 3, 4, 5) AP

P10–1A   The following transactions occurred in Wendell Company in the year ended December 31:

1. Wendell purchased goods for $120,000 on December 23, terms n/30, FOB shipping point. The goods were shipped on December 27.
2. Weekly salaries of $60,000 are paid every Friday for a five-day (Monday to Friday) work-week. This year, December 31 is a Wednesday. Payroll deductions include income tax withholdings of $18,000, and CPP of $3,000, and EI of $1,000.
3. Wendell is the defendant in a $500,000 negligence suit. Wendell's lawyers estimate that Wendell may suffer a $95,000 loss if it loses the suit. In the lawyers' opinion, the likelihood of success in the case cannot be determined at this time.
4. Wendell issued a $500,000, five-year, 6% note payable on July 1. The note requires payment of the principal in instalments of $100,000 each June 30 for the next five years. Interest is due monthly on the first of each month.
5. The company received $25,000 from customers in December for services to be performed in January.
6. Wendell issued a mail-in purchase rebate on one of its specialty inventory items sold between September 1 and November 30. Each item was sold for $45 and had a $4 rebate attached to it. A total of 4,500 items were sold in that period. Wendell estimates that 25% of the customers will request a rebate. By December 31, Wendell had issued $3,900 in rebates.
7. The company has a $100,000 operating line of credit. No money is owed on this line of credit to date.

Instructions

Identify which transactions above should be presented in the current liabilities section and which in the long-term liabilities section of Wendell's balance sheet on December 31. Identify the account title(s) and amount(s) for each reported liability.

Taking It Further

Indicate any information that should be disclosed in the notes to Wendell's financial statements.

P10–2A The current liabilities section of the December 31, 2010, balance sheet of Learnstream Company included notes payable of $14,000 and interest payable of $490. The note payable was issued to Tanner Company on June 30, 2010. Interest of 7% is payable at maturity, March 31, 2011.

Record note transactions; show financial statement presentation.
(SO 1, 5) AP

The following selected transactions occurred in the year ended December 31, 2011:

Jan. 12 Purchased merchandise on account from McCoy Company for $20,000, terms n/30. Learnstream uses a perpetual inventory system.

    31 Issued a $20,000, three-month, 5% note to McCoy Company in payment of an account. Interest is payable monthly.

Feb. 28 Paid interest on the McCoy note (see January 31 transaction).

Mar. 31 Paid the Tanner note, plus interest.

    31 Paid interest on the McCoy note (see January 31 transaction).

Apr. 30 Paid the McCoy note, plus one month's interest (see January 31 transaction).

Aug. 1 Purchased equipment from Scottie Equipment by paying $11,000 cash and signing a $30,000, 10-month, 6% note. Interest is payable at maturity.

Oct. 30 Borrowed $100,000 cash from the First Interprovincial Bank by signing a 10-year, 5% note payable. Interest is payable quarterly on December 31, March 31, June 30, and September 30. Of the principal, $10,000 must be paid each September 30.

Dec. 31 Paid interest on the First Interprovincial Bank note (see September 30 transaction).

Instructions

(a) Record the transactions and any adjustments required at December 31.

(b) Show the balance sheet presentation of notes payable and interest payable at December 31.

(c) Show the income statement presentation of interest expense for the year.

Taking It Further

Why is it important to correctly classify notes payable as either current or non-current in the balance sheet?

P10–3A On January 1, 2011, Shumway Software Company's general ledger contained these liability accounts:

Record current liability transactions; prepare current liabilities section.
(SO 1, 2, 4, 5) AP

Accounts payable	$42,500
Customer loyalty program liability	4,500
CPP payable	1,340
EI payable	702
HST payable	11,400
Income tax payable	2,915
Unearned service revenue	15,000
Vacation pay payable	7,680

In January, the following selected transactions occurred:

Jan. 2 Issued a $50,000, four-month, 7% note. Interest is payable at maturity.

    5 Sold merchandise for $8,800 cash, plus 13% HST. The cost of this sale was $4,600. Shumway Software uses a perpetual inventory system.

    12 Provided services for customers who had made advance payments of $8,500. Assume HST is not charged for these services.

    14 Paid the Receiver General (federal government) for sales taxes collected in December 2010.

    15 Paid the Receiver General for amounts owing from the December payroll for CPP, EI, and income tax.

    17 Paid $20,000 to creditors on account.

    20 Sold 500 units of a new product on account for $55 per unit, plus 13% HST. This new product has a one-year warranty. It is estimated that 9% of the units sold will be returned for repair at an average cost of $10 per unit. The cost of this sale was $25 per unit.

29 Provided $2,300 of services for customers in exchange for customer loyalty rewards redeemed in the month. Assume that HST of 13% is included in $2,300.

31 Recorded and paid the monthly payroll. Gross salaries were $16,000. Amounts withheld included CPP of $720, EI of $277, and income tax of $3,215.

Instructions

(a) Record the transactions.
(b) Record adjusting entries for the following:
1. Interest on the note payable
2. The estimated warranty liability
3. Employee benefits for CPP, EI, and vacation pay (accrued at a rate of 4%)
4. Estimated property taxes totalling $7,560 in 2011
(c) Prepare the current liabilities section of the balance sheet at January 31.

Taking It Further

Explain when the company should reduce its vacation pay liability.

Record warranty transactions.
(SO 2) AP

P10–4A On January 1, 2009, Hopewell Company began a warranty program to stimulate sales. It is estimated that 5% of the units sold will be returned for repair at an estimated cost of $30 per unit. Sales and warranty figures for the three years ended December 31 are as follows:

	2009	2010	2011
Sales (units)	1,500	1,700	1,800
Sales price per unit	$150	$120	$125
Units returned for repair under warranty	75	90	105
Actual warranty costs	$2,250	$2,400	$2,640

Instructions

(a) Calculate the warranty expense for each year and warranty liability at the end of each year.
(b) Record the warranty transactions for each year. Credit Repair Parts Inventory for the actual warranty costs.
(c) To date, what percentage of the units sold have been returned for repair under warranty? What has been the average actual warranty cost per unit for the three year period?

Taking It Further

Assume that at December 31, 2011, management reassesses its original estimates and decides that it is more likely that the company will have to service 7% of the units sold in 2011. Management also determines that the average actual cost per unit incurred to date (as calculated in (c) above), is more reasonable than its original estimate. What should be the balance in the warranty liability account at December 31, 2011?

Record customer loyalty program and gift card transactions; determine impact on financial statements.
(SO 2) AP

P10–5A Save-Always Stores started a customer loyalty program at the beginning of 2010 in which customers making cash purchases of gasoline at Save-Always Gas Bars are issued rewards in the form of grocery coupons. For each litre of gasoline purchased, the customer gets a grocery coupon for 3.5 cents that can be redeemed in Save-Always Food Stores. The coupons have no expiry date. Save-Always Stores began selling gift cards in 2011 that do not have expiry dates.

The following are selected transactions in 2010 and 2011:
1. In 2010, the Gas Bars sold 3.5 million litres of gasoline, issuing grocery coupons for these sales.
2. In 2010, customers redeemed $45,000 of the grocery coupons in the Food Stores while purchasing $1.8 million of groceries, paying the balance in cash.
3. In 2011, the Gas Bars sold 4.25 million litres of gasoline, issuing grocery coupons for these sales.
4. In 2011, customers redeemed $52,500 of the grocery coupons in the Food Stores while purchasing $2,230,000 of groceries, paying for the balance in cash.

5. In 2011, customers purchased $75,000 of gift cards, and $45,400 of the cards were redeemed by the end of the year.

Instructions

(a) Indicate if the following items will increase, decrease, or have no effect on each of revenues, expenses, and profit:
   1. Issuing grocery coupons
   2. Redeeming grocery coupons
   3. Issuing gift cards
   4. Redeeming gift cards
(b) Record the above transactions.
(c) What balances will be included in current liabilities at December 31, 2010 and 2011, regarding the customer loyalty program and gift cards?

Taking It Further

What factors should management consider in determining if current liabilities are correctly valued at December 31, 2011?

P10–6A   Mega Company, a public company, is preparing its financial statements for the year ended December 31, 2011. It is now January 31, 2012, and the following situations are being reviewed to determine the appropriate accounting treatment:

Discuss reporting of contingent liabilities and assets.
(SO 3, 5) AP

1. Mega Company is being sued for a possible malfunction of one of its products. In July 2011, a customer suffered a serious injury while operating the product. The company is vigorously defending itself as it is clear the customer was intoxicated when using the product.
2. In a separate lawsuit, Mega is being sued by an employee who was injured on the job in February 2011. It is likely that the company will lose this lawsuit, but a reasonable estimate cannot be made of the amount of the obligation.
3. Since June 2009, Mega has guaranteed a bank loan for one of its main suppliers. In September 2011, the supplier started experiencing financial difficulties, which have continued. On December 16, 2011, the bank called Mega Company to confirm that if the supplier is unable repay the loan in January 2012, the bank will be seeking payment from Mega Company under the guarantee.
4. On January 7, 2012, a potential customer injured himself when he slipped on the floor in the foyer of Mega Company's office building. Mega Company did not have appropriate floor mats in place and melting snow from the customer's boots made the floor very dangerous. Mega has negotiated a potential settlement with the individual's lawyer.
5. If Mega loses the lawsuit mentioned in part 2 above, then its insurance company will likely pay it a portion of the damages.

Instructions

For each of the above situations, recommend whether Mega Company should (a) make an accrual in its December 31, 2011, financial statements; (b) disclose the situation in the notes to the financial statements; or (c) not report it. Provide a rationale for your recommendations.

Taking It Further

What are the differences between accounting for contingencies under IFRS versus Canadian GAAP for Private Enterprises?

P10–7A   Atom Construction Company is in the second year of a three-year construction schedule to build a nuclear plant for the Province of Ontario. The province has agreed to pay the company a bonus if the plant is completed on time and on budget. Atom Construction Company has never missed a deadline and also has a history of completing projects on budget.

Discuss reporting of contingent liability and asset.
(SO 3, 5) AP

Instructions

(a) What should the Province of Ontario record or disclose in its financial statements in this situation? Explain why.

(b) What should Atom Construction Company record or disclose in its financial statements in this situation? Explain why.

Taking It Further

Why are there differences in how contingent liabilities and contingent assets are accounted for?

Prepare payroll register and record payroll.
(SO 4) AP

P10–8A Sure Value Hardware has four employees who are paid on an hourly basis, plus time-and-a-half for hours worked in excess of 40 hours a week. Payroll data for the week ended March 14, 2011, follow:

Employee	Total Hours	Hourly Rate	CPP	EI	Income Tax	United Way
I. Dahl	37.5	$16.00	$26.37	$10.38	$ 89.70	$ 7.50
F. Gualtieri	42	15.00	28.60	11.16	99.35	8.00
G. Ho	44	14.50	30.68	11.54	108.00	5.00
A. Israeli	46	14.50	32.83	12.29	122.75	10.00

The first three employees are sales clerks (store wages expense) and the other employee does administrative duties (office wages expense).

Instructions

(a) Prepare a payroll register for the weekly payroll.

(b) Record the payroll on March 14 and the accrual of employee benefits expense.

(c) Record the payment of the payroll on March 14.

(d) Record the payment of employee benefits on April 15.

Taking It Further

Does the owner of a proprietorship need to deduct CPP, EI, and income taxes on his or her drawings?

Record and post payroll transactions.
(SO 4) AP

P10–9A The following payroll liability accounts are included in the ledger of Drumheller Company on January 1, 2011:

Canada Pension Plan payable	$ 5,454
Canada Savings Bonds payable	2,500
Disability insurance payable	1,050
Employment Insurance payable	3,050
Income tax payable	16,800
Union dues payable	1,250
Vacation pay payable	6,450
Workers' compensation payable	5,263

In January, the following transactions occurred:

Jan. 8 Sent a cheque to the insurance company for the disability insurance.

10 Sent a cheque for $1,250 to the union treasurer for union dues.

11 Purchased Canada Savings Bonds for employees by writing a cheque for $2,500.

12 Issued a cheque to the Receiver General for the amounts due for CPP, EI, and income tax.

20 Paid the amount due to the workers' compensation plan.

31 Completed the monthly payroll register, which shows office salaries $24,600; store wages $38,700; CPP withheld $2,845; EI withheld $1,095; income tax withheld $15,620; union dues withheld $950; Canada Savings Bond deductions $1,200; and long-term disability insurance premiums $1,100.

31   Prepared payroll cheques for the net pay and distributed the cheques to the employees.

At January 31, the company also made the following adjusting entries for employee benefits:

1. The employer's share of CPP and EI
2. Workers' compensation plan at 5% of gross pay
3. Vacation pay at 4% of gross pay

Instructions

(a) Enter the beginning balances in general ledger accounts.
(b) Journalize and post the January transactions and adjustments.

Taking It Further

What is the purpose of an employee's earning record?

P10–10A   Kangaroo Media Inc. reports the following current assets and current liabilities at December 31, 2008 (in thousands):

Prepare current liabilities section; calculate and comment on ratios.
(SO 5) AP

Accounts payable and accrued liabilities	$1,993
Accounts receivable	897
Cash and cash equivalents	9,266
Short-term investments	160
Current portion of long-term debt	3,199
Deferred revenues	211
Inventories	128
Prepaid expenses	128

Instructions

(a) Prepare the current liabilities section of the balance sheet.
(b) Calculate the current and acid-test ratios.
(c) At December 31, 2007, Kangaroo Media Inc. had current assets of $27,177 thousand, cash plus short-term investments plus accounts receivable of $25,662 thousand, and current liabilities of $6,813 thousand. Did the current and acid-test ratios improve or weaken in 2008?

Taking It Further

What other factors should be considered in assessing Kangaroo Media's solvency?

*****P10–11A**   Western Electric Company pays its support staff weekly and its electricians on a semi-monthly basis. The following support staff payroll information is available for the week ended June 5, 2009:

Calculate payroll deductions.
(SO 6) AP

Employee Name	Weekly Earnings	Claim Code
Chris Tam	$ 945	2
Terry Ng	1,135	4
Olga Stavtech	1,135	1
Alana Mandell	1,067	1

The electricians' salaries are based on their experience in the field, as well as the number of years they have worked for the company. All three electricians have been with the company more than two years. The annual salaries of these employees are as follows:

Employee Name	Annual Salary for 2009
Sam Goodspeed	$40,840
Marino Giancarlo	60,760
Hillary Radley	70,480

Instructions

(a) Determine the mandatory payroll deductions and net pay for each of the support staff. Calculate the CPP and EI deductions using the formula provided in Appendix 10A. Use the tables in Illustration 10A-3 to determine federal and provincial income taxes.

(b) Calculate the CPP and EI deductions for each of the electricians for their June 15, 2009, semi-monthly payroll.

(c) In which semi-monthly pay period will each of the electricians reach their maximum CPP and EI payments for 2009?

Taking It Further

Why are there separate payroll deduction tables for determining weekly, semi-monthly, and monthly income tax deductions?

Problems: Set B

Identify liabilities.
(SO 1, 2, 3, 4, 5) AP

P10–1B The following transactions occurred in Iqaluit Company in the year ended April 30:

1. Iqaluit purchased goods for $12,000 on April 29, terms n/30, FOB destination. The goods arrived on May 3.
2. Weekly salaries of $90,000 are paid every Friday for a five-day (Monday to Friday) work-week. This year, April 30 is a Thursday. Payroll deductions include income tax withholdings of $27,000, and CPP of $4,500, and EI of $1,500.
3. Property taxes of $40,000 were assessed on March 1 for the calendar year. They are payable on May 1.
4. The company purchased equipment for $35,000 on April 1. It issued a six-month, 5% note in payment. Interest is payable monthly on the first of each month.
5. Iqaluit offered a two-year warranty on one of its new products. It estimated it would cost $45 to honour each warranty and that 5% of the units sold would be returned for replacement within the warranty period. By April 30, 10,000 units of the product had been sold and customers had returned 100 units under the warranty.
6. The company has a $225,000, 20-year mortgage payable; $9,250 of the principal must be paid within the next year.
7. Iqaluit was named in a $1-million lawsuit alleging negligence for an oil spill that leaked into the neighbouring company's water system. Iqaluit's lawyers estimate that the company will likely lose the suit and expect the company will have to pay $250,000 in restoration costs.

Instructions

Identify which transactions above should be presented in the current liabilities section and which in the long-term liabilities section of Iqaluit's balance sheet on April 30. Identify the account title(s) and amount(s) for each reported liability.

Taking It Further

Indicate any information that should be disclosed in the notes to Iqaluit's financial statements.

Record note transactions; show financial statement presentation.
(SO 1, 5) AP

P10–2B MileHi Mountain Bikes markets mountain-bike tours to clients vacationing in various locations in the mountains of British Columbia. The current liabilities section of the October 31, 2010, balance sheet included notes payable of $15,000 and interest payable of $375 related to a six-month, 6% note payable to Eifert Company on December 1, 2010.

During the year ended October 31, 2011, MileHi had the following transactions related to notes payable:

2010
Dec. 1 Paid the $15,000 Eifert note, plus interest.

2011

Apr. 1 Issued a $75,000, nine-month, 7% note to Mountain Real Estate for the purchase of additional mountain property on which to build bike trails. Interest is payable quarterly on July 1, September 1, and at maturity on December 1.

   30 Purchased Mongoose bikes to use as rentals for $8,000, terms n/30.

May 31 Issued Mongoose an $8,000, three-month, 8% note payable in settlement of its account (see April 30 transaction). Interest is payable at maturity.

July 1 Paid interest on the Mountain Real Estate note (see April 1 transaction).

Aug. 31 Paid the Mongoose note, plus interest (see May 31 transaction).

Oct. 1 Paid interest on the Mountain Real Estate note (see April 1 transaction).

   1 Borrowed $90,000 cash from Western Bank by issuing a five-year, 6% note. Interest is payable monthly on the first of the month. Principal payments of $18,000 must be made on the anniversary of the note each year.

Instructions

(a) Record the transactions and any adjustments required at October 31, 2011.

(b) Show the balance sheet presentation of notes payable and interest payable at October 31, 2011.

(c) Show the income statement presentation of interest expense for the year.

Taking It Further

Why is it important to correctly classify notes payable as either current or non-current in the balance sheet?

P10–3B On January 1, 2011, Zaur Company's general ledger had these liability accounts:

Record current liability transactions; prepare current liabilities section.
(SO 1, 2, 4, 5) AP

Accounts payable	$52,000
Customer loyalty program liability	2,150
CPP payable	1,905
EI payable	850
HST payable	11,390
Income tax payable	4,640
Unearned service revenue	16,000
Vacation pay liability	9,120
Warranty liability	5,750

In January, the following selected transactions occurred:

Jan. 5 Sold merchandise for $15,800 cash, plus 13% HST. Zaur uses a periodic inventory system.

  12 Provided services for customers who had previously made advance payments of $7,000.

  14 Paid the Receiver General (federal government) sales taxes collected in December 2010.

  15 Paid the Receiver General for amounts owing from the December payroll for CPP, EI, and income tax.

  16 Borrowed $18,000 from HSBC Bank on a three-month, 6% note. Interest is payable monthly on the 15th day of the month.

  17 Paid $32,000 to creditors on account.

  20 Sold 500 units of a new product on account for $60 per unit, plus 13% HST. The cost of the product sold is $25 per unit. This new product has a two-year warranty. It is expected that 6% of the units sold will be returned for repair at an average cost of $10 per unit.

  30 Customers redeemed $1,750 of loyalty points in exchange for services. Assume that HST of 13% is included in this amount.

  31 Issued 50,000 loyalty points worth $1 each. Based on past experience, 10% of these coupons are expected to be redeemed.

31 Determined that the company had used $875 of parts inventory in January to honour warranty contracts.

31 Recorded and paid the monthly payroll. Gross salaries were $22,500. Amounts withheld include CPP of $1,027, EI of $289, and income tax of $5,135.

Instructions

(a) Record the transactions.
(b) Record adjusting entries for the following:
    1. Interest on the note payable for half a month
    2. The estimated warranty liability
    3. Employee benefits, which include CPP, EI, and vacation pay that is accrued at a rate of 4%
(c) Prepare the current liabilities section of the balance sheet at January 31.

Taking It Further

Explain when the company should reduce its vacation pay liability.

Record warranty transactions. (SO 2) AP

P10–4B On January 1, 2009, Logue Company began a warranty program to stimulate sales. It is estimated that 5% of the units sold will be returned for repair at an estimated cost of $25 per unit. Sales and warranty figures for the three years ended December 31 are as follows:

	2009	2010	2011
Sales (units)	1,200	1,320	1,420
Sales price per unit	$100	$105	$110
Units returned for repair under warranty	60	70	80
Actual warranty costs	$1,275	$1,600	$1,960

Instructions

(a) Calculate the warranty expense for each year and warranty liability at the end of each year.
(b) Record the warranty transactions for each year. Credit Repair Parts Inventory for the actual warranty costs.
(c) To date, what percentage of the units sold have been returned for repair under warranty? What has been the average actual warranty cost per unit for the three year period?

Taking It Further

Suppose at December 31, 2011, management reassesses its original estimates and decides that it is more likely that the company will have to service 7% of the units sold in 2011. Management also determines that the original estimate of the cost per unit is the appropriate cost to use for future repair work. What should be the balance in the warranty liability account at December 31, 2011?

Record customer loyalty program and gift card transactions; determine impact on financial statements. (SO 2) AP

P10–5B Caribou County Service Station started a customer loyalty program at the beginning of 2010 in which customers making cash purchases of gasoline at the gas bar are issued rewards in the form of coupons. For each litre of gasoline purchased, the customer gets a coupon for 2.5 cents that can be redeemed in the service department toward such things as oil changes or repairs. The coupons have no expiry date. Caribou County Service Station began selling gift cards in 2011 that do not have expiry dates.

The following are selected transactions in 2010 and 2011:

1. In 2010, the gas bar sold 750,000 litres of gasoline, issuing coupons for these sales.
2. In 2010, customers redeemed $5,950 of the coupons in the service department while purchasing $23,800 of repair services for their vehicles, paying the balance in cash.
3. In 2011, the gas bar sold 810,000 litres of gasoline, issuing coupons for these sales.
4. In 2011, customers redeemed $9,500 of the coupons in the service department while purchasing $30,230 of repair services for their vehicles, paying for the balance in cash.
5. In 2011, customers purchased $3,950 of gift cards, and $1,500 of the cards were redeemed by the end of the year.

Instructions

(a) Indicate if the following items will increase, decrease, or have no effect on each of revenues, expenses, and profit:

1. Issuing coupons
2. Redeeming coupons
3. Issuing gift cards
4. Redeeming gift cards

(b) Record the above transactions.
(c) What balances will be included in current liabilities at December 31, 2010 and 2011, regarding the customer loyalty program and gift cards?

Taking It Further

What factors should management consider in determining if current liabilities are correctly valued at December 31, 2011?

P10–6B Big Fork Company, a private company that follows Canadian GAAP, is preparing its financial statements for the year ended December 31, 2011. It is now February 15, 2012, and the following situations are being reviewed to determine the appropriate accounting treatment:

1. Since 2004, Big Fork has guaranteed a bank loan for one of its main customers, Little Fork. Little Fork has always made all of its payments in a timely fashion.
2. The company is being sued for a possible malfunction of one of its products. In March 2011, a customer suffered a serious injury while operating the product. The company is defending itself but it is clear that there was an error in the published operations manual for the product. It is likely that the company will lose this lawsuit, but a reasonable estimate cannot be made of the amount of the obligation.
3. Big Fork is being sued by an employee for wrongful dismissal and defamation of character. The employee was fired on August 2, 2011. The company is vigorously defending itself because the employee had a long and documented history of poor performance and being intoxicated at work.
4. If Big Fork loses the lawsuit mentioned in part 2 above, then its insurance company will likely pay it for a portion of the damages.
5. On January 7, 2012, a sales representative from one of the company's suppliers injured herself on a visit to Big Fork's offices. She tripped over equipment that had not been properly stored and will be unable to work for several months as a result of her injuries. A claim against Big Fork has been filed by the sales representative's insurance company.

Instructions

For each of the above situations, recommend whether Big Fork Company should (a) make an accrual in its December 31, 2011, financial statements; (b) disclose the situation in the notes to the financial statements; or (c) not report it. Provide a rationale for your recommendations.

Taking It Further

What are the differences between accounting for contingencies under IFRS versus Canadian GAAP for Private Enterprises?

P10–7B On March 4, a fire destroyed the chemistry building on the College of Learning's campus. The college, a private institution, has filed a claim with its insurance company. At March 31, the college's year end, the claim has not been settled.

Instructions

Under each of the following independent assumptions, explain what the college should record or disclose in its March 31 financial statements:
(a) The insurance claim is likely to be successful.
(b) The insurance claim is unlikely to be successful because the insurance company believes the fire is suspicious.
(c) The college receives written confirmation from the insurance company that the claim will be paid in full, but it will not happen before the financial statements are issued.

Margin notes:

Discuss reporting of contingent liabilities and assets.
(SO 3, 5) AP

Discuss reporting of contingent asset.
(SO 3, 5) AP

Taking It Further

Why are there differences in how contingent liabilities and contingent assets are accounted for?

Prepare payroll register and record payroll.
(SO 4) AP

P10–8B Scoot Scooters has four employees who are paid on an hourly basis, plus time-and-a-half for hours in excess of 40 hours a week. Payroll data for the week ended February 15, 2011, follow:

Employee	Total Hours	Hourly Rate	CPP	EI	Income Tax	United Way
P. Kilchyk	40	$12.75	$21.91	$ 8.82	$66.20	$5.00
B. Quon	42	14.00	26.47	10.41	81.95	7.25
C. Pospisil	40	15.25	26.86	10.55	83.55	5.50
B. Verwey	44	13.50	27.41	10.74	85.10	8.25

Instructions

(a) Prepare a payroll register for the weekly payroll.
(b) Record the payroll on February 15 and the accrual of employee benefits expense.
(c) Record the payment of the payroll on February 15.
(d) Record the payment of the employee benefits on March 15.

Taking It Further

Does the owner of a proprietorship have to deduct CPP, EI, and income taxes from his or her own drawings?

Record and post payroll transactions.
(SO 4) AP

P10–9B The following payroll liability accounts are included in the ledger of Amora Company on January 1, 2011:

Canada Pension Plan payable	$ 8,878
Canada Savings Bonds payable	2,420
Employment Insurance payable	3,723
Income tax payable	22,500
Union dues payable	1,200
United Way donations payable	750
Vacation pay payable	10,704
Workers' compensation payable	5,676

In January, the following transactions occurred:

Jan.   7   Issued a cheque to United Way.
      10   Sent a cheque to the union treasurer for union dues.
      12   Issued a cheque to the Receiver General for the amounts due for CPP, EI, and income tax.
      17   Purchased Canada Savings Bonds for employees by writing a cheque for $2,420.
      20   Paid the workers' compensation plan.
      31   Prepared the monthly payroll register, which showed office salaries $41,200; store wages $50,300; CPP withheld $4,168; EI withheld $1,583; income tax withheld $21,700; union dues withheld $1,250; United Way contributions $750; and Canada Savings Bonds deductions $1,210.
      31   Prepared payroll cheques for the net pay and distributed them to employees.

At January 31, the company also made the following adjusting entries for employee benefits:

1. The employer's share of CPP and EI
2. Workers' compensation plan at 7% of gross pay
3. Vacation pay at 4% of gross pay

Instructions

(a) Enter the beginning balances in general ledger accounts.
(b) Record and post the January transactions and adjustments.

Taking It Further

What type of information does an employer keep track of for each employee?

P10–10B Shoppers Drug Mart Corporation reports the following current assets and current liabilities at January 3, 2009 (in thousands of dollars):

Prepare current liabilities section; calculate and comment on ratios.

(SO 5) AP

Accounts payable and accrued liabilities	$1,018,505
Accounts receivable	448,476
Bank indebtedness	240,844
Cash	36,567
Commercial paper	339,957
Dividends payable	46,709
Future income tax asset	83,279
Income taxes recoverable	8,835
Inventory	1,743,253
Prepaid expense and deposits	64,054
Short-term debt	197,845

Instructions

(a) Prepare the current liabilities section of the balance sheet.
(b) Calculate the current and the acid-test ratio.
(c) On December 29, 2007, Shoppers had current assets of $2,150,137 thousand, cash plus short-term investments plus accounts receivable of $399,894 thousand, and current liabilities of $2,158,320 thousand. Did the current and acid-test ratios improve or weaken in 2008?

Taking It Further

What other factors should be considered in assessing Shoppers Drug Mart's liquidity?

*P10–11B Slovak Plumbing Company pays its support staff weekly and its plumbers on a semi-monthly basis. The following support staff payroll information is available for the week ended May 8, 2009:

Calculate payroll deductions.
(SO 6) AP

Employee Name	Weekly Earnings	Claim Code
Dan Quinn	$ 995	1
Karol Holub	1,030	3
Al Lowhorn	1,074	1
Irina Kostra	940	4

The plumbers' salaries are based on their experience in the field, as well as the number of years they have worked for the company. All three plumbers have been with the company more than two years. The annual salary of these employees is as follows:

Employee Name	Annual Salary for 2009
Branislav Dolina	$75,760
Henrietta Koleno	64,980
Aida Krneta	41,180

Instructions

(a) Determine the mandatory payroll deductions and net pay for each of the support staff. Calculate the CPP and EI deductions using the formula provided in Appendix 10A. Use the tables in Illustration 10A-3 to determine federal and provincial income taxes.
(b) Calculate the CPP and EI deductions for each of the plumbers for their May 15, 2009, semi-monthly payroll.
(c) In which semi-monthly pay period will each of the plumbers reach their maximum CPP and EI payments for 2009?

Taking It Further

Why are there separate payroll deduction tables for determining income tax deductions for weekly, semi-monthly, and monthly pay periods?

Continuing Cookie Chronicle

(*Note:* This is a continuation of the Cookie Chronicle from Chapters 1 through 9.)

Recall that Cookie Creations borrowed $2,000 on November 16, 2010, from Natalie's grandmother. Interest on the note is 3% per year and the note plus interest was to be repaid in 12 months.

Natalie is considering paying back her grandmother before the note becomes due in November 2011.

Instructions

(a) Calculate the total interest expense recorded in 2010. Calculate total interest expense to be incurred in 2011 if the loan is repaid on its due date.

(b) If Natalie's grandmother's loan were to be repaid at the end of August 2011, calculate Cookie Creations' cash savings.

(c) Identify to Natalie some of the advantages and disadvantages of repaying the loan before it becomes due.

(d) Prepare the journal entry to record the loan repayment at the end of August 2011. Recall that a monthly adjusting journal entry was prepared for the months of November 2010 (half month), December 2010, and January 2011.

Cumulative Coverage—Chapters 3 to 10

The unadjusted trial balance of LeBrun Company at its year end, July 31, 2011, is as follows:

LEBRUN COMPANY Trial Balance July 31, 2011		
	Debit	Credit
Cash	$ 17,400	
Petty cash	200	
Accounts receivable	38,500	
Allowance for doubtful accounts		$ 2,000
Note receivable (due December 31, 2011)	10,000	
Merchandise inventory	40,900	
Prepaid expenses	16,000	
Land	50,000	
Building	155,000	
Accumulated depreciation—building		10,800
Equipment	25,000	
Accumulated depreciation—equipment		12,200
Patent	75,000	
Accumulated amortization—patent		15,000
Accounts payable		78,900
Mortgage payable (due August 1, 2026)		124,200
S. LeBrun, capital		127,690
S. LeBrun, drawings	54,000	
Sales		750,000
Cost of goods sold	450,000	
Operating expenses	181,220	
Interest revenue		400
Interest expense	7,970	
Totals	$1,121,190	$1,121,190

Adjustment data:

1. The July 31 bank statement reported debit memos for service charges of $45 and a $650 NSF (not sufficient funds) cheque that had been received from a customer for the purchase of merchandise in July.
2. Estimated uncollectible accounts receivable at July 31 are 10% of gross accounts receivable.
3. The note receivable bears interest of 8% and was issued on December 31, 2010. Interest is payable the first of each month.
4. A physical count of inventory determined that $39,200 of inventory was actually on hand.
5. Prepaid expenses of $5,500 expired in the year (use the account Operating Expenses).
6. Depreciation is calculated on the long-lived assets using the following methods and useful lives:

> Building: straight-line, 25 years, $15,000 residual value
> Equipment: double diminishing-balance, five years, $2,500 residual value
> Patent: straight-line, five years, no residual value

7. The 7% mortgage payable was issued on August 1, 2001. Interest is paid monthly at the beginning of each month for the previous month's interest. Of the mortgage principal, $1,680 is currently due.
8. Accrued liabilities for salaries at July 31 are $1,975.

Instructions

(a) Prepare the adjusting journal entries required at July 31. (Round your calculations to the nearest dollar.)
(b) Prepare an adjusted trial balance at July 31.
(c) Prepare a multiple-step income statement and statement of owner's equity for the year, and a balance sheet at July 31.

BROADENING YOUR PERSPECTIVE

Financial Reporting and Analysis

Financial Reporting Problem

BYP10–1   Refer to the financial statements of The Forzani Group Ltd. and the Notes to Consolidated Financial Statements in Appendix A.

Instructions

Answer the following questions about the company's current and contingent liabilities:
(a) What were Forzani's total current liabilities at February 1, 2009? What was the increase (decrease) in total current liabilities from the previous year?
(b) Which specific current liabilities did Forzani present on the February 1, 2009, balance sheet?
(c) Calculate Forzani's current ratio, acid-test ratio, receivables, and inventory turnover ratios, and operating cycle for 2009 and 2008. For 2008, beginning accounts receivable was $65,543 thousand and beginning inventory was $302,207 thousand. Comment on Forzani's overall liquidity.
(d) Does Forzani report any contingent liabilities? If so, where are they disclosed? Explain the nature, amount, and significance of Forzani's principal types of contingent liabilities, if any.

Interpreting Financial Statements

BYP10–2 Saputo Inc. reported the following information about contingencies in the notes to its March 31, 2009, financial statements:

SAPUTO INC.
Notes to the Consolidated Financial Statements
March 31,2009

Saputo

NOTE 18 COMMITMENTS AND CONTINGENCIES
The Company guarantees to certain lessors a portion of the residual value of certain leased assets with respect to operations which mature until 2014. If the market value of leased assets, at the end of the respective operating lease term, is inferior to the guaranteed residual value, the Company is obligated to indemnify the lessor, specific to certain conditions, for the shortfall up to a maximum value. The Company believes that the potential indemnification will not have a significant effect on the consolidated financial statements.

Claims
The Company is defendant to certain claims arising from the normal course of its business. The Company is also defendant in certain claims and/or assessments from tax authorities in various jurisdictions. The Company believes that the final resolution of these claims and/or assessments will not have a material adverse effect on its earnings or financial position.

INDEMNIFICATIONS
The Company from time to time offers indemnifications to third parties in the normal course of its business, in connection with business or asset acquisitions or dispositions. These indemnification provisions may be in connection with breach of representations and warranties and for future claims for certain liabilities, including liabilities related to tax and environmental matters. The terms of these indemnification provisions vary in duration. At March 31, 2009, given that the nature and amount of such indemnifications depend on future events, the Company is unable to reasonably estimate its maximum potential liability under these agreements. The Company has not made any significant indemnification payments in the past, and as at March 31, 2009 and 2008, the Company has not recorded a liability associated with these indemnifications.

Instructions

(a) Why would Saputo Inc. disclose information about these legal disputes in the notes to the financial statements instead of accruing an amount for these as liabilities in its accounting records?

(b) Where should Saputo Inc. record the legal costs incurred to date (i.e., the costs before going to trial) on the disputes (claims)?

(c) In the first paragraph above, Saputo Inc. provides an explanation of an obligation it has with respect to certain leased assets. What factors might cause the market value of the leased assets to decline significantly?

Critical Thinking

Collaborative Learning Activity

Note to instructor: Additional instructions and material for this group activity can be found on the Instructor Resource Site.

WILEY PLUS
Working in Groups

BYP10–3 In this group activity, you will work in pairs to review the accounting for notes payable and its relationship to the accounting for notes receivable (Chapter 8).

On September 1, 2011, a borrower signs a 6-month, 5.5% note payable in exchange for $10,000 cash. Interest is payable at maturity. Both the borrower and lender have a December 31 year end and adjustments are made only annually.

Instructions

(a) In your pair, decide who will play the roles of lender and borrower.
(b) Based on your role, record the journal entries for:
    1. issue of the note
    2. year-end adjustments
    3. maturity of the note
(c) Compare your answer to that of your partner. If they are different, explain how you decided on your journal entries.
(d) You may be asked by your instructor to write a short quiz on this topic.

Communication Activity

BYP10–4 The Show Time movie theatre sells thousands of gift certificates every year. The certificates can be redeemed at any time since they have no expiry date. Some of them may never be redeemed (because they are lost or forgotten, for example). The owner of the theatre has raised some questions about the accounting for these gift certificates.

Instructions

Write a memo to answer the following questions from the owner:
(a) Why is a liability recorded when these certificates are sold? After all, they bring customers into the theatre, where they spend money on snacks and drinks. Why should something that helps generate additional revenue be treated as a liability?
(b) How should the gift certificates that are never redeemed be treated? At some point in the future, can the liability related to them be eliminated? If so, what type of journal entry would be made?

Ethics Case

BYP10–5 Nice Nuke Corporation, which owns and operates a nuclear plant, recently received notice from the provincial government that it has to find a new disposal site for its radioactive waste. The company was also told that it is responsible for the environmental cleanup of the old site. The vice-president of engineering and the vice-president of finance meet to discuss the situation. The engineer says that it could take many years to clean up the site and that the cost could be considerable—a minimum of $50 million and perhaps as much as $100 million.

The vice-president of finance says that there is no way that the company can afford to record this liability. He says he is not even sure that he wants to disclose the potential liability, because of how this could affect the company's share price.

Instructions

(a) Who are the stakeholders in this situation?
(b) What are the alternative reporting options that the company can use?
(c) What is the likely impact of each alternative on the company's financial position?
(d) Is there anything unethical in what the vice-president of finance suggests doing about this potential liability?
(e) What do you recommend the company do?

"All About You" Activity

BYP10–6 In the "All About You" feature, you learned who is responsible for remitting income tax, CPP, and EI to the CRA if you are an employee or self-employed. You also learned that the CRA has strict guidelines as to whether someone is self-employed or an employee.

Assume that as a new graduate you are accepting a position where you will be providing consulting services to a company. You have agreed to provide the services for $3,000 a month. The company's manager of human resources suggests that you may want to be considered self-employed rather than an employee of the company. Before you make your decision, you need to better understand the CRA's guidelines and the financial implications.

(a) Go to Canada Revenue Agency's website www.cra-arc.gc.ca and search for document RC4110 "Employee or Self-Employed?". What are the factors that should be considered when determining if a worker is an employee or self-employed?

(b) Assume you are an employee and you are paid monthly and that the following is deducted from your gross earnings:

CPP	$134.06
EI	51.90
Income tax	429.84

What is the amount of cash you will receive each month? What is the total amount of cash you will receive in a year?

(c) Based on the information in (b), what is the total CPP you will pay in a year? What is the total EI you will pay in a year?

(d) Assume you are self-employed, and you have chosen to pay EI. What is the amount of cash you will receive each month? What is the total CPP you will have to pay in a year? What is the total EI you will have to pay in a year?

(e) Assuming that you will pay the same amount of income tax as you would if you were an employee, calculate the amount of cash you will receive if you are self-employed.

(f) Based on your answers to (c) and (e), do you want to be self-employed or an employee of the company? Explain.

(g) If you had the opportunity to provide consulting services to another company in your spare time, would your answer in (f) be different? Explain.

ANSWERS TO CHAPTER QUESTIONS

Answers to Accounting in Action Insight Questions

Across the Organization Insight, p. 565

Q: A company's marketing department is responsible for designing customer loyalty programs. Why would Shoppers' marketing department add the option of donating points to charity?

A: Most customer loyalty programs were designed under the assumption that customers are motivated by cost savings. Shoppers realized that some customers have enough disposable income that cost saving is not a motivation. But many of these customers are motivated by the desire to help others. Thus the option to donate points has the potential to appeal to a wider base of customers and increase the program's success.

Business Insight, p. 569

Q: Environmental contingencies are generally considered to be harder to estimate than contingencies from lawsuits. What might be the reason for this difference?

A: The requirement to account for environmental contingencies is relatively new compared with the requirement to account for contingencies from lawsuits. Although it is difficult to predict whether the company will win or lose a lawsuit and what type of settlement may be involved, there is a vast history of case law that can be used to help a company form an opinion. Environmental regulations, in contrast, are still evolving and there is often no system (e.g., regulatory compliance audits or environmental site assessment data) that would help a company estimate the possible cost, or even the existence, of environmental contingencies for many years.

All About You Insight, p. 577

Q: If you are providing services to a company, what are the advantages and disadvantages of being a self-employed consultant versus an employee of the company?

A: As a self-employed individual, your monthly cash received from the company would be higher as no CPP, EI, and income tax will be deducted. On the other hand, you will have to make quarterly instalment payments of CPP, EI (if you choose to pay it) and income taxes. If you are self-employed, you may be able to deduct certain expenses to reduce your income tax.

  However, some individuals may not manage their cash properly and may be unable to make the remittances when required. In addition, you will have to pay twice as much for CPP and you will not qualify for EI benefits. If you are self-employed, you would not qualify for other benefits offered to employees by the company either.

Answer to Forzani Review It Question 2, p. 579

The Forzani Group reports only three current liabilities: (1) current indebtedness under its revolving credit facility, (2) accounts payable and accrued liabilities, and (3) the current portion of long-term debt. The three liabilities may be listed in order of maturity, but we don't have enough information to determine this.

Answers to Self-Study Questions

1. d 2. c 3. a 4. b 5. a 6. d 7. b 8. b 9. d *10. b

Remember to go back to the beginning of the chapter to check off your completed work!

←